Dr Claire's
LOVE
your
DOG

WOODSLANE
PRESS

Woodslane Press Pty Ltd

10 Apollo Street

Warriewood, NSW 2102

Email: info@woodslane.com.au

02 8445 2300 www.woodslane.com.au

First published in Australia in 2020 by Woodslane Press

A catalogue record for this book is available from the National Library of Australia

Printed in China by Asia Pacific Offset

Cover images: By Richard Weinstein courtesy of Hypro Premium

Book design by: Christine Schiedel and Cory Spence

For Sasha

Contents

Dogs & Me ♥

'Please, please can I have a dog?'

I was totally in love with dogs from the time I was a small child, but my dad was not a dog person and the answer to the question, 'can I please have a dog' was always no. He was a general practitioner but also a conservationist and an environmentalist. I grew up in Kuranda, a beautiful rainforest village on the Tablelands in Far North Queensland. We had acreage and a Balinese-style eco-friendly house built up off the ground; the semi-open lower floor attracted a veritable wildlife zoo. It was not unusual to find pythons and giant green tree frogs hanging out in the kitchen or white-tailed rats in the toilet. Everything we did was about living sustainably and caring for the wildlife, including wallabies and the endangered cassowaries that lived in the forest. Consequently, dogs did not fit into Dad's plan for the environment.

My two sisters were eight and seven years older than me and during their teenage years they lived in a little flat away from the main house; although I desperately wanted to hang out with them they didn't want much to do with me at that age, so I remember often feeling lonely. I was allowed to have chickens and they sort of became my friends. I'd incubate the eggs and when they hatched the chicks would follow me around thinking I was their mummy. But chickens were no substitute for a dog.

No matter how much I begged, Dad would not budge. 'Dogs stink,' he said. I had a stuffed fluffy toy spaniel with floppy ears which I took to bed with me every night and I knew that was exactly the sort of dog I wanted. I called it Sasha and decided that when I got a real dog it was going to sleep with me too. My dreams and waking hours were about a real dog that looked like Sasha.

'When I get a dog, it's going to look just like Sasha,' I told Mum, thus affirming my belief that I would one day have one.

Pester power must have worn Dad down because when I was nine, a chink appeared in his armour. He said a dog was a big responsibility and I had to show commitment by walking a neighbour's dog every day for three months. So, every day after school I walked the neighbour's dog to prove to my father that I was responsible. I liked the neighbour's dog but it wasn't my dog.

'Oh, for goodness sake, get the poor kid a dog,' my mother finally told Dad.

The day we drove for hours to collect my puppy from the breeder remains imprinted on my memory. The real-life Sasha was a beautiful little floppy-eared Cavalier King Charles Spaniel and I bonded with her immediately. When we got home, Dad said the puppy would not be allowed to sleep in the house but then relented and said she could sleep downstairs. On the first night I lay upstairs listening to the puppy whimpering until I couldn't stand it anymore. I ran into Mum and Dad's bedroom begging to be able to bring the puppy up. They said no.

The second night I thought, right, if the puppy can't sleep with me, I'll sleep with the puppy. I crept downstairs with my doona and pillow, terrified of the wildlife noises in the darkness outside and curled up with Sasha. She quickly went to sleep followed instantly by me. In the morning my parents stood over me and the cuddled-up puppy and asked what on earth I thought I was doing.

'Sasha was scared and I'm going to sleep down here with her,' I said determinedly. I felt it was Sasha and me against the world. It didn't last long as my father reluctantly agreed that Sasha could sleep upstairs with me. My father grew to acknowledge that Sasha was a special part of my life – accepting Sasha just so long as she didn't get too close to him.

When I was 11, Dad, being an adventurous environmentalist, built a 40-foot catamaran for us to circumnavigate Australia. Mum, not entirely enthusiastically, agreed to go on this journey and as long as I could take Sasha, I was happy to go. My cabin was over the engine and Dad made a little hole with a flap-door in the cockpit so Sasha had access to my room. She had a special bed with a Perspex barrier to keep her off my bed but as soon as Dad was asleep, she would jump over it and sleep with me.

Sasha adapted very well to life at sea – she was an adventurous little pooch, but she had to be. She used to go to the toilet on the canvas trampolines between the hulls although found peeing on board unpleasant and one day after we had been at sea for a few days we pulled into a harbour and Sasha, thinking a large patch of floating seaweed was grass jumped off and landed in the drink.

I found shipboard life a bit lonely, but I learnt to entertain myself and I read a lot. Mum was home schooling me and was obviously unhappy; I never heard my parents fighting but the atmosphere was tense probably amplified by the closeness of shipboard life. We had started out on the Gold Coast where the boat had been fitted out and just over a year later we reached the northern coast of Western Australia where somewhere near Broome, Mum, Sasha and I jumped ship.

Perth was Mum's hometown, so we made our way there where we lived with her mother and Mum enrolled me for a term in a local school. We eventually went back to Kuranda where my parents had another go at making the marriage work. It didn't and Mum and I moved to Cairns.

Sasha was a constant through all these unsettling changes in my life – my sisters leaving home, life on the boat, my parents' divorce. When things were a bit yuk, I'd just walk with Sasha or give her a cuddle. When I was small and had some anxieties around going to sleep Mum would tell me to picture something that made me feel calm. After I got Sasha, it was the thought of her that soothed me and as I got older I knew her face so well I came to rely on it as a calming mechanism. There are many studies that show dogs can reduce anxiety and even today I can still picture her when I go to sleep.

Sasha has her own hero dog story. Mum and I hand-reared two cockatiels in Cairns and one or the other would sit on my shoulder when I was doing my homework. When we were home the cage would be left open and the cockatiels would just hang out around the house. One day one went missing and the other one went nuts. We looked everywhere and Sasha started barking and digging at the filter at the corner of the swimming pool.

Sasha would find me in the lower cabins through the hatches; she was always looking for a smooch

Because we were so engrossed in our search we ignored her at first until we realised she was trying to tell us something. We took the lid off the pool filter and there was the cockatiel, still alive, although it probably had aspiration pneumonia. The bird had flown into the pool and had been sucked into the filter. It lived and my little Sasha saved it.

In my younger years if you asked me what I wanted to do when I left school I would have said a dog trainer or zoo keeper. Dad said I could be a vet, but I didn't know exactly what a vet did! So, while still in primary school I volunteered to help out at the Kuranda veterinary clinic and from then on I knew it was exactly what I wanted to do. I did further work experience, during high school holidays, at another local vet clinic in Cairns.

Dad was a natural educator. Everything was a lesson in medicine or science. He said if I liked animals I needed to learn about animals. If I told him that Sasha was itchy he would not only tell me it was dermatitis but would break it down – 'derm' means skin and 'itis' means inflammation — so from a young age I understood and used the correct term for things.

Veterinary science is a five-year course, but I didn't get in straight away so I did a year of general science first– human and animal biology at Queensland University in Brisbane. I was only 17 when I moved to Brisbane and initially I lived in a share house with a friend from school and my boyfriend; Sasha stayed with Mum in Cairns and it was the first time I had been separated from Sasha since she was a puppy and eight years is a long time in a dog's life.

Vet school was huge – not just the number of students but the sheer size of the campus. Everything was big; think about the size of a table you need to dissect a horse! Vet school was also a shock to the system, both academically and emotionally. Students are animal lovers with a rosy outlook about life as a vet; they go in wanting to make a difference to the lives of animals but for most the reality of learning how to care for sick animals was a slow desensitising process.

Before my years at vet school I had never seen so much death – it was a real baptism of fire. While I was inspired to become a vet by my emotional connection with Sasha, my love of one dog actually extends to all dogs, in fact all animals and nature. This is known as biophilia – a love of life and all living systems and made some aspects of studying veterinary science challenging.

V eterinary science students study all species, but the more common animals such as dogs, cats, horses and cows are studied in more detail. The anatomy physiology, structure and function of mammals is basically the same and shared across the mammal species – from cats to dogs to horses to humans. The dog is generally the animal that is studied in great detail first as it's the most common patient for the majority of vets. After the dog the student moves on to other species and learns the differences. For example, because cats don't eat plant material, they have a different dentition and gastric mucosa to dogs and shorter intestines while bovines have an entirely different digestive system to either of them. By studying dogs first, students understand how each body system works and are able to compare the various characteristics of each species.

Regardless of what sort of vet you want to be, you still have to study every animal and when it came to farm animals, we had to spend three-week stints on different types of rural properties. While I recognised the necessity for a vet to have a broad knowledge of animal husbandry, I had only ever wanted to be a dog and cat vet and found those group farm stays a bit of a trial. When it came to the cattle work practicum I chose dairy rather than beef. Our group of four slept in bunks in the staff quarters and had to get up at 3am to do the milking which one of my friends took to with relish. But as I didn't want to be a bovine vet I spent a lot of time with the farm's dogs.

The wife of the couple who owned the farm-bred chocolate Labradors, a very trendy dog at the time. One of our jobs after the early milking was to spend the morning cleaning, grooming and feeding this woman's dogs. Among the litter was a runty little sick puppy which was not getting enough food because it was being pushed out by the rest of the litter. While I was doing the feeds, I grew to love and protect this little dog. I asked the owner what she planned to do with it. She said she was never going to get any money for it, so Ralph will have it.

Ralph was a farm worker who lived next door and gave off bad vibes. I didn't want Ralph to have it.

'Do you want it?' she asked me. My heart was going 'I want it' but my head was saying 'you can't have a dog, don't be ridiculous'. I wasn't in position to have a dog, but I knew she would give it to me if I said yes.

The day we loaded up the car to leave and were saying our goodbyes, the breeder approached the car with the puppy.

'I'm surprised this little dog is not in the car with you,' she said.

'I really want to take it, but I can't.'

'She's going to have a much better life with you; if you want to give her a chance, take it,' she said holding it out towards me.

'Okay. Quick,' I said, snatching the puppy into the car before we drove off. Not only had I not prepared my boyfriend for dog ownership – I was returning with a diseased pure-bred puppy grabbed on impulse. By then I had been a vet student for three years and I knew I was getting myself into something most people wouldn't know about. This was not the way you choose a dog.

I called her Java; she was gorgeous, but she was never a well dog. She had terrible hip dysplasia and other problems and by taking her I gave her a chance at life that she probably would not have had otherwise. Nevertheless, I was young and wanted to travel as a vet after I graduated and couldn't bear to think what I would do with Java when it came time to leave so I put those thoughts aside.

Not long before I graduated, I was required to do some work experience in a veterinary clinic and I chose the one in Malanda in the Tablelands not far from Kuranda. While I was there my darling Sasha died of congestive heart failure. She was 13 by then and I was lucky to have a week with her before she died; Mum said Sasha had waited until I came back so I could say good-bye and be there to bury her. I was devastated and cried my eyes out. My dad still lived in the old Bali eco-house where we had first brought Sasha home and I went up there and walked down to the Barron River where I sat and thought about the joy she had brought to my life. Mum and I said a little prayer and buried Sasha on the block where Mum still lives today.

Java on her bed outside my bedroom door during my university days.

By the time I graduated I was burnt out – I had only ever wanted to be a small animal practitioner and it was a long and tiring mission through a wide spectrum of animals to get there. Some things were horrific; one practicum involved a stint at the abattoirs. My friend and I happily made our way in totally unprepared for what confronted us: a dead horse hanging from several large hooks in its spine being skinned in preparation for us to study its musculoskeletal system. We had to wear big boots to keep our feet out of the blood and flushing water; my friend who was a serious horse person burst into tears and started vomiting.

Not all students lasted the distance; many dropped out over the years and a lot became vegetarians. I wanted to get away as soon as possible and just be a dog and cat vet. First, I had to re-home my own dog Java, and Toby, a tabby cat I had fostered and ended up adopting. It was a heart-wrenching process and when I think about it now it still upsets me. I did find them a good home where the people adopted them together but leaving them tore me apart.

After I broke up with my boyfriend I had moved in with a Zimbabwean student for a couple of years. She invited me to go back to Africa with her for a month after we graduated. Africa was a place I had fantasised about since I was a child; I imagined being free in this natural environment surrounded by native animals. I had read about the animals and fell in love with Jane Goodall and her wild chimpanzees in Tanzania from documentaries. I was the only one in my class who didn't wait around for the graduation ceremony, a decision that astounded my family; they couldn't believe that after six years of hard work I had no desire to don the cap and gown. I just wanted to get out of there. Africa beckoned.

Africa was wonderful and my friend introduced me to lots of welcoming people in Zimbabwe. When you are a young vet in Africa everyone wants to take you under their wing and I went under lots of wings. There seemed to be never-ending invitations to see wildlife; people would say 'Get in the truck and let me take you out to see the rhinos' – or hippos or lions or whatever. I said yes to everything and saw some amazing things. It was fun and exciting, and I just kept on extending – one more safari, one more safari. I knew when I went back to Australia I would have to join the real world and get a job.

After three months I returned to Cairns and moved in with Mum. One of the things I had been thinking carefully about since I finished vet school was getting a job in a small animal hospital in London. Every small animal vet who lectured us at university told us to go and do the UK thing because their veterinary medicine was very advanced, and it would be a valuable experience as it was quite different to working as an Australian vet. But first I had to replenish my savings after my African adventure, and my first job where I was able to practice what I'd learnt and get paid for it was at the same vet clinic where I had done work experience in high school.

About a year later, I was sitting on the Cairns Marina looking out over the panoramic views of the ocean and mountains when a handsome man entered my view and asked me if I wanted a drink. His name was Christian, a South African marine engineer working on a luxury yacht that was in port for some repairs. This was how I unexpectedly met my future husband and changed my immediate plans.

Shortly after meeting Christian, I temporarily shelved going to London in favour of travelling back to Africa with him. We were staying in a small town on the Garden Route of South Africa near where his family lived and I heard that once a month the town's vet headed out to the local villages or townships, where the very poor live, to treat the local animals. Eager to seize any veterinary opportunity that came my way I volunteered my services. The experience was both exciting and confronting.

The consultations were carried out in a local hall provided for the vet's use. People came from far and wide with their animals; quite a crowd gathered outside the hall, but some were there just to watch out of curiosity. These were very poor mainly rural Africans and I was stunned by the array of bizarre containers in which they transported their sick animals to us; one woman brought in an injured dog wrapped in a kanga (African sarong) inside an old tyre – I unwrapped the kanga not sure what I might find. All the animals were malnourished and unkempt and I was never sure if they were strays or pets or a bit of both.

Most of the many hours of work we did involved desexing and stitching up wounds all done in the most unsanitary conditions using a mish-mash of donated and second hand supplies and surgical equipment.

The correct position to spay a dog is on their backs and I would normally have used a specially-made cradle; here the locals created a v-shaped cradle from a couple of towel rails and a wooden block. It was an ingenious contraption made out of necessity from scraps and the beginning of my naive 23-year-old's realisation of the sheltered, privileged white life I had led. How lucky I was to be Australian.

After Africa I went to work in London and Christian went back to working on the yachts in the Mediterranean. Working at a vet hospital in London was a totally different experience to working in one in Australia. Most people have pet insurance in the UK which opens opportunities for a lot more advanced surgical procedures on a daily basis whereas less than 50 per cent of

Australian pet owners have pet insurance which means a vet is often doing the most affordable treatment or euthanising the animal if the owner cannot afford an expensive operation.

Another point of difference was the training of vet nurses; their education requirements are very high. The nurses carry out a range of things a vet would normally do in Australia such as placing urinary catheters, applying dressings and bandages and some even do wound stitch-ups; this enabled the vet to focus on the more advanced procedures. At the hospital where I worked there were seven vets on duty at the one time and the waiting room brimmed with cats, dogs, birds, ferrets, rabbits and various reptiles. It was often bedlam.

My stint in London was a fabulous experience; it was also the first time I was bitten by a dog. It was a Rottweiler. They're lovely dogs but I find them a bit hard to read. The dog was not meant to be my patient, but its own vet was called away urgently and so the nurse asked me to take over. She said it had been health checked, just needed its vaccination – she didn't mention anything

The positioning cradles we made from towel rails – in the local hall where we set up our makeshift surgery

about it being aggressive. So I quickly walked in, picked up the needle and approached the dog assuming it would be friendly. But the dog obviously saw me as a stranger rushing in and grabbing a needle. As it attacked me, I fell back and the nurse managed to get him off me before he did any major damage. My hand bled a bit and didn't need stitches, but it was a scary experience. It was a lesson for an inexperienced vet about keeping the radar switched on at all times.

Christian visited me regularly in London and it was a good life but after three years I knew it was time to return to Australia and move to the next phase in my career. I bypassed Cairns

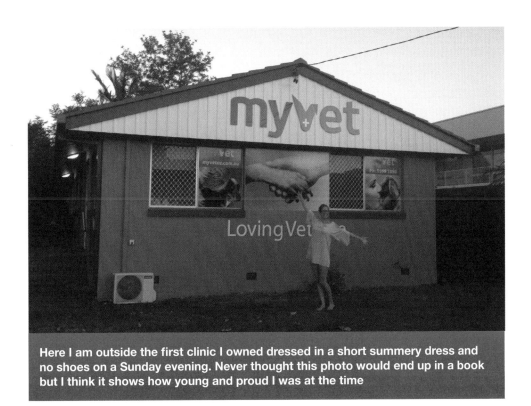

Here I am outside the first clinic I owned dressed in a short summery dress and no shoes on a Sunday evening. Never thought this photo would end up in a book but I think it shows how young and proud I was at the time

as a place to base myself and headed for the Gold Coast where I had friends from vet school. There I was introduced to established veterinarian Geoff Wilson, a meeting that was to become a turning point in my career. I had gone to London as a new graduate with not a lot of confidence, but I had come back a good vet, really energetic, with the high practice standards that had been drummed into me.

At first I worked for Geoff and within six months he offered me a partnership in his clinic, which became very successful. He also taught me about running a business and we ended up owning three clinics together.

When Christian and I got married my mother made a memorable speech. She told the assembled guests that when I was a little girl I had advised her that I wanted to be 'rich vet' – apparently I saw myself as exceedingly wealthy driving myself to work in a red convertible with a beautiful Golden Retriever sitting next to me in the front seat (must have been some movie image). I was going to cuddle animals and save lives all day. It caused much laughter at the reception, but the fact is that many people do have this romanticised idea of a vet's life and that was mine too.

Contrary to the perception that vets must be 'rolling in it' you'd be hard pushed to see the average vet driving around in an expensive convertible – more likely a battered four-wheel drive with a mixed breed mutt or two in the back. However, the life of a vet is not without its rewards – making good medical decisions and alleviating suffering is what we are trained to do and is immensely satisfying. For me the real pleasure comes from helping people understand the needs of animals and showing them how to be advocates for their much-loved pets who do not have a voice of their own.

Writing this book has been a way for me to pass on to other dog lovers the many things I have learnt as a vet from our four-legged friends. Love Your Dog was initially inspired by the deep connection I had with Sasha from the day I brought her home as a puppy. This canine connection was especially important to me as a child; today I am still fascinated by this human-animal bond which I see as stronger than ever as dog ownership has steadily increased over the years and people begin to appreciate the meaning of having a dog in their lives.

I hope *Love your Dog* will help you to better understand and communicate with your dog, further strengthening the incredible bond that you already share together.

CHAPTER 1

The Modern Dog

Domestication of the dog

The mysterious history of the dog has been revealed primarily through archaeological research. The evidence of pre-historic dog-like creatures traces the evolution of the dog back millions of years. In fact, the transition of the wolf into the dog probably began about 100,000 years ago while the domestication of the dog could have started anywhere between 15,000 and 30,000 years ago. Guy Hull in his book The Dogs that Made Australia cites an international study of canine DNA in 2009 which concluded that the taming of the she-wolf began about 16,000 years ago with the world's first dog emerging from an Eurasian canid in central China which became extinct about 100,000 years ago.

The domestic Asian dog population spread throughout the world over the next several thousand years as they accompanied Neolithic people on their travels beyond mainland Asia. Guy Hull believes the creation of the Asian dog from the wild wolf was the greatest investment prehistoric man ever made. As it made its way south, the Asian dog's herding and hunting abilities would have been an indispensable aid to the people colonising the Southeast Asian archipelagos. Through island hopping with its sea-going Chinese explorers the dog is thought to have finally reached Australia around 4,000 years ago, more than 55,000 years after the first Aboriginal people arrived.

Although not highly domesticated by today's standards, the first Asian dogs to arrive in Australia were nevertheless not wild either. The indigenous people may have thought they were related to the native carnivorous thylacine or Tasmanian Devil. However, unlike the thylacines and Devils, they did not fear and avoid humans although they maintained an air of independence. In the early days they would have had to scavenge for much of their food and as the population grew and they adapted to the harsh Australia environment, they grew into the wild canine we know as the dingo, but which still came and went among the indigenous people.

England was a nation that created many of the original dog breeds that we know today by other names and a variety of these dogs arrived in Australia with the First and subsequent Fleets. The dogs were mostly the companion animals of officers and they were breeds such as terriers and early Greyhounds. As it became apparent that the growing colony needed sheep-guarding and hunting dogs, working breeds were brought in such as Newfoundlands and the Scottish Deerhound. The Deerhound was later cross bred with the Greyhound to make a dog with both speed and stamina to kill kangaroos, which came to be known as the kangaroo dog and for the next hundred years or so was a very useful animal for the farming colonialists. It eventually fell into disrepute due to the nature of its work and a reputation for aggressiveness and disappeared from the urban landscape.

As more British domestic dogs arrived and bred and interbred without restraint during the early years of New South Wales colonisation, there was little way of controlling them; the number of pet dogs increased to such an extent that they became a bit of an unruly menace and many bred with dingoes and became feral packs. By the end of the nineteenth century, better standards of living enabled Australians to devote more time to their pet dogs. Thus, began Australian's love affair with dogs, which continues to this day. Like our British ancestors, we became dog mad and started importing various dog breeds from all over the world and crossbreeding them for certain looks and traits. The human-canine bond has blossomed and strengthened down the years.

Probably the most obvious thing dogs give us is companionship and devotion. They help us relax and keep us active. But dogs love to have a job and they will happily work for humans in many ways: as service dogs for the police and military, as search and rescue dogs, as guide dogs and guard dogs, as cattle dogs and as therapy dogs. In return dogs will thrive through our love and care; we provide food, shelter, health care and exercise. It's a win-win arrangement.

Australian Dingo in the wild

Guy Hull believes that way back when the first wolves decided to align themselves with humans, both parties had an unspoken agreement: 'The wolf agreed to become a dog and help humans dominate nature. But in return the people had to provide it with food, water, shelter, care, control and, most importantly, a job'. Over thousands of years, the evolution of this 'agreement' crystallised into the modern dog's bond with humans. I think Guy might be on to something.

Learning from a dog's philosophy

It is a recognised fact that dogs can improve our health and mental wellbeing – every day I see examples of how dogs have saved or changed lives. Dogs offer a loyal companionship like no other; when every other aspect of our lives seems to be falling apart, we can count on our dog. I regularly see dogs helping people get through tragic and difficult times. I find that the love shared between dogs and the elderly, the blind, the disabled and children particularly profound.

Dogs help us focus on the needs of something other than ourselves; they teach us empathy. Caring for your dog draws you away from your problems. When we see their little expressions and non-verbal cues, we think about what they might need and how we can help them – thinking about others is the best way to get yourself out of a rut.

Kindness is an energetic currency with a ripple effect. The more kindness we give out, the more kindness we experience and the more kindness there is in the world. When we do something out of kindness, such as loving and caring for a dog, it releases oxytocin, the happy hormone. It makes us feel good and improves our health. Sometimes it's all we need to pick ourselves up after a knock.

Dogs can inspire us to be better people. You can become the type of person the dog already thinks you are by adopting some dog traits – loyalty, dependability, kindness and wisdom. Yes, dogs are wise; the wisdom of a dog is medicine for the soul. Oscar's Wilde's famous quote 'Life is too important to be taken seriously' could easily have been said by a dog.

Since becoming a vet I've come to understand that dogs have a simple but cheerful way of looking at the world. It's what I call a dog's philosophy – a life that revolves around lots of good things – eating, sleeping, love and affection, running and playing, smiling and really just living in the moment. Imagine living a happy dog's day?

Dogs are amazing teachers and can show us a lot more than any of the aforementioned dog philosophies. I'd like to take you through a few.

Dogs show gratitude. Over and over I see and hear stories of rescue dogs that show their owners such a huge amount of love and gratitude that they feel like the rescued ones. Dogs are great at saying thank-you, even for the smallest gift. Humans tend to look to the future, waiting for something better to come along – we think 'If I just had that then I'd be happy.' Acknowledging life's every little miracle, like dogs do, is a good lesson to learn.

Good morning! What a wonderful day it is! Yummo; time for breakfast. I love this food – eating is the best, so is sleeping; I'm going to have a sleep soon, over there in that spot in the sun. But first, can I have a good scratch? Please give me a scratch! That feels good – maybe we should go for a run now. I love running! Fresh air smells so good and the wind – isn't it lovely? I love being outdoors with you – thanks for being my leader. Oh, do you want to play with those kids over there. I love kids. Right now is the greatest moment ever, don't you think? I do.

Dogs live in the now. Humans exist in the present, attached to the past and intent on controlling the future. Dogs on the other hand, are not thinking about something they could have done better yesterday or what the weather might be tomorrow, they only care about the relationship they have with us in the now. They only care if you are going to take them for a walk now; promising to take them for a walk tomorrow means nothing today. We can learn a lot about living in the now. Each day could be the last so don't waste time with unimportant things; make everyday matter and channel your intentions and attitudes from your heart.

Dogs don't have egos. Your dog doesn't care if his dog bed is more expensive than the neighbours' dog bed or if their collar is encrusted with jewels. They only care if you spend time with them. At the end of the day, love is all that matters, and the best memories are the ones we share with people or animals we love!

Dogs have no concept of planning. A dog would never contemplate getting through a list of chores before getting out and enjoying life. A dog's life embraces the joy of living regardless of time. Life passes us by when we are not paying attention; make the most of the time you have now because you can't control it and what you lose you can never get back.

Dogs don't hold back their love. A dog won't wait until it is sure you love it. He will just bound in and go for it regardless, tail wagging optimistically. Love is the basis of loss and grief. The more love you give the more loss you will feel but this shouldn't stop you from loving in the first place. People often hold back their love out of fear of getting hurt; this concept is completely foreign to a dog. The loss may be profound but only because the love was.

Dogs are vulnerable. Dogs can be hurt, ignored and even neglected and yet still roll over when offered a tummy rub or a scratch behind the ear. Vulnerability brings more love – being vulnerable enables us to receive more love.

Dogs will share your sadness. A dog will sit close while you cry; they will be present with you and their quiet presence is the sort of therapy money can't buy. During the unsettling events in my childhood Sasha would just sit with me. Dogs can show you how to be with others when they are sad. If you don't know what to say, say nothing; if you do know what to say, still say nothing. Being open to sadness is human. It helps you feel the love that surrounds you. Dogs seem to be intuitive – they sense when we are low and comfort us in a way that we need, snuggling up or giving us a gentle nudge, that says, 'It's okay that you're not okay. I love you'.

Dogs accept loss. Dogs mourn loss too, but they don't get stuck in their grief. Dogs that lose their owners to death or through other circumstances that removes them from their lives will miss them but will happily transfer their love and devotion when rescued by a new owner. Mourning a lost future stops us from acceptance and appreciating what we have – love and memories.

Dogs have no self-judgement. Dogs are very good at looking after their emotions when they need to; they retreat and curl up when they need to self-soothe. They have no need to beat themselves up over something they regret they did – just a good snuggle up is good enough. Dogs are accepting, they allow us to be as we are, even when we are not at our best; there is no judgement, just love. The lesson we can learn from this is that we too can self-soothe by having compassion and practicing forgiveness for ourselves.

CHAPTER 2

How Dogs Perceive the World

We live in a 21st century world full of technological development; as humans we can understand and rationalise the constant changes going on around us but what do dogs make of all those sights and sounds? As dogs can't rationalise between cause and effect of all our modern contraptions it must seem like 'magic'.

In his book 'A Modern Dog's life' veterinary animal behaviourist Professor Paul McGreevy refers to all the modern boundaries and surfaces a dog must negotiate such as polished floors, electric fences and even elevators. 'Stairs, especially those with open spaces between steps, can take a bit of getting used to. Then there are lifts that must feel, to a dog, like earth tremors as they come to rest.'

A dog must surely think it was pretty weird to go into a lift and exit through the same door to be confronted by an entirely different set of stimuli.

Different doors also present challenges – there are ones that open quietly, slam shut with the wind or even slide into a wall. And what do they make of glass doors they can see through and mesh fly screens they can not only see through but possibly smell through as well? Then there are all those mysteriously differently shaped door handles which humans use to somehow make the door open. I have known crafty dogs that through trial and error have learnt how to unravel the mystery of opening a door.

In the early 20th century when dogs on the streets were not required to be on a leash and cars were a bit of a noisy novelty, they would often chase them. Today they probably still appear as a type of noisy box but one where they get in at one place and emerge at an entirely different place, often at a park or beach where they can run around and explore new smells – very exciting. Many dogs love going for a jaunt in the car and it can be even more exciting for dogs large enough to see out the window and gaze at things flashing past – trees, walking humans, other dogs, and other noisy boxes.

In my introduction I wrote about what was the greatest car ride of my life – the day we brought Sasha home from the breeder. She was only eight weeks old but never made a whimper. I think she enjoyed travelling in cars from then on. I like to think her love of riding in cars was linked to her attachment to me as she rode home with me that day as a puppy. In Chapter 14, I cover everything you need to know about travelling with and transporting dogs.

Dogs learn to recognise differences between one car and another by associating it with recognisable humans. Or even the job of the recognisable human – we have all heard stories about the wayward dog who avoids the ranger's van. Professor McGreevy writes that it's intriguing how dogs can attach importance to the cars that important humans depart in rather than arrive in. 'It's almost as if they can make an association between the noise the car makes once the significant human is inside it. The alternative is that they make the association retrospectively after that significant human has emerged from it.' But McGreevy says this would require the dog to log all the sounds of all of the cars just in case a significant human emerged from one of them – a taxing and time-wasting occupation. This skill is fascinating because it implies evolution has assisted dogs to in associating a particular noise with a disappearing member of the pack.

So how do dogs make sense of the world around them? Dogs have the same five senses as humans, and they use these senses to make sense of the world. However, some of these senses are more highly developed in dogs, while others are not as developed compared with those of humans. Let's take a closer look at your dog's five senses and see how these impact the way he perceives and interacts with the world around him.

Smell

The power of a dog's sense of smell should not be underestimated. It is their primary sense and has been tested at being up to 100,000 stronger than a human's sense of smell, but it could actually be even ten times more than that.

The millions of scent receptors in a dog's nose enable it to sniff out and identify an endless range of odours. The vomeronasal organ — a long pouch-like structure which sits unseen in the roof of the dog's mouth, behind the upper incisors — plays an integral

A dog's nose is its primary sense

part in the way dogs analyse smell. Its main role is to detect chemical messages, known as pheromones, deliberately left behind by other dogs for mating or other social purposes. The cells that detect these pheromones relay them to the dog's amygdala and hypothalamus the parts of a dog's brain responsible for emotion and behaviour. Urine is full of pheromones which is why dogs spend so much time sniffing the urine of other dogs and marking it with their own.

SCENT MARKING

This is instinctual behaviour and there's so much to say about it that I could write a whole chapter on it and call it the Pee-mail Chapter. The dog's instinct is to mark his territory or to leave a message for other dogs, yet despite the fact that I am not a dog, I have had many, many dogs cock their leg in the consulting room and wee on my leg leaving me to smell of dog piss for the rest of the day. They also scent mark on my computer leads, in the waiting room and on the nurses – in fact throughout whole building.

When they wee on me the embarrassment of the owners can be profoundly funny; while I'm assuring them that it's okay and 'no problem at all', they just don't know what to do, where to look and how to continue. It's usually the first thing the dog does to introduce himself and we have to get through the rest of the consultation. Intact (non-de-sexed) males are the worst offenders; testosterone informs the male brain to tell the female dogs of the world that they are sexually available and to claim their territory.

Dogs can get a lot of information about other dogs who have peed in one spot including how many dogs were there and how long ago, the gender of the dog, if they have been de-sexed, state of their health and even their stress levels. A dog can determine if a bitch is on heat by the smell of her urine. Intact dogs and those with higher social status are more likely to pee over another dog's scent; female dogs tend to leave their message nearby as opposed to marking over another dog's pee-mail. Dogs low in the pecking order sniff but are less likely to pee over another dog's mark although little dogs often have a 'stuff you' attitude and will try as hard as they can to stretch up to over pee.

While urine is the most common form of scent marking, dogs also use faeces to leave a message; without being able to 'read' the message humans don't know exactly what it says but it may just be to show what the other dog had for dinner. Faeces themselves do not contain pheromones but they are smeared with it by the dog's anal glands as the dog defecates. These anal sacs expel a powerful stomach-churning, foul odour. Dogs can also use their anal glands to express fear which may also alert other dogs to danger. I have had many a dog 'express fear' in my consulting room too. Phew, vets are not overly fond of this smell – it can hit you like a ton of bricks!

BOTTOM SNIFFING

Dogs love walks because walks not only mean smells but the opportunity to interact with other dogs where more sniffing takes place. When your dog meets another dog, your dog will have a role – as either the sniffer or the sniffed. Sniffing each other's bottoms is a dog's version of a handshake. The hormones excreted by the glands surrounding their genitalia offer a lot of important information about the dog – such as its diet, gender and emotional state.

The sniffed will usually have its ears pinned back while the sniffer starts communication beginning at the rear – the sniffed is in a vulnerable position and alert for any signs of trouble so he can move quickly away. Dogs with higher status can move out of the sniffed role to the sniffer role at the speed of light. The challenge for two dogs on first encounter is negotiating how the roles are changed. Moving too fast from one to the other can bring on some aggressive or bullying behaviour which may include biting. By observing the body language of both dogs, you will understand what's going on and by using the three-second 'hello' rule you can usually keep everyone safe and happy. The rule goes like this: count in your head 'One sniff, two sniffs, three sniffs and go...' and if either dog looks wary go sooner.

Two dogs sniffing each other's' bottoms is a necessary and informative ritual no matter what we humans might think about it; to not allow your dog to do this is denying him his instinctive behaviour. If you are ever tempted to stop your dog from greeting another dog with a bottom sniff, please remember that it could create undue stress and anxiety when he meets other dogs in the future.

DETECTING CHANGES

When we think about detector dogs we tend to think of the ones that sniff our bags at airports but these specially-trained dogs are also used in a range of other detector roles such as tracking missing people, searching for buried bodies and detecting mines and booby traps during wars. And we now know that a dog's sense of smell can even detect cancer. They have the impressive ability to pick up disease by sniffing the distinctive chemicals produced by cancer cells in the human skin and urine in bladder cancer and even on the breath of sufferers of breast and lung cancers. If you have a cut somewhere your dog can smell it, even through your clothes.

Dogs can even detect an oncoming seizure in people suffering from epilepsy. They do this by exhibiting attention-getting behaviour such as pawing, whining or anxious barking up to 12 hours before the episode. Dogs have also been known to alert someone to an approaching heart attack by using the same anxious behaviour. How they do this is a mystery. These dogs, which appear to be neither age nor gender specific, appear to be born with this remarkable ability – it can be taught but takes years of vigorous training before a therapy dog can be homed with a seizure patient. Some researchers and trainers believe the dog can detect or smell subtle changes in a person's behaviour or their sweat prior to an episode but so far these theories have not been proved.

> **SMELLY FEELINGS**
>
> *Your dog can smell your feelings by picking up subtle changes in your scent. By smelling your perspiration your dog will know if you are nervous or fearful.*
>
>

And just as we can smell changes in the air when it rains, so can dogs, but they know the weather is changing long before we do. People with storm phobic dogs tell me they start to pace and get anxious before the owner is even aware one is on its way. While these amazing abilities are mainly linked to a dog's superior smell, they are probably all the canine senses working together.

Both my dogs paired their incredible sense of smell with their ferocious appetites, digging and nose-diving into every crack and crevice, looking under beds, down the back of couches and into cupboards, all for a minuscule crumb that would be barely visible to most humans.

WET NOSES

A dog with a wet nose can smell even more effectively than a dry one and a wet nose also cools your dog down on hot days, similar to the way panting helps regulate their body temperature by evaporation.

There is a common myth is that dog is sick if he has a dry nose, but this is not necessarily the case. There are plenty of healthy dogs that have a dry warm nose, and plenty of sick dogs with wet noses, so a dry nose can't be used as a reliable indicator of a dog's health and wellbeing.

There are four common reasons why your dog's nose might be dry.

1 **Your dog was napping.** Sleeping dogs don't usually lick their noses, so they may wake up with warm dry noses.

2 **Dehydration from illness or exercise.** Strenuous exercise is dehydrating, which can lead to a dry nose.

3 **Exposure to the elements.** Exposure to sunlight, wind, or cold can dry your dog's nose, and, in some cases, may result in chapped or sunburned snouts. Lying next to a source of heat, like a fire or a heater, can also cause dry skin on your dog's nose. Protecting dogs that are susceptible to sunburn is important because repeated sunburn can lead to skin cancer; white haired dogs with pink noses are most susceptible. Get advice from your vet about what sort of sun cream lotion to use on your dog.

4 **Age.** Some dogs develop dry noses with age. A hot, dry nose doesn't always mean trouble, but it can certainly be a sign of fever, dehydration, or even conditions like dry eye. If your dog's dry nose is accompanied by other symptoms, like lethargy, vomiting or diarrhoea, or changes in activity or appetite, contact your vet for advice. Looking and touching your dog's gums and noting their colour can give a lot more accurate information about his health and hydration than his nose. If gums are moist, that's a sign of good hydration. If they're very dry, or tacky, it could be a sign of dehydration. If gums are a nice pink, like yours, it's a good sign. Pale or whitish gums could be an indication of anaemia or low blood pressure. If your dog has pale pink-white, bright red or bluish gums, he should be examined by a vet right away.

Vision

A dog does not reach visual maturity until it is about four months old. Put a puppy in front of a mirror and watch its reaction. The puppy runs towards it and performs all sorts of antics in front of it but the puppy behind the mirror never comes out to play. As the dog in the mirror becomes older and seems permanently trapped, the two become less interested in each other until they finally give in and ignore each other completely.

A dog's sight is not as good as ours, but it can see shapes in considerable detail. Recent studies have dispelled the myth that dogs are colour blind, but rather they have dichromatic colour perception. Unlike humans who have three different colour sensitive cone cells in their retina (red, green and blue) dogs have only two (yellow and blue). This means that dogs cannot distinguish green, yellow or red objects based on their colour. They are better at identifying different shades of grey than humans and see much better at night than we do.

An intense stare

Is television a mystery for the modern dog? Humans sit and watch it engrossingly – but what about dogs? How much interest a dog takes in television probably depends on the dog's personality, but all dogs can and do respond to onscreen images and sounds and some dogs love it! DOGTV is an American high definition cable channel designed for dogs and according to the channel, it captures the attention of canines because it has a much higher number of frames per second and is specially coloured to accommodate dogs' dichromatic vision. In the UK, a pet food manufacturer used a high frequency noise only detected by dogs in its TV dog food advertisements; a bunch of dogs were filmed sitting around in front of the TV engrossingly watching the advertisement. Anthropomorphism at its best!

Sound

Puppies are born deaf, but their hearing quickly surpasses our hearing abilities. Dogs can hear higher pitched sounds detecting a frequency range of 67 to 45,000 KHz (cycles per second) which is more than twice that of humans at between 64 to 23,000 KHz. Before domestication, such acute hearing was most likely used to catch small prey such as rats and mice which communicate through high-frequency sounds. But dogs are also sensitive to loud noises, such as fireworks. Huge numbers of dogs hide or run away after becoming seriously distressed with our New Year's Eve fireworks. Dogs can also get stressed with thunder, especially loud thunderclaps.

The varying sizes and shapes of the ears of different dog breeds can affect their ability to detect sound. Some dogs are born clinically deaf, especially those with hypopigmentation which is particularly common with merle-patterned coats – mottled patches of different colours and patterns. Congenitally deaf dogs can be trained to obey signals. I recommend that once a normal hearing dog has been trained in the response to a single verbal signal that is also trained to respond to a visual cue as well. This will help if the dog loses its hearing when it gets old. The upper range of hearing decreases with age in both dogs and humans but there are no hearing aids for dogs.

Sometimes when I'm home alone at night I get a little anxious but I was never worried during my share house days at vet school when Java was in my life because I knew she would be up in flash if there was even the softest sound at the door or window.

Boston Terrier

Touch

Most dogs love being touched, and it has been documented that, like humans, the more touching they receive as pups the more they thrive. In fact, both Sasha and Java went the extra mile in the affection department which I didn't mind at all. My children and fur babies are my number one source for cuddles.

Dogs have little hairs called vibrissae that sense touch, and these hairs are located above their eyes, on their muzzle and under their chins. In fact, their whole body is covered with touch sensitive nerve endings, but despite this, both my dogs were clumsy clots. Because Java was born a runt with deformed hips, she became over-excited when she spied anyone she thought would give her love and forgot to factor in her hip problem before making her way over to show her love. And I don't know Sasha's excuse for clumsiness; it is said that our pets mirror their owners and my friends tell me I lack coordination so maybe I'm the problem?

Apart from a few, mostly rare, breeds of hairless dogs, most dogs have a layer of hair to protect their skin. The length of hair varies between the short-haired and long-haired breeds, but each is protected to some extent from wind, cold and rain by their fur buffer. Clipping a dog's fur can not only change a dog's appearance, if it is done correctly (and with care) it can sometimes result in a marked difference in a dog's behaviour. I have seen newly-clipped dogs frolicking, spinning and racing about like loons. I'm not quite sure why some dogs act like that – maybe it makes them feel light and free, especially during the warmer months. We call it the 'post groom zoom'.

How a dog reacts to professional grooming is probably more likely to be related to the age the dog is introduced to the grooming experience and how gentle the groomer is with young dogs as they need to get used to the clippers and the noise of the hairdryer. Dogs forced to be clipped or that get nipped during the process will never forget it. It can be a pretty stressful experience so if it's not done correctly in the beginning using positive reinforcement it's natural for them to become fearful.

The thick leathery footpads and nose tip are designed to be tough and resilient. The leather cover on the nose tip helps prevent injuries during fighting and protects it during intense ground sniffing. A dog's foot pads are much tougher than the soles of our feet as they have to withstand a variety of surfaces that could damage them. During summer when temperatures in some regions reach heat wave proportions dog owners should consider their dog's paws when walking them over searing hot paths, roads and even sand.

SEEN BY A WHISKER

Your dog's whiskers help him 'see' in the dark. Okay, it's not quite night vision but the whiskers pick up even subtle changes in air currents providing The dog with information about the size, shape and speed of nearby things. This gives the dog a better sense of approaching dangers or prey.

Taste

The average dog consumes food with such speed that it's hardly likely to come into contact with the range of taste buds on the tongue. Dogs, bless their hearts, will wolf down the most disgusting things. A human won't eat something if it smells bad but for a dog, the smellier the better. Sasha's favourite munch was road kill; fortunately, she only rolled around on the dried up dead cane toads — of which there were hundreds where I was growing up in Far North Queensland – because cane toads are toxic to dogs. Loving her as much as I did, I managed to overlook the fact that she smelt like the rotting carcass she'd been rolling in or snacking on and continued to let her lick me every day. It was little wonder that my father said that dogs smelt!

Apart from eating smelly things that seem totally gross to us, dogs can also ingest things that don't appear to have any smell or dietary appeal whatsoever. It's not unusual to see a dog eating grass but the range of objects vets find in the stomachs of dogs is extraordinary: cotton reels, socks, underwear, corn cobs, fishhooks, and even mobile phones. I have also removed a g-string, a tampon, chewed up plastic toys, a fishing line sinker, even wire! I once removed pieces of a pink plastic toy from a Labrador's intestines – Labs are the worst, they eat everything. Sharp objects, such as sticks, bones, wire and glass, can threaten a dog's life by perforating its stomach and cause blockages.

As if all this isn't bad enough, a very nasty situation can arise when the foreign body the dog eats is a string or of similar linear structure. Imagine a pair of drawstring pants or drawstring bag and tie a knot in one end of the drawstring so that it cannot move and pull on the other end. You will see that the fabric wads up along the string channel. If the string is pulled hard enough and the knot still will not budge, the string will actually rip right through the string channel. Now imagine this linear foreign body scenario in a dog; the foreign body lodges somewhere in the gastrointestinal (GI) tract and will not move. The strings, however, dangle forward in the GI tract like a drawstring; the intestine attempts to move them forward but because the foreign body is lodged, the bowel ends up inching up the strings similar to the drawstring on the pants. This type of folding is called 'plication' and if the foreign body is not removed, the strings will cut through the intestine leading to life-threatening peritonitis.

No-one knows why dogs eat — well, mostly swallow — these indigestible items. Could it be the item smells deliciously like its owner — think socks and underwear — or the dog is plain bored? Eating things that have no nutritional value is known as pica and I cover this in more detail in Chapter 6.

While most dogs are inclined to eat their food as if was their last meal, others will turn their noses up to whatever is served. Picky behaviour is learned behaviour in most cases and I'm probably going to be very unpopular saying this, but I think owners can only blame themselves for a dog with a fickle appetite. Dogs can, however, develop an aversion to certain foods and the association may last a lifetime. They may associate danger with foods that cause nausea. We are all familiar with the frustration of trying to medicate a dog with a tablet; that crafty little pooch will repeatedly avoid the pill no matter what delicious morsel you hide it in. I explain how to give your dog tablets in Chapter 10.

When talking about taste it's important not to overlook the part it plays in the rituals around mating. A dog will deliberately transfer pungent odours from urine into its nose with its tongue. If a dog is looking for a bitch's readiness to mate, he will lick her ears and lips to assess her tolerance for sex and her genitals for physiological readiness.

COPROPHAGIA

Sometimes dogs eat things so unpalatable to us they can make us literally gag. No self-respecting dog owner would like to see their precious pooch eat their own poo or that of another dog or cat, but certain dogs love eating the faeces of cats, probably because it tastes like cat food! Eating their own or other's poo is called coprophagy, however, an American study found that only 16 of 100 dog owners had seen their dogs eat other canine faeces six or more times and 77 per cent had never seen their dogs do it. Several key factors such as age, gender, diet, whether the dog had been de-sexed, housetrained, weaned or removed from its mother too early, appeared to have no effect on whether the dog was a poo-eater.

Coprophagia is normal behaviour in a bitch with puppies. The mother will ingest her pups' poo while she's cleaning up the nest and also clean any poo off the pups by licking them; she'll also lick their bottoms to encourage them to poo. But coprophagia is to be discouraged in adult dogs; if they are eating their own poo they can recycle infections and reinfect themselves – and us if they lick us afterwards — with bacteria and intestinal worms . And if they are eating another dog's faeces, they'll pick up other intestinal worms and bacteria.

The majority of coprophagia appears to be behavioural but if an owner tells me their dog is eating a lot of poo, I check that there's no underlying medical problem in the gut that may be causing it, such as the malabsorption of nutrients. I check with the owner to ensure worming is up-to-date and if I'm concerned that the patient is under weight or its faeces are abnormal, I'll do some diagnostic tests.

Most cases of coprophagia are purely behavioural – for more information on how to deal with this see Chapter 12.

What dogs like

Dogs are the ultimate opportunists. One owner told me about how his dog, possibly disappointed in the lack of food or action at home, disappeared for a short time one Sunday before reappearing with an entire cooked and still warm roast fillet of beef in his mouth. Obviously, the wafting aroma from a neighbour's Sunday lunch as it rested on the kitchen table was irresistible. That was a nice bit of opportunist filching for which the dog, tail wagging, obviously expected a reward.

REWARDS

Dogs love to be rewarded; food is definitely a reward, so is water – sometimes people forget what joy a dog gets from a bowl of water. However, the ultimate reward for a dog is having fun, even more than food and I think we overuse food to reward and don't use enough fun. A dog is happiest when it has had heaps of fun – chasing sticks and balls, splashing in the sea, playing with other dogs in the dog park or racing across open spaces – until they are exhausted. Happiness is a worn-out pooch.

A happy tired pug

WORKING

Unlike many of us who drag ourselves off to work, dogs find great pride and delight in their work. They actually love to work for a living, and I'm not only talking about the working farm dogs or those trained to guard, guide and seek, but also the average pet dog. You can train them to bring your things, such as slippers and that missing remote, or fetch their own things like their toys or their lead. Their 'work' doesn't have to be productive; it can involve play such as getting them to jump on a stool or wave a paw.

Selfies have brought out the inner model in dogs; some owners just have to say the word 'selfie' and the dog will run up and strike a head on paw pose. This is work to a dog and they love it, especially being acknowledged and rewarded with a neck scratch and a treat. Dogs will become very disappointed if they have worked hard and don't get a reward afterwards.

FOOD

Of course dogs love food but humans have fallen into the trap of believing dogs need a broad diet with a variety of food with lots of yummy rewards thrown in, just like us. Supermarkets devote aisles to hundreds of different types of dog food and the specialist pet supplies outlets, often huge barns, promote a bewildering array of canine food. The truth is that dogs thrive on one good quality complete and balanced diet – it's good for their digestion and bowels.

Dogs are usually on their best behaviour at mealtimes and will sit waiting expectantly, tail busy, until dinner is served, after which they will wolf it down. When it comes to food, a dog's extreme opportunism appears to confirm that they have no understanding that there will be any future mealtimes. If the food is there now, most dogs will scoff it all now although some breeds, such miniature poodles will eat a bit here and a bit there outside their main meal. Some breeds have no moderation and the most food-obsessed breeds I've ever known are Cavalier King Charles Spaniels, Dachshunds and Labradors. Genetically, the Labrador has three genes that don't switch off when they've had a meal which causes them to keep eating without feeling satisfied so they're constantly hungry and prone to weight gain. In Chapter 6, I discuss the other end of the spectrum – the notoriously fussy eaters – as well as how to feed your dog correctly.

HAPPY CHATS

Dogs are really good at reading your face and the tone of your voice – you don't even have to move to make a dog happy; just use fun in your language and facial expressions. When dogs were stuck in a cage waiting for a procedure or recovering from one in my vet clinic, we would talk to them in a happy, chatty way and their tails would start going mad. Dogs love a friendly yarn.

RULES

Dogs are happy to have rules and a dog who understands the rules is a very happy dog. They thrive when they know where the boundaries are, but they don't understand exceptions to rules such as why they are allowed to jump on you when you are wearing casual clothes but not when you are dressed up. Dogs don't understand that it's okay to lie on the furniture after a bath but not after coming in from a rolling around in the mud. So, it's important that when you say 'no' to your dog for breaking a rule that you also do something to help your dog stop the behaviour. You can read more about positive reinforcement in Chapter 12.

GROOMING

A well-delivered bit of grooming is like a trip to heaven for a dog because it releases happy endorphins. But I'm not referring to dropping the dog off at the professional groomers, which for some dogs can be quite stressful. The sort of grooming I'm talking about is sitting quietly on the sofa with your dog, brushing and stroking and inspecting their ears, removing any goop from the corners of their eyes; dogs find that attention really calming and relaxing. They especially like being stroked on the chest area between the collar and front legs. Most dogs also love to be stroked on their backs and scratched behind their ears and other hard to reach places. For more on grooming your dog's coat see Chapter 8.

BONES AND CHEWING

Dogs love bones and chewing. When you watch your dog chewing blissfully on a bare bone that he's already chewed off any stray meat scraps, you might wonder what he's getting out of what appears to be non-nutritional dead tissue. Well, the action of spending hours grinding, crushing and chewing does several things for dogs; it's a source of comfort and a way of keeping them busy while home alone. Chewing makes life better for dogs and is soothing for puppies when they are teething.

> ### ONE UPMANSHIP
>
> *Dogs have ten more teeth than humans – 42 versus 32*
>
> *So while the evolutional survival behaviour in chewing a bone to get to the source of fat has become a pleasurable occupation for the domestic dog giving them a great deal of satisfaction, many vets are now advising against both raw and cooked bones because of the various dangers they pose.*
>
> *As a vet I do appreciate the enjoyment dogs get from chewing bones but I'm also reluctant to wholeheartedly recommend them having seen so many bone-related illnesses and teeth and mouth damage in dogs. For more information on bones and chewing see Chapter 6.*

He may be very pleased with his raw chicken bone, but his vet would disagree

Bones have played an important part in the evolution of carnivores, including the early dog. When times were lean, they could find fat — which was more important to survival than protein — in the bones of their prey. Bone marrow is particularly rich in fat; in addition, it bonded with the calcium of the bone itself forming 'bone grease' which, although less digestible, was still a substantial source of fat. Getting to the bone marrow involved a lot of grinding and gnawing to access as it's at the core of the bone. Our modern dogs have to work a lot harder at the bone because they don't have the specialised bone-crushing teeth of some of the extinct canines.

POSSESSIONS

Dogs adopt ownership over things just like we do although we are less likely to protest if someone wants to share our food. Some dogs will guard a pig's ear or a juicy bone as if his life depended on it – you may have heard your dog give a guttural growl when another dog approaches their food or an unattended possession. There are a lot of things a dog may become hooked on– shoes, an old bag, an item of clothing, a blanket, a chair leg.

Anyone who has had a puppy will know the seemingly endless period of chewing. It's normal behaviour but when it involves a new pair of expensive shoes (or worse, just one of the pair) you despair! Chewing everything is part of a puppy's neurosensory exploration and they will usually grow out of it. Until then no amount of scolding when you find your new book completely shredded will stop this little menace from finding new things to chew – or stop your heart from melting when you look down at that cute puppy face. For more on coping during this period in your dog's life see Chapter 4.

Dogs get bored just as we do but by providing them with a variety of toys we can divert attention from certain behavioural issues such as digging, destructive chewing and whining. Dogs can get extremely attached to their toys and like to have a special spot for them such as a basket, bed or corner. By using toys to interact with our dogs, such as throwing balls or chucking flying disks we can add extra value to them. Devices for throwing balls increase the distance a dog has to run to fetch it – good exercise for the dog (if not its owner).

Your dog needs active 'people time' to let off steam especially if he has spent time in a confined space. Rope toys are fun for playing tug-of-war, but the rope should be dedicated to this particular exercise to avoid your dog grabbing anything else in your hand that looks tuggable. Some owners spin in a circle while holding on to the rope, this circular force coupled with the dog's persistent grip means the dog lifts off the ground and spins around in the air with the owner – while this looks like fun it can cause serious damage to the dog's jaw and dentition. So a gentle tug-of-war with all your dog's four paws planted on the ground is a safer way to play that game. When you don't have time to play, invest in a few distraction items such as hard rubber toys for chewing and gnawing. Edible chewing toys or food delivery toys which a dog must manipulate or solve puzzles to get at some kibbles or a small treat are also a good distraction and exercise your dog's brain.

Welsh Corgi nervously protecting his blanket

TOYS FOR COMFORT

Toys should not be overlooked as a source of comfort. Soft stuffed toys are not suitable for dogs that would eat them– Labradors, for example, would most likely tear it open, eat the stuffing and need an operation to remove it all! Soft stuffed toys can provide comfort for some dogs and be a plaything they can toss about; it should be small enough to carry around and can be used as a special toy reserved for when you leave the house or bedtime. Dirty laundry such

Toys are a source of comfort

as an old shirt, towel or blanket (especially if it smells like you) can also be very comforting. It's a good idea to use a variety of both interactive and distraction toys; don't have more than about four or five out at the same time and rotate them weekly to prevent boredom.

Special toys, clothes and blankets can be a source of comfort when your dog has a sleep-over at a friend's, staying in a boarding kennel or unwell and requiring a lengthy vet stay. I used to give both Sasha and Java one of my pyjama shirts if they had any overnight stay at the vet's. I know how scared dogs can be in foreign environments, so the familiar smell of their owner can go a long way. I did the same with my babies when transferring them from co-sleeping to their cots.

Remember when choosing toys it's important that they are appropriate for your dog's current size; toys that are too small are easily swallowed or may lodge in your dog's mouth or throat. I once had to remove a chew toy that was wedged across the hard palate at

A puzzle toy with kibble can provide hours of entertainment for some dogs

the top of the dog's mouth where it had become stuck after a vigorous chew. The owners actually didn't know what was wrong, just rushed the dog to see me after they found it freaking out and running around anxiously in the backyard, rubbing his face and whining. It only took one quick look in the mouth to diagnose the problem. One vet I knew removed a dog toy lodged in the back of a dog's mouth. The dog only lived because the toy had a narrow hole in it – one that you put treats in – which enabled it to breathe on the way to the vet.

Buy toys that are 'dog proof' or make sure you remove any ribbons, strings or button eyes that the dog might swallow and get rid of any toys that have bits coming off them. Ask your vet about the safety of chewable toys such as puzzle toys, pig's ears and rawhides.

What dogs don't like

Even the most laid-back dog will dislike some of the things humans do. No two dogs are exactly the same, even with the same breed, so what one dog hates another dog may enjoy. You may know what your dog hates but not necessarily what other dogs don't like and it's a good idea to have some general knowledge about things that often annoy dogs and how to avoid doing them.

HEAD PATTING

Being patted on the head is not an act that most humans enjoy, even if it's done lovingly, but for some reason most people think dogs like being patted on the head. They don't. They prefer a neck rub or scratch. Many dogs will put up with a head pat if it's someone they know and trust, but you may observe that the dog pulls away slightly. It's a good idea to teach children not to pat a dog's head but direct them to stroke on the dog's back. For more on the do's and don'ts for children around dogs see Chapter 15.

Owners need to get up close and personal with their dogs when they ear clean and brush their teeth. Poking and prodding should be done slowly and gently and after the dog has endured the indignities it's a good idea to reward him with loving words and a treat. Dogs dislike it when humans get in their faces. Avoid putting your hands on a dog's face, standing over them in an aggressive way or rushing towards them, especially if the dog does not know you well. Most dogs don't like having their faces blown on either – something important to tell the kids.

HUGGING

Although most dogs like being touched, many don't enjoy being hugged, especially by strangers; putting arms around a dog's neck or body may be perceived as threatening. We usually hug dogs because we enjoy hugging each other and it seems logical that our dogs will like it too; most dogs tolerate gentle hugs from trusted humans, but that doesn't mean they actually like them. It's best to let the dog get close on his own terms and to pat him along the back and on the chest, especially if you don't know the dog well.

Of course, some dogs do love to be hugged which is why it's important to understand the limits of your dog; always be guided to his body language. If he leans away, averts his eyes, yawns, has a worried look, or shows other avoidance gestures he's probably uncomfortable.

An even more serious issue is children hugging dogs; children are the victims of most dog bites and this is often due to children handling dogs in ways that make their canine friends uncomfortable. For more on Children and Dogs see Chapter 15.

ROUGH HANDLING

Dogs are often subjected to handling that they find stressful. Having strangers and even people they know reaching their hands down right into a dog's face in an attempt to pet their head can feel very intimidating from a dog's point of view. Dogs that haven't been properly desensitised to other forms of handling, such as grooming, nail trimming and vet visits can find these situations extremely frightening. It's important to work with dogs, particularly as puppies, to get them to enjoy handling and to make vet and grooming visits more pleasant in the future. Some people think dogs like to be tackled, pushed, pulled and thrown about but often this is stressful and a bit confusing for a dog.

FORCED SOCIALISING

Just like us, dogs have favourite friends and those they don't like. Being pack animals their interaction with other dogs is usually related to where they are in the canine social pecking order. Dogs are generally happy to hang out in the pack, racing, rolling, sniffing, scent marking, but if your dog is disinclined to play with certain dogs don't push it because these other dogs may be bullies. So, while we all like to see our dogs frolicking in the dog park with the rest of the neighbourhood gang, be alert to cues that your dog might want to be somewhere else.

More subtle cues that indicate your dog does not want to socialise, include general avoidance or signs of nervousness, and lip licking. Retreating behind your legs, tucking tail under legs, baring their teeth and growling are more obvious cues. Don't force your dog to allow strangers to touch or pat it if he looks uncomfortable because he may sense something in the stranger he doesn't like. I'm suspicious of people who don't like dogs, but I trust a dog when it doesn't like a person!

RUSHED WALKING

The unkindest thing you can do when walking a dog is to rush it through as if it was just a quick piddle and poo drop. For a dog, a walk is not just a walk for a bit of exercise; it is pure bliss. It gives him a chance to explore the outside world, sniff the messages left by other dogs and leave little messages in return. But they like to have the time to have a really good 'sniff' at the interesting messages along the way. Dogs save up their pee at home, hanging on to a full bladder until they have the opportunity to post their messages on the daily walk. I always feel sorry for a dog when I see its owner dragging and tugging on the lead to pull the pup mid-sniff off a lamppost or tree. Dogs hate not being able to have a bit of a free rein around the usual haunts but to also sniff out a few new environments. Give your dog a chance to smell the roses.

PUNISHMENT

I am a firm believer that smacking and hitting dogs – well, actually all animals –is not appropriate. Just as we discovered that punishing children puts them in a state of fear it's the same with dogs. Fear does not equal respect; learning through fear is not as effective as using positive reinforcement which will strengthen the relationship between you and your canine friend. While a stern 'no' needs to be said as soon as the bad behaviour occurs in reality you probably won't always be there when it happens. Even if you discover a ripped-up newspaper five

Australian Cattle Dog cross looking rather sheepish

minutes later and growl at the dog, he might know he's in trouble but he won't know what you're talking about. You can reprimand your dog hours after the event thinking he knows what he's done is wrong because he cowers and looks guilty but the general consensus among animal behaviourists is that the dog is more likely responding to the shouting and the negativity in the pack leader's voice – that's you.

Although studies have shown that shame is not a canine emotion, as it's a very complex emotion which dogs have never needed or developed, I would argue that dogs do feel shamed when they are being told off and they hate it. They may not understand the words we are saying but they sense our emotions when we are talking sternly and get the drift that they're getting into trouble. Dogs find this confusing and unclear and by repeating your same old angry method of dealing with bad behaviour your dog may eventually become immune to it and keep on doing whatever he wants. See more about positive reinforcement in Chapter 12.

INCONSISTENCY

When a dog's leader or their entire household is inconsistent with them, it makes it much harder for a dog to work out exactly what we want. Make sure you, and anyone else involved with the dog, are all on the same page about hand signals, voice cues and the rules that allow the dog to live happily in your house. Giving mixed signals isn't fair to the dog – imagine if you had one person in your household encouraging you to sit on the couch while others yelled at you when they see you sitting there! Put up a chart or use a whiteboard on your fridge with the 'house rules' and right cues for the dog and go over it with the whole family.

DRESSING UP

Many dogs will tolerate outfits or costumes – tolerate being the operative word because there's a good chance your dog detests being dressed up. If the pooch is being dragged off to puppy parties in a pink tutu it might not be what the dog wants to do. You may think your dog looks cute, but do you really know what your dog thinks? Then again, I once saw a dog wearing Batman ears which some children had put on him for Halloween and he was the happiest dog ever because he was involved with the kids!

When I'm asked about putting clothes on dogs, I tell owners they should always put the comfort and wellbeing of their dog first. Dressing their dog may not be a comfortable experience for the dog; dogs are not humans and dressing a dog in miniature human clothes is for the human's benefit, not for the dog's. Attributing human traits, emotions and intentions to your pet is called Anthropomorphism. For more on this see Chapter 12.

What about winter coats? I know of dogs who love their little winter jumpers and run and jump on the owner's lap when the coat comes out, excited to get into it, holding their paws out to go into the sleeves. Little short-haired Chihuahuas are famous for snuggling up in a warm coat.

English Bull Dogs dressed but not impressed

However, dogs that are made for the cold have an extra layer of insulating fur and adding an extra layer might overheat the dog. Exactly how cold your dog gets will depends on the breed, size and age. Suitability for a well-fitted coat might apply to smaller, lighter dogs; those with thin or shorthair; a dog with a fresh haircut; and old or sick dogs. Make sure the coat has no fancy trimmings or buttons which could become a hazard if swallowed. One thing many people don't consider when dressing up their dog in restrictive clothing is how this might interfere with their ability to communicate with other dogs.

TIGHT LEADS

Dogs hate a tight lead because it raises a level of stress, frustration and dampens what should be an exciting time sniffing and leaving messages. Most people who have their dog on a tight lead do it because they say their dog is pulling them and it's the only way they can maintain control. What a tight strip of canvas that attaches you to your dog conveys is the message that you are tense, nervous or annoyed and the dog responds accordingly. We don't like to be pulled around and nor does your dog. A dog on a tight lead is usually tense or over-excited and more inclined to bark and jump up on people, even in normal social situations. When you teach your dog how to walk on a slack lead it gets the message that you are calm, relaxing your dog reassuring him that everything is hunky-dory. For more on walking your dog on a slack lead see Chapter 12.

I recommend head halters and dog harnesses as the preferred alternative to attaching the lead to the dog's collar. If a dog repeatedly pulls on a lead when attached to its collar this can cause them to cough and eventually may even cause permanent damage to their trachea (windpipe).

That being said, my Java was an absolute nut case of a dog and it took years to train her to walk calmly on a slack lead. Active dogs or dogs with exuberant and boisterous natures need longer and more frequent walks or runs and extra hours of training before you can even think about a calm walk on a slack lead.

Belgian Shepard on tight lead

Often, they need to let off steam in a dog park or dog beach especially if they've been climbing the walls all day waiting for you to finish work. Maturity is also a factor – some dogs don't grow out of there rebellious puppy or teenage years until they are two or three! Sasha was easy but Java was a fruit loop and she didn't settle on walks until she was about three.

CHAPTER 3

Responsible

♥ Pet

Ownership

Dog ownership is a proven way to improve our physical and mental wellbeing. There are many reasons dogs are good for humans: our sense of purpose increases when we have a pet to care for; our stress levels are reduced; and we get surges of dopamine, the 'feel good' hormone, by doing simple things like taking our four-legged best friend for a walk in the sunshine.

But before I move on to the various breeds and what might be a suitable one for you and your family either as a pure-bred puppy or a rescue dog, I want to talk about the responsibility of owning a dog. Responsible dog ownership is far more than simply loving your dog or succumbing to the pleas of children and taking home that cute puppy in the pet shop. Remember how my father drummed into me that having a dog was a serious commitment and made me walk the neighbour's dog for three months before I was allowed to get Sasha?

Time, energy and commitment

Owning a dog takes time and energy so before you decide to get one, ask yourself if you would be a conscientious owner. Be honest. Is the time right? For instance, the time might not be good if you are pregnant or have a young baby in the house. What about if you have the added stress and responsibilities of caring for an elderly or an unwell relative? Then there are the various issues that come with owning a dog. What happens during holidays or work-related trips if you are the sole carer? Are you prepared or can you afford to feed your dog good quality food? Can you allocate time to train and walk your dog for exercise? What about the amount of dog poo you will have to pick up during those walks? Signing up to owning a dog also means you will have to be the dog's medical advocate and there will be vet bills and the cost of pet insurance.

Many people get a dog and later become stressed by the responsibility. You need to be in it for the long haul; the natural life of the dog will depend on the breed, but dogs can live up to 15 years, even 20 and beyond. According to the Guinness Book of Records the record holder for the oldest dog is Bluey, an Australian Cattle Dog who lived to the ripe old age of 30 and died in 1939.

Getting a dog is not like buying a car; you can't just trade it in when it gets old or return it if it has too many maintenance problems. If your circumstances change and you have to move to a place where you cannot take your dog (such as overseas, into an apartment or retirement village) or if illness prevents you from looking after your dog properly you must consider the best future for him either by finding him a responsible short-term carer or finding him a suitable new permanent home.

As far as I am concerned, euthanasia is not the right option for a healthy dog and I'm sure most vets feel the same. I had one really lovely client who used to bring her little dog in for vaccinations and check-ups and over the years we got to know each other quite well and I knew how much she loved that dog. One day her adult children came to me with the dog and asked me to put it down because their mother was in hospital with a serious illness; they said she might not come out and there was no-one to look after the dog. I told them we couldn't possibly put the dog down; it was their mother's 'everything'. What would happen if she came out of hospital and found that her dog was dead?

I offered to keep the dog at the clinic for a few weeks until we knew what was happening with their mother. No, that wasn't what they wanted. I think they were finding their mother's illness overwhelming and the dog was just another problem they didn't want to deal with. Unfortunately, I had no choice; a vet must comply with the wishes of anyone who has ownership of the pet because that's the law. I did not see the woman again so it's possible she didn't survive but that healthy little dog had plenty of life and love in him and should have been re-homed.

In another case, I met a couple who had settled in Australia from Japan and got themselves a dog. When they decided to return to Japan, they wanted me to euthanise the dog. I suggested they find a new home for the dog, but they said the dog had bonded with them and they didn't want to surrender it to us or have it to go to anyone else. Again, another dog with plenty of love left to give to another owner.

Bonding is not something you do once and call it finished. Maintaining the bond is a lifelong process and if you have to cut that bond and relinquish your dog for whatever reason, make sure you give the dog a shot at bonding with someone else by finding a new home yourself or giving it to an animal shelter that will hopefully re-home it.

I know from personal experience how easy it is to make a bad decision when we have a scrumptious puppy in our arms. I adopted Java knowing that once

I finished university I would likely be moving overseas. I don't regret it but re-homing her was really traumatic experience even though I found her a beautiful loving home. Dogs are for life and I learned that the hard way.

When parents get a dog for their children, they will generally emphasise the responsibilities that go along with it, just as my father did to me – the walking, feeding, and the cleaning up. But as most parents will admit, with an eye roll, one of them will end up doing all those things and more if you add in the costs associated with owning a dog. So if you are preparing to give a child a dog, remember it will most probably become the responsibility of the whole household.

Exercising your dog

After food the next most important responsibility you have to the dog is walking it. Dogs need exercise to help keep their weight where it should be, maintain their cardiovascular fitness, to slow the loss of muscle that goes along with advancing years and to strengthen their body. There's another bonus to exercise — just like it does for us, exercise puts your dog in a good mood by releasing serotonin in the brain.

Along with all these positive benefits, exercise also strengthens your bond with your pooch and helps with his behaviour because when you're engaging your dog in physical activity, you're right there with him, paying attention to him and keeping him from becoming bored or lonely. When dogs are more in sync with their owners they are more willing to do what is asked of them and follow their leader's cues.

If you don't have the time to exercise your dog, you have to make the time or arrange an alternative for him. If you don't have the physical ability, then you need to invest in a professional dog walker. While you are out at work, socialising or shopping remember your dog is at home waiting for you. Time spent walking, grooming and playing with your dog is essential for a happy dog,

Jack Russell terrier mid-flight and living the best life

because apart from the exercise, walking has the added benefit of strengthening the bond between you and the dog.

Weather can sometimes be a factor in being able to walk a dog, especially if it's very cold or very hot. In Australia we do have extreme weather events – floods, fires and cyclones– but it is not common for them to last for long periods so there's no excuse for extended periods of no walking.

While on the subject of wild weather it might be good to mention that as many areas of our vast continent are prone to natural disasters people in high risk areas are encouraged to have an emergency evacuation kit. It's a good idea to prepare one for your pets too; take some dried food for the dog, a pig's ear, a lead and a favourite toy.

So just how much exercise does your dog need? The amount of physical activity that is right for your dog depends on his time of life, his breed and his health. Let's look at the four stages of a dog's life.

PUPPYHOOD

Although puppies have tons of energy, they also need lots of down time. They can be playing and running around like loonies one minute, then literally fall asleep at your feet the next. Just like human children they're growing rapidly and their little bodies need lots of rest. It's best not to take your puppy on long walks; in fact, long walks can be hard on a puppy's developing bones and joints. Puppies will be happy with short bursts of exercise – say five to ten minutes at a time – throughout the day. And indoor exercise, such as throwing a ball across the room, is perfectly fine as well. Outside you can just chase each other around the backyard – he'll love that too. Best of all, he'll love being with you.

THE ADULT DOG

When I talk about an adult dog I mean one who has not reached 'senior' status which could be anywhere from five or nine years of age depending on their breed. For instance, a small dog will not become senior until he passes the age of eight, nine or even ten. Generally, a two-year-old dog is going to have more energy that he wants to run off than, say, a seven-year-old, so to some degree you are going to have to work out for yourself your dog's exercise limit. But unless your adult dog is in poor physical health, two 20-minute walks daily is not always enough, particularly for sporty-type breeds such as Labradors, retrievers, spaniels, German Shepherds, collies and setters who need somewhere between

60-90 minutes of vigorous exercise each day, such as running and playing with other dogs.

The working dogs, bred for energy and stamina, are the ones needing 90 minutes of vigorous exercise a day, which in reality very few people are able to maintain, me included! Siberian huskies – designed to drag a sled many kilometres over ice – absolutely must have their need for exercise satisfied or they become depressed. As a result of their cattle and sheep herding background, Australian shepherds and collies have very high energy levels and exercise requirements. These dogs make great cycling and running companions and star at the dog shows in agility competitions, disc games and of course, sheepdog trails.

Vizslas, Labradors, pointers and Golden Retrievers are pointing and retrieving dogs designed to travel and hunt for hours on end. A 20-minute walk for Vizsla pup would be a warmup! A Dalmatian is another great companion for long distance runners and cyclists because they too have a running instinct and impressive stamina. And Weimaraners, another hunting breed, will play fetch for hours and love swimming!

MISSING YOU

Your dog does have a sense of time and misses you when you're gone. If you think your dog knows when it's timefor dinner or a walk, you're right; dogs pick up on our routines and habits and they also sense how much time has passed.

If you have more time for your dog on weekends, that's great but bursts of strenuous exercise at weekends is not ideal for his body; muscles and joints that are unused during the week and worked to capacity at weekends can make them prone to injury and strains. Leaving an adult dog alone in the house all day while you go off to work can also make the poor dog bored out of his mind, so it's a good idea to think of ways to keep his body and mind happy by using dog walkers and doggy day care.

THE GERIATRIC YEARS

An older dog requires less exercise than a young adult or middle-aged one; around 20-60 minutes a day broken up into two sessions is a good rule of thumb.

Two walks a day is ideal and dogs like some variety in their routine, so try to vary your routine by trying new routes as even old dogs need some stimulation. However, it's important to remember that many older dogs have stiff limbs and arthritic pain, so ensure their exercise doesn't add to their pain. If you see your dog is uncomfortable during his walks talk to your vet about pain medication and other remedies that may relieve stress on his joints.

Cleaning up your dog's poo

Anyone who has walked the streets of Paris will know the hazards of walking around the vast amount of Parisian dog deposits. No-one likes dodging doggie-do-do or worse, stepping in it; I know of people who will throw out shoes that have dog poo on the soles. But no point in turning up our noses at French dog poo. Until Australian town and city councils began to introduce laws to penalise dog owners' who didn't pick up their dogs' waste the problem was literarily of Olympic proportions. The Brisbane City Council estimated that every year Brisbane dogs deposited enough poo in public places to fill one and a half Olympic-sized swimming pools and a Victorian survey found that the one million dogs in that State managed to push out around 33,000 tonnes of the stuff annually.

Laws and the size of fines differ from state to state but all require the person in charge of the dog to pick up after it. Some states still operate under existing litter or old pooper scooper laws but newer legislation requires dog owners to carry at least two suitable plastic bags to pick up and dispose of their dog's waste. This is a much better option as it is contained properly for disposal; some city and local councils even supply dispenser bags and special collection bins.

Picking up your dog's waste is important for community health as some dog droppings contain harmful bacteria. Rain can wash dog waste through the stormwater system into natural waterways and into our ocean outfalls, contributing to excessive E. coli pollution readings on beaches following heavy rainfall. Toxocara Canis, the roundworm found in the faeces of infected puppies or adult dogs, can also be passed onto humans. Children, people with compromised immune systems and field sports players are most at risk of infection.

The word has been out for decades about the necessity of whoever is walking the dog to clean up after it, yet I'm constantly surprised that many people still don't get the message; I've spotted people ignoring the evidence (and the law) walking off quickly hoping it won't be noticed. A dog off-leash in a dog park does not absolve its owner from picking up his dog's poo.

Keeping your dog healthy

While a balanced diet, plenty of exercise and a warm safe shelter are the most obvious ways of keeping your dog happy and mentally well he will also need annual vet visits. If your dog is over seven years old (or five for giant breeds) or suffers from a particular condition or illness they will need to see the vet more often; be guided by your vet's advice about this.

Caring for a dog means making sure it's up to date with all the necessary vaccinations and preventative treatment against fleas, ticks, intestinal worms and heartworm. It will also need to be micro-chipped for identification purposes and registered with your local council.

Unless you plan to breed from your dog, all dogs must be de-sexed. It will keep your dog healthier and calmer and will reduce the number of unwanted dogs that end up in dog shelters.

Pet Insurance

Compared with US, Canadian and British pet owners, Australians have a relatively low rate of pet insurance. According to Roy Morgan Research in 2018, just 7.1 per cent of the 5.4 million registered dog owners in Australia have insured their dogs. Australians have a very good socialised health system if they get sick or have an accident and don't have private health insurance – Medicare. Dogs get pretty much all the same diseases and degenerative health problems as humans but there's no equivalent to Medicare for pets.

As a practicing vet I have seen pet insurance policies save the lives of hundreds of dogs, particularly in emergency situations where the costs of surgeries, hospitalisation, rehabilitation and other medical costs have been through the roof and the owners were only able to provide this life saving veterinary care thanks to their pet insurance. But equally, I have seen many frustrated owners, who didn't read the fine print or understand how pet insurance works and were horrified to find their claims were rejected. I have also seen the sad outcome for those without pet insurance who couldn't afford a necessary operation or treatment and euthanasia has been the best option. In one such case at my clinic, a beautiful pure-bred Rhodesian Ridgeback puppy about five months old came in with a broken leg. The owner, who must have paid a lot of money for this dog, couldn't afford the surgery, which was fairly simple but expensive. He couldn't get a loan and there was no way I could put that puppy down. In the end the owner signed papers surrendering the dog to the clinic.

Every policy and insurance company is different so do your research. Here are some points I think every pet owner should know before buying pet insurance.

- Pet insurance doesn't cover costs upfront. Typically, you will need to pay your veterinarian for all services rendered and then submit your claim to the insurance company.

- The majority of pet insurance policies are for illness, injury and emergencies and they usually do not cover preventative care and annual health checks or things like vaccinations, flea and tick treatments, worming and prophylactic dental procedures. Some insurance companies offer wellness plans for additional fees which may help you with these costs. Remember to read the fine print! Some vet clinics now offer memberships or healthy pet programs, so always ask.

- I recommend all puppies with no known health problems get pet insurance. This is because healthy puppies are pretty cheap to insure and my goodness do they get themselves into trouble. I've known plenty of owners who have come in cheery-eyed with their brand new puppy for its first vaccination, only to return a week later with a puppy that's broken it's leg falling down the stairs, been hit by a reversing car or suffering from diarrhea and vomiting because they've swallowed something they shouldn't, such as an entire cheesecake! Puppies are bonkers and they very commonly get themselves into trouble in the first year or two.

- If you have an older dog, consider the available policies more carefully. Older dogs cost more to insure because just like us they suffer from more health problems. If you have an older dog and he/she hasn't been previously insured then the insurance company will not cover any pre-existing conditions when you take out the policy. I have known clients who forgot their dog had a bout of achy joints or a lump removed many years back and were shocked to find cancer and arthritis were therefore not covered under their policy. In the case of older dogs, you might find it better to set aside this money in a savings account rather than taking out an insurance policy.

- Don't get burned! Not all insurance policies are equal. Do your research to avoid being ripped off. Compare premiums, deductibles and payouts for each policy.

- Get clear on what is covered and what isn't. Some policies exclude major health conditions such as some cancers or hip dysplasia — I suspect they aren't too keen on paying for radiation and chemotherapy and hip replacements. Also be aware that some pet insurance companies do not cover conditions that are genetically linked to certain breeds. I talk more about these genetic links in Chapter 10.

- A list of Australian pet insurance agencies can be found at the back of the book.

Quality of life

Another part of responsible dog ownership is something none of us like to think about: what to do when your dog has reached old age and is suffering from debilitating health issues. You need to be emotionally prepared to make the right decision about the quality of your dog's life (or the lack of it) and not prolong it for the wrong reasons which may be that you cannot bear to say goodbye. For more on this subject see Chapter 17.

Being a good neighbour

Most of us have lived in a neighbourhood where there is an incessant barking dog that drives us mad. You don't want to become the owner of 'that dog'. Dogs do have an impact on others in your street or in your apartment block if it allows dogs. Do not ignore the issue if your dog is incessantly barking when you're not home; continuous barking is unfair to your dog and annoying to neighbours. The Darwin City Council recently introduced a by-law on the amount of barking is permitted before a ranger will visit when a neighbour complains: six minutes of barking per hour is allowed during the day and three minutes per hour at night.

Barking is usually a sign that the dog is bored or anxious; you need to train your dog not to whine or bark when left at home alone. For more on this see Chapter 12.

Chihuahuas howling

Out and about with your dog

Responsible dog ownership means being in charge of the dog's behaviour at home and in public. By law you must register your dog with your local council and look after it properly; if you don't look after your dog, you could be fined and banned from owning animals. Make sure your yard is well-fenced so your dog can't escape and roam around the neighbourhood. He should always be on a lead when out walking, and when he is allowed off lead in a dog park you need to keep your eye on him at all times. Even though your dog is micro-chipped it should also wear a collar with an ID tag with a name and current contact details in case it gets lost.

The goal should be to have your dog properly socialised and under control when you take it out for walks so the only remarks people make are about its appearance - 'What a beautiful dog' - and good manners — 'What a good dog'.

A well-behaved dog is less likely to upset people and pets in public places and will be more welcome at social gatherings — 'Yes, please bring the dog with you.' If your dog's misbehaviour results in any sort of accident or injury, you will have to take full responsibility for the outcome. A well-trained dog is a happier dog because they have more freedom to come along with you wherever you go and more than that, they actually enjoy the sense of structure.

A content well-behaved beagle

Responsible breeding

If your dog is suitable for breeding and you decide to breed your dog, you need to understand what you are embarking on, follow responsible protocols and be a responsible breeder. I recommend that you find out as much as you can about breeding standards and become involved with a network of responsible breeders. Dog breeding is a serious business and a reputable breeder with years of experience can guide you. And find a vet who has an interest in canine reproduction.

There are a few myths around letting a dog have a litter of puppies before she is desexed. One is that it will calm her down. Actually, your dog's temperament depends on a variety of factors, including the genes she has inherited, the way you manage her, and her maturity. A lot of female dogs do grow a little calmer with advancing age, but this has nothing to do with having babies as male dogs also grow calmer with age. If your dog is a bit hyperactive, having puppies won't change her personality but her litter will most likely include a number of excitable puppies who take after their mother. If my experience is anything to go by, motherhood only makes you more strung out!

Some people believe allowing their dog to have the experience of having a litter of puppies because 'it's natural' or that it will be good for the children. Doubtless half a dozen or so happy, healthy puppies would bring joy to the family, but life is not always that straightforward. A lot of things can and do go wrong in the natural world: dogs do die in labour; puppies can be stillborn or die after birth; the mother will have difficulties feeding her pups after a caesarean. There is also the time, stress and mess of looking after a litter of puppies, especially runty, sickly ones you have to hand-rear. These are not easy things for anyone to cope with.

A lot of people are motivated by the idea of making money from a litter of puppies. But often the costs involved outweigh any income a dog owner might gain from a single litter. In fact, there's a good chance you might end up considerably out of pocket. Anyone breeding puppies has a moral obligation to do their best to ensure that the puppies produced are healthy and ready to grow into happy, good-tempered, trainable dogs. This can be an expensive and time consuming responsibility.

The range of costs to take into account when breeding from your female dog for the first time include: health clearances involving blood tests; worming and veterinary antenatal care; extra food for your pregnant and lactating dog; a whelping box and plenty of soft washable bedding; heat pads for pups to cuddle up to when the mother dog is not with them; access to money if a caesarean or other emergency care is necessary; worming treatment for puppies; food for weaning; first vaccinations and vet checks; advertising costs and the cost of extra care for any unsold pups after eight weeks. The number of puppies available outstrips demand and no matter how beautiful your dog is, the fact is that you may be left with a few puppies long after they have outgrown their cute tiny puppy stage.

A tall order

Good breeders offer new owners support after they have taken their puppies home and will usually offer a guarantee to take the puppy back if it has health problems or if the new owner can't cope. An amateur breeder who may not be prepared to do this, risks the dog being relinquished to a rescue shelter, adding to the tragic mountain of unwanted dogs in rescue centres throughout Australia. It is not unheard of for rescue centres to be given an entire litter of 12-week old puppies that the owner has simply been unable to sell and does not have the resources to house now that they have outgrown their puppy pens. All those people who eagerly expressed an interest in taking one of the puppies once they were born may get cold feet later.

As a responsible dog owner, you need to think very carefully about the ramifications of allowing your dog to have a litter before she is de-sexed. There is certainly no advantage to her physically and this is something I don't recommend.

Vaccinating your dog

We vaccinate our pets because we love them. Dogs are our protectors, helpers and mates and we want to keep them happy, healthy and full of life. There's nothing like a smiling dog with shining eyes. Vaccines exist to provide immunity from a range of infectious diseases which can affect not only their health but that of you and your family. If you have an adult dog and are unsure if it needs a vaccination you can ask your vet about a titre test or serology, an affordable blood test that measures the amount of anti-bodies present in the dog's system which will tell you if it needs an immune booster.

In order to be effective, vaccines need to contain an agent similar to the micro-organism responsible for the disease, or a low dose of the actual pathogen itself — a live vaccine. The injected agent stimulates the dog's immune system enabling it to recognise it as a threat; this causes the immune system to attack the foreign agent and remember it in case the body is exposed to the same disease in the future.

If there is a mild adverse reaction such as sensitive skin or a swelling at the vaccination site or a fever it usually shows up in the first 24 hours and generally passes within a couple of days. If reactions are more serious such as breathing difficulties, vomiting, loss of appetite and diarrhoea, you need alert your vet immediately. The most severe vaccination reaction is known as anaphylaxis, a life-threatening allergic reaction and the vet will likely need to administer adrenalin. This reaction occurs within seconds to minutes of administering the vaccination. Anaphylaxis is a very rare in dogs, in fact I have never seen an anaphylactic reaction from a vaccine and as a vet I've given thousands. It's important to keep any adverse reactions in perspective. Side effects are considered far less risky than exposing your dog to serious illnesses if they remain unvaccinated.

The World Small Animal Veterinary Association (WSAVA) has listed core vaccines as those that all dogs and cats must receive regardless of age, environments, habits and breeds to help prevent them from contracting life-threatening diseases which have a global reach. Core vaccines are those for canine distemper virus, canine adenovirus and canine parvovirus and are commonly given with one injection. I recommend it be given to every adult dog, every year. The recommendation for non-core vaccines – parainfluenza virus, Bordetella bronchiseptica and lepotspira interrogans – usually depends on the dog's environment and geographic location. Having said that, I vaccinate all dogs against Kennel Cough (parainfluenza and bordetella), as it is not just spread in kennels or the pound; it is very contagious and can be caught anywhere other dogs have been. I also recommend repeating this vaccination annually to maintain protection. The vaccination can be given as either drops into the nose or mouth, or as an injection.

To give you an idea of the dangers to your dog by not having it vaccinated I'd like to explain the diseases.

CANINE DISTEMPER

This is a fatal disease that attacks a dog's nervous system and can lead to paralysis. Puppies and younger dogs tend to be more susceptible to this virus. Fortunately, this is now very rare in Australia thanks to increased vaccination, however outbreaks still occur in low-vaccinated areas. While I have never seen Canine Distemper in Australia I did see it while volunteering in South Africa as it's a country with huge numbers of unvaccinated dogs. This highly contagious disease is devastating as it takes many dogs' lives.

CANINE ADENOVIRUS

Also known as infectious canine hepatitis, this is a really horrible disease that attacks a dog's liver and subsequently its eyes and kidneys. It can't be transmitted to humans but is a deadly illness for a dog.

CANINE PARVOVIRUS

This is another deadly virus which is one of the most common in the world and one of the hardest to eradicate. This disease is characterised by vomiting, bloody diarrhoea, anorexia, lethargy and fever or hypothermia. Parvovirus vaccinations are usually started at six to eight weeks in combination with adenovirus and distemper virus vaccines.

KENNEL COUGH

Kennel Cough is caused by parainfluenza virus and Bordetella brochiseptica. These upper respiratory infections, similar to flu, can occur in dogs especially when they are in contact with a large number of other dogs, such as shelters, dog parks and kennels. A symptom of kennel cough is usually a dry cough which may be accompanied by a significant nasal discharge. In severe cases the dog may stop eating and even vomit due to an excessive hacking cough. This can cause many owners to rush in thinking the dog has something caught in its throat as a result of all the coughing and dry retching. These symptoms ease after about seven to 14 days. The RSPCA and other shelters vaccinate against kennel cough however some dogs may contract it before the vaccine fully kicks in. If your adopted dog has severe signs of kennel cough seek advice from your vet because antibiotics are often required. Dogs can still get kennel cough after they have been vaccinated (and often do), they just get a much milder form and recover much faster than they would if they were unvaccinated.

CORONAVIRUS

This is a highly contagious, hard to eradicate virus that primarily attacks the intestinal tract. The disease is spread from dog to dog through contact with faeces and leads to diarrhoea, vomiting, loss of appetite and fever. The coronavirus vaccine is not a core vaccine.

CANINE LEPTOSPIROSIS

This bacterium affects organ function and is transmittable to humans. It is commonly given to young dogs that live in a susceptible geographical region such as farming areas. The leptospirosis vaccine is a non-core vaccine as it is a rare disease and the vaccination does not protect against all serotypes so may not provide adequate protection to at risk dogs.

RABIES

Rabies is a very contagious disease, fatal to both dogs and humans, in which infected animals act as carriers. Fortunately, Australia is rabies-free so it's not a core vaccine here, but it still affects many countries, including the US. If you are planning to take your dog overseas, it may need to be vaccinated against rabies depending on the country. You must see an Australian Quarantine and Inspection Service (AQIS) officer or an accredited AQIS vet for advice on ensuring your dog is ready to travel overseas. Only these vets can administer rabies vaccines and sign off documentation for import and export animals, pets included.

Worm, flea and tick treatments

Vaccinations are not the only way we keep our dogs healthy and happy. There are a number of other nasties we need to protect our dogs from using preventative treatments regularly.

INTESTINAL WORMS

You don't want your dog to become infested with intestinal worms because apart from making your dog feel unwell many can also transfer to humans. The range of worms is stomach-churning – roundworms, hookworms, whipworms and tapeworms. These can cause diarrhoea (sometimes with blood), vomiting, weight loss and a general poor appearance. A dog should be wormed regularly throughout its life. Ask your vet about the most suitable worming product.

HEARTWORM

This nasty little parasite is spread by mosquitoes and the adult worms live inside the heart and pulmonary artery of dogs; it can have very serious health consequences. The presence of heartworm varies throughout Australia and rescue dogs are not routinely tested by shelters. I recommend you discuss with your vet the necessity of a blood test to determine its presence before commencing any treatment.

FLEAS

Your dog may be the cleanest, healthiest dog in the neighbourhood, but it can still get fleas! Flea bites can cause a very marked allergic reaction in much the same way that mosquitoes affect humans by sucking blood when they bite; heavy infestation can result in significant blood loss in a dog, especially puppies. When severely irritated the dog may scratch and bite damaging the skin and causing a secondary infection, commonly known as hotspots. So if you don't actually see the irritating little blood suckers don't be fooled– fleas spend only a limited period of their life cycle on a dog and you may underestimate the impact they've had. They are the most common external parasite and there's a range of simple-to-use products available for the prevention and treatment of infestation. Have a chat with your vet to see what they recommend.

TICKS

There are two species of paralysis ticks in Australia: the Australian paralysis tick and the Tasmanian paralysis tick, both of which can be life-threatening to your dog because just one attached paralysis tick can kill it. Ticks are blood-sucking parasites that can only survive on the blood from an animal or 'host' to grow, develop and reproduce. They have four different life stages – egg, larva, nymph and adult – and all except the egg must find a host to take blood from at which time they inject a neurotoxin into the bloodstream of their host. This toxin causes progressive paralysis of muscles throughout the body.

The paralysis tick is common in many areas of Australia and adult ticks are most active in spring and summer, which is the tick season, but they can be found all year round particularly in tropical and subtropical regions. Ticks like dense bush, long grass and anywhere else inhabited by their natural hosts, which are bandicoots, possums, koalas and kangaroos. Ticks damage the skin of animals when they embed, creating wounds susceptible to secondary bacterial infection. Ask your vet to recommend a good paralysis tick prevention product.

There are two other types of ticks in Australia — the brown dog tick and the bush tick – which are both non-venomous. The brown dog tick usually hangs about in the environment of its host, usually a kennel, backyard or house. It can irritate your dog's skin and cause 'tick worry', which is a general state of unease and irritability, and a heavy infestation could cause anaemia due to blood loss. They can also cause tick fever.

Bush ticks prefer cattle, but they also bite dogs and can cause 'tick worry'. Check your dog for ticks every day, even if he has had tick treatment. If you find a tick don't panic but act fast as this could be a life-threatening emergency. Remove the tick immediately, making sure there aren't any more. Use a pair of fine-point tweezers or a tick hook to effectively remove the tick. Grasp the tick as close to the skin as possible and very gently pull straight upward, in a slow, steady motion. This will prevent the tick's mouth parts from breaking off and remaining embedded in the skin. I think the best method is to use a tick removal hook. You simply put the prongs on either side of the tick and twist, lifting upward. Keep the tick in a plastic container or zip lock bag for identification by your vet. If the vet identifies it as a paralysis tick, your dog will need to be seen immediately, so take your dog with you! For more on tick paralysis see Chapter 10.

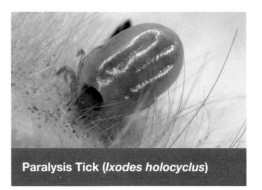

Paralysis Tick (*Ixodes holocyclus*)

CHAPTER 4

Getting a Dog

Once you have decided that you are ready to be a responsible dog owner, or you've lost your other dog and now it's time to bring a new one into your life, the next step is the fun part – choosing the right one. However, it takes time, planning and lots of research as you consider both your own needs and that of the animal you are bringing into your life.

The advent of the internet means you can trawl through websites and size up the various options on offer, decide whether you want a pure-bred or a selective mixed-breed, such as a Labradoodle or Cavadoodle. You can check-out the dogs for sale online and if you decide to take the adoption option, roam through the dog shelter websites which are absolutely bursting at the seams with beautiful dogs waiting to be rescued. For advice on the pros and cons of various breeds see Chapter 5.

The adoption option

I'm a huge fan of people choosing a rescue dog as a way of giving an animal a second chance. It's really the gift of life as the estimated annual euthanasia rate of 43,000 dogs at shelters and pounds across Australia is sadly way too high. Every year the RSPCA takes in many thousands of dogs that are no longer wanted, many being the aftermath of impulse purchases of the cute puppy in the pet shop. When looking at rescuing a dog don't overlook an older one. Dogs that have entered the final third of their lives, say around 7 to 10 years are considered seniors. They can be an excellent choice for the right people because unlike excitable pups, older dogs have calmer natures and are long past inappropriate behaviours. While senior dogs still need exercise, they are more content with shorter strolls which make them particularly suitable for older people. With a senior dog, you'll know what you are getting – they won't grow any bigger and you'll see their special personality straight away!

The RSPCA has some strict criteria around people purchasing one of their rescue dogs, including being over the age of 18 and not having a conviction for animal cruelty. The dog is not to be used solely as a commercial guard dog and must not be bought as a present for another person without their knowledge. The rules for purchase laid down by animal shelters come under the Domestic Animals Act 1994 and cover a variety of conditions including agreeing to provide the dog with all food, water, shelter and veterinary treatment for the life of the animal and that the animal will not be used for experimental and research purposes of any kind.

Dogs adopted from the RSPCA and other registered shelters come to you de-sexed, wormed and vaccinated. Your rescue dog will have also been micro-chipped, a permanent method of electronic identification; it is a tiny implant about the size of a grain of rice which is implanted between the dog's shoulder blades and contains the contact details you have given the shelter. The nine-digit code is your dog's unique identification which can be accessed by all vets, pounds and councils with a barcode scanner; a data base enables the dog to be tracked to you if it escapes so it's important to have up-to-date contact details on it at all times. Micro-chipping is compulsory in all States and the Australian Capital Territory. It is not compulsory in the Northern Territory.

The cost of the micro-chipping, worming, vaccination and desexing are paid by the person adopting the dog. In order to control canine over-population all shelters have a strict policy of desexing every un-desexed dog before they leave. Keep the vaccination certificate for your vet and the desexing certificate to get a concession from the council when you register the dog, which should be done as soon as possible.

After volunteering at a shelter in South Africa and seeing the devastating effects of over population, I am passionate about adopting dogs

When you get to the shelter it might be tempting to take more than one dog home when you look at those big eyes melting your heart and longing to love you, but again it's important to ask yourself how well you could manage more than one dog. Multiply by two everything I have written about in this chapter. The possible exception would be if two dogs came from the same home. The dogs would already be under some stress from being removed from their usual environment but at least they have each other; to separate them would likely cause more stress.

Bringing your rescue dog home

I mentioned stress and there's no doubt that an animal shelter can be an unsettling place for many dogs, in spite of the company of other dogs and the caring staff who look after them. Once you take your chosen dog home you will need to give it some 'settling in' time. Your newly-adopted dog has just gone through a time of great change and uncertainty so be prepared to spend some time mending a damaged soul. If the dog has recently undergone surgery such as desexing it will also need some recovery time and if it still has stitches make sure you know when they are due for removal and ask about any post-operative care necessary at home. For instance, if the dog is on any medication it's important to follow the instructions until the course is finished.

Any children in the house should be cautioned to curb their enthusiasm and 'be gentle' for awhile. Let the new member of the household investigate and sniff out his new surroundings and get to know members of the family individually. Be on the watch constantly to ensure this process is proceeding smoothly. If your property has a yard, make sure the fencing is secure before letting the dog off its lead. When you take him off the property he should always be on his lead and even in an off-lead area until you feel comfortable that your new dog will respond obediently to your calls.

I have put together a bare essentials list of doggie things you will need before you bring your new furry friend home:

- Food and water bowls
- Dog basket, kennel and bedding
- Collar and ID tag
- Dog lead
- Dog or puppy food (ask your vet or local pet supplies shop for advice)
- Toys
- Reward treats
- Poo bags
- Brush or comb for grooming
- Flea, tick and worm control products

House training a rescue dog

Initially your new dog won't know what's expected of him so don't get cross or annoyed while he is learning. Getting angry could back-fire, slowing down the settling in and learning period. Give simple, clear and consistent commands followed by praise and reward treats so he gets to understand what's expected of him. Have an agreed plan about your training methods with the rest of the family. A dog's behaviour is the result of both inherited traits and learned responses; many behaviours can be modified by training and positive reinforcement. Your new dog may not have had much training before he came to you and it may take several weeks or months to instil basic commands such as 'sit', 'stay' and 'come'.

If the dog is intended as an inside dog, you need to start toilet training as soon as you bring your dog home. It may have been trained in its former home, but your home is new and you can't assume it will know what to do where. Dogs usually want to go to the toilet as soon as they wake up or after food and you need to watch for telltale signs such as sniffing or circling; get in quick and say 'toilet', immediately taking it outside. After it has peed or pooped tell it how wonderful it is and give it a reward treat and take it back inside.

If the dog has an accident in the house please don't shout at the poor animal or punish it as it is likely to make it anxious; instead clean up the mess with a paper towel, take it outside with the dog, let the dog sniff the towel and praise him. Use a non-ammonia-based cleaning product to avoid the dog being attracted to the same spot.

Toilet training takes patience and commitment but follow the same rules using positive reinforcement often enough and the dog will get the message. Right here I would like to reiterate that I am absolutely against any form of physical punishment. No hitting, no way. Aversion therapy or negative reinforcement by punishing the poor dog has the potential to tip into the realms of animal cruelty. At the back of this book there is a list of things that the RSPCA constitutes as animal cruelty.

Settling in a rescue dog

Some rescue dogs become unsettled and stressed by all the changes including a new diet and they may stop eating, so offer a range of different foods to encourage your dog to eat. Or they may get an upset tummy and diarrhoea in which case you should feed small amounts of bland food such as boiled chicken breast and rice for a few days. If an adult dog's upset tummy persists for more than 24 hours, you should seek veterinary attention; puppies on the other hand need to be seen immediately, don't wait. Read more about transitioning your dog to a new diet in Chapter 6.

If you have an existing dog, you can expect some tension while they get to know each other and establish their seniority. It's probably a good idea to introduce them to each other on neutral territory i.e. away from your

Accidents happen

home. Provide your new dog with an area of his own for eating and sleeping and remove anything the two dogs are likely to compete over such as bones, toys or food. In fact, I suggest that you feed them separately until you are sure that food will not be a source of conflict. Start with short walks together and share reward treats and try not to over-compensate by spending more time with one dog than the other.

If you have a cat, the initial introduction should be carefully supervised, and the dog should be on a lead. Dogs like to chase cats and while you can't force them to love each other you can minimise opportunities for conflict. I have witnessed household cats and dogs that genuinely seem fond of each other and even sleep snuggled up, however it's far more common that the cat learns to tolerate the dog. If your dog wants to chase the cat you need to start training it out of the inclination by using reward treats for good behaviour.

Puppy love

If you have your heart set on a puppy I would first check with your local RSPCA or other reputable animal rescue organisation as there are many beautiful surrendered puppies looking for a good home. But if you want a particular breed you will need to find a responsible breeder and do some research about where your dog is actually coming from.

It's important that you don't source your puppy from a backyard breeder.

Often a litter of puppies arrives due to ignorance or neglect where a pet dog becomes pregnant because the owner has failed to have her desexed. If breeding has been accidental, the owner is often unaware of the special requirements for the mother and her puppies before and after their birth. Inadequate nutrition, fleas and worms are common in backyard breeding. In other cases, animals are deliberately bred so the animals can be sold.

What distinguishes backyard breeders from responsible breeders are the standards that the breeder meets and whether there is a known demand for puppies before they are bred. Backyard breeding contributes to the unwanted companion animal population in the community. Uncontrolled breeding and overpopulation inevitably lead to the euthanasia of healthy unwanted animals.

While States and Territories are introducing mandatory desexing of pets and/or registration of breeders to help prevent over breeding of dogs and cats, there are no national mandatory requirements for breeders to be registered in Australia. The term 'registered breeder' can mean either that they are members of a breed association or a club which operates a stud book or register or that the breeder is registered with the local council as a breeder. Registration with an association/club or local council does not necessarily indicate that a breeder is responsible or meets good animal welfare standards. The RSPCA supports compulsory legislated registration and mandatory standards to regulate the breeding, supply and sale of companion animals and help to stamp out puppy farms.

A litter of mixed breed puppies having out grown the 'cute' phase have ended up homeless and in the local shelter – a common story

A puppy farm – also known as a puppy factory or puppy mill – is an intensive dog breeding facility operated under inadequate conditions that don't meet the dogs' behavioural, social and/or physiological needs. They are usually large-scale commercial operations, but less than adequate conditions may also exist in small volume breeding establishments which may or may not be run for profit. Any dog can come from a puppy farm – purebred, crossbreeds, mixed breeds – so it's impossible to judge whether a dog has been bred in a puppy farm based on the breed or type of dog. The only way to be sure is to visit the breeding facility and check out the conditions.

After you have settled on the sort of dog you want and sussed out who breeds them you will most likely end up with a hobby breeder, which is someone who loves that particular breed. When you visit the breeder you should go equipped with a bunch of questions. Among the things you should ask are how long they have been breeding dogs and why they started breeding, what health checks they do (ask to see the certificates), do they offer a guarantee if the puppy turns out to have health problems at their first vet check, the age at which you can take the puppy home, and what follow up services the breeder offers. You will be the puppy's new owner, but most good breeders will be happy to give advice if you need it later.

Important questions for the breeder

There are breeders for whom breeding puppies is a business and, in some cases of very popular breeds, a lucrative one. And as I have already advised, you need to take the time to visit the place where the puppies are bred so you can see for yourself how much proper care the puppies (and their mothers) are getting during the important few weeks of the pups' lives e.g. warm blankets to sleep on, toys, and lots of gentle interactions with their human caretakers. Before you visit a potential breeder, I have suggested three questions which should help you know if the breeder is the right choice for your puppy.

1 How many bitches do you own? A breeder that owns two or three bitches producing two to four litters a year will be able to give the puppies the right individual care and attention; the more bitches the breeder has each producing regular litters the more it begins to sound like a puppy farm.

2 Where are the puppies born? I'd be suspicious if the answer to this question was 'In the garage' or 'We have special shed up the back'. If your dog is going to become a family pet it needs to start the process of socialisation with humans as early as possible. A more acceptable answer would be that the breeder had a dedicated area attached to the house or the mum was allowed to choose her own birthing spot.

3 How often are the puppies in the company of people? Puppies will have an easier time adapting to humans of all shapes and sizes if people are frequently coming and going and paying loving attention to the dogs.

Bringing your puppy home

Buying a puppy is exciting but also daunting; when you finally get to bring your puppy home it will need a lot more care and attention than an adult dog. It's also is a big deal for a puppy – not just the strange environment and new people, but if it comes straight from a breeder, it is away from its mother and littermates for the very first time.

You will be removing your puppy from a temporary mini society in which he created social bonds as he played and learned to communicate with other pups. The pups got comfort and warmth as they cuddled up and slept together. They also began to develop their position in the pecking order and whether a pup develops a dominant, sub-dominant or submissive personality will depend, in part, on the relationship it forms with its littermates. Until your puppy comes to you, the first eight to ten weeks of his life will be the only time in his life in which natural canine pack behaviour was allowed to develop. When you become the pack leader in his life, he will apply the knowledge he acquired in his dog pack environment to the relationships he will develop in his new 'human' pack.

You will be able to take the puppy home between 8 to 10 weeks, at which stage the breeder should have organised his first vaccination and, ideally, started toilet training. There's no doubt that your puppy's health and behaviour will have been heavily influenced by the way the breeder has cared for it. A good breeder will provide a positive environment for puppies so that they begin life in the best possible physical and mental health.

There are a few things you need to do before you bring your new family member home such as finding the right vet if you haven't had one before. Depending where you live you may not have a choice of vets, but if you have friends with pets, ask around. You will have also set out a special place for the puppy to sleep and toys for him to play with. If he had a special comforter blanket at his original home, bring that home with your puppy. Remove everything of value around the house that he might want to chew on once he starts exploring and teething – shoes, electrical cords, TV remotes (a favourite chew toy), decorative items from the coffee table and food from the lower shelves of the pantry. Roll away any heirloom Persian rugs while he is toilet training and provide a variety of his own toys for chewing because his chewing period can go on until he is at least a year old.

The breeder is responsible for weaning pups off their mother's milk and onto a safe nutritious food. Continue to use whatever food the breeder has been using when you first bring the puppy home. Once your puppy is settled and passing well-formed healthy stools you can start weaning it onto another complete and balanced puppy diet. You can read more about feeding your puppy in Chapter 6.

This adorable eight-week-old Dogue de Bordeaux puppy will soon weigh more than me! They grow to a whopping 50-68kg

The first few weeks at home are an important time for your puppy because what they learn and experience now will shape their future behaviour. For behavioural reasons and pack hierarchy it's not advisable to let the puppy sleep on your bed; he should have his own bedding, blanket and toys. You'll need to put towels or pads in the rooms he has access to because he will use the floor as a toilet. And expect the little darling to keep you up all night as he will cry like the baby he is, missing his mother and the comfort of his littermates. I recommend crate training as soon as you can after bringing the puppy home and you'll need to buy the right crate.

Crate training

The best way to train a puppy is in a crate. And it's not cruel. Before dogs were domesticated it was natural for dogs in the wild to seek out small 'dens' where they could shelter, feel safe and care for their puppies. Providing a crate for your dog from a young age is a great way to house train him – he won't want to go to the toilet on his own bed. But if he has full reign of the house, he probably won't think twice about having a pee in some far corner when he's not fully toilet trained and you're not watching him. A crate can also prevents anxiety in a puppy who might find a great big house a bit challenging especially when no-one's home.

Choose a large well-ventilated crate that is not only big enough for your puppy to stand up and turn around but will also hold him when he's fully grown. If he's a larger breed the crate will be too big while he's a puppy so you can use a divider to make it smaller for the time being. Many pet supply outlets sell dividers. Size is important because if it's too small the dog will be cramped.

Make the crate cosy with blankets and some toys and pop the puppy in the crate for little naps (babies need sleep) and quiet time away from the excitement of playing with you and the family. At first put him in for short periods, slowly increasing the length of time he's in the crate over a few weeks and give him a treat each time. Every time you take him out of the crate give him a little walk outside so he can go to the toilet; he'll get the message that after crate time is toilet time. Remember, puppies have tiny bladders so he might not be able to wait for the next crate break; if he starts whining and scratching take him outside quickly and praise him after he's does his business and give him a reward. Try not to let him do it in the crate because you don't want him to get the idea that it's a good thing.

A six-month-old puppy can reasonably be expected to hold on for about six hours and should be able to sleep overnight in the crate but take him out before you go to bed and first thing in the morning. However, no two dogs are the same and the length of time it takes to learn how to control their bowels and bladder will depend on the dog. Be patient – learning takes time. If there is no-one home during the day who can take the puppy for crate breaks, you could use puppy pads or paper in an approved place in the home until it is mature enough to learn how to hold on for long periods and to always do their business outside.

Crate training must be a positive experience for the puppy. It should become a happy, safe place where they have food, water and toys. Using a crate from an early age means you can reduce anxiety when using it for transport or if your dog has to spend time in a crate or cage at the vet's; it's also handy as a safe haven if they turn out to be storm phobic.

Socialisation

Socialisation of your puppy is an important part of learning to be a well-behaved happy dog. The word 'socialisation' doesn't mean taking the puppy to the pub to meet your mates or local cafe for a puppychino; it means gradually exposing him to the world so he sees it in a positive way and discovers all sorts of new and awesome things.

Once people know there's a new puppy in your house, everyone will want to come over to see the 'gorgeous little dog'.

Meeting a lot of new people quickly may not be the best idea when you have just brought him home, especially if the puppy is shy. So keep this in mind, and only let children pat him gently on his back – tiny hands patting lightly should not be a problem as long as they give the puppy a chance to rest between play sessions. Interaction with other dogs should also be monitored carefully; large rough dogs could frighten a small or timid dog and not be a very positive initial experience.

One person you should introduce your puppy to is your chosen vet; keep in mind that this will be the person that you are entrusting your precious dog to carry out vaccinations, health checks and look after any illness or accidents throughout the dog's life; a good vet will try to make this initial visit a positive experience. Good breeders often offer a money back guarantee if there is a serious problem on their first health check, so people often take their puppy to the vet for a health check as soon as they have collected it. I check for congenital conditions such as heart murmurs, cleft palates, umbilical hernias and more minor things like retained deciduous canines and unattached dewclaws and we make appointments for future vaccinations.

A health check for a rescue dog is less urgent because they have usually been checked over by a vet at the shelter to make sure they are suitable for re-homing; having said that, a second opinion is never a bad idea.

When I know someone is getting a new puppy I encourage them to pop in for a fun visit – so the puppy can get some cuddles from the staff, have a sniff around and snack on some treats. Making the first trip to the vet a positive experience is a great idea, but I suggest calling the vet clinic first to ensure they can accommodate a fun visit on that day. There may be certain times when a 'fun visit' could not be accommodated such as a contagious case in the hospital, staff snowed under with emergencies or a euthanasia situation with grieving owners at the clinic.

When your puppy is about three months, one way to boost his confidence is to enrol him in a good puppy school to begin some professional training. Puppy classes are an excellent way to help you sort out positive associations for him. Be guided by the puppy trainer on how to reinforce at home what he's taught in

DIDUMS DOGGIE

Like human babies, puppies respond better to high-pitched human speech than to low tones. But by the time they become adult dogs they no longer prefer the higher pitch.

class. Knowing your puppy's favourite food or toys can help to motivate him during training but he's still a baby and growing and learning is tiring so let him rest regularly and keep training sessions short and fun. If he has a crate, let him retreat to that for time out.

Vaccinations courses vary slightly from vet clinic to vet clinic and between brands of vaccinations; injections are usually given at 6, 8 and 10 weeks. Of course it's important to protect a puppy that's not fully vaccinated yet from the dangers of parvovirus and kennel cough but you can plan your outings after his second vaccinations, taking him to public places for short periods of time and avoiding dog parks and over-populated areas until your vet gives you the all clear. Discuss this with your vet before taking your puppy out into the big world as this advice can vary. Groom him gently, so he gets used to having his ears, eyes and other body parts checked. Introduce him to travelling in the car, ensuring he is properly restrained. You can read more about this in Chapter 14.

Keep on training him and reinforcing his good behaviour with praise and treats. Everything you do from the time you get the puppy home should be consistent: rules and a routine established; rewards given after toileting outside; good behaviour rewarded and bad behaviour ignored. Nip separation anxiety in the bud by leaving the puppy alone for short periods to get him used to being without you. Take him out for a toilet break before you go, leave a treat for him and take him out again when you come back. Remember a reward treat can be a tiny piece of dried liver or a single piece of kibble, chat to your vet to be sure you're not over feeding them.

By the time he's six months old he will probably be ready for more advanced obedience training. In terms of a dog learning boundaries and where they stand in the family pack, the first year is a critical period in your dog's life. There are obedience schools and most vets have a puppy pre-school where puppies who have been appropriately vaccinated learn socialisation and basic commands such as 'sit' and 'stay' as well as awareness of different sounds like clapping. The dogs are provided with a graduation certificate and some schools even have photos taken of the puppies wearing mortar boards – very cute!

A number of breeds are very intelligent and easy to train – the more eager they are to please the more trainable they are. Labradors in particular are so desperate to please so they are often the star pupils. Golden Retrievers also have easy to train temperaments. You can tell the dogs that have been well-trained; they're the laid-back ones who sit confidentially outside a supermarket waiting patiently for the owner to re-emerge without barking or looking anxious. For more about the trainability of various breeds see Chapter 5.

As your puppy gets older, his dietary needs will change and he should be gradually moving on to adult food. Most veterinary-recommended diets say the

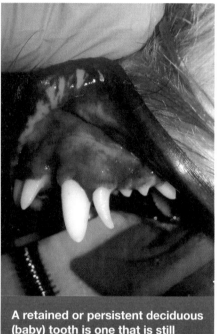

A retained or persistent deciduous (baby) tooth is one that is still present despite the eruption of the permanent tooth, usually between three to seven months of age

puppy should be fed a puppy diet until it is 12 months old. At 12 weeks he should have finished the vaccination course or had at least the first two vaccinations and after that he can be out and about with you, meeting other fully vaccinated dogs, new people and experiencing different sights and sounds. What fun!

When you take your puppy to the vet for his second vaccinations ask about on-going worming, tick and flea treatment, and desexing. This is probably the best time to have him micro-chipped, although you can have them done as early as eight weeks. Some vets prefer to do it when the dog is being de-sexed because it will be anaesthetised and won't feel any pain or discomfort. After micro-chipping you will need to register your new dog with your local council which is done with the help of the receptionist or nurse at the vet clinic.

Desexing

This subject is a biggie. Dog owners ask me a lot of questions about it and as a general rule I recommend desexing for both males and females if the dog's owner has no intention of breeding from it. The term desexing covers both spaying, which is the removal of a female dog's ovaries and uterus, and castration or neutering, which is the procedure to remove male testicles.

When surgical desexing first became a common practice around 50 years ago, dogs were usually de-sexed at about six months old. But over the past 10-15 years, early-age desexing (EAD) has become the norm with the RSPCA now recommending the desexing of dogs as early as eight weeks and at a minimum weight of one kilo, regardless of breed. The RSPCA bases its decision to advocate EAD on the considerable scientific evidence that it is safe. One of its key objectives is to prevent unwanted litters ending up in shelters and pounds; another is to reduce the time a young animal needs to spend in a shelter. EAD makes it possible for breeders to have puppies de-sexed before they sell them, thus avoiding owners forgetting to get their maturing dog de-sexed, although this is rare.

SMARTY PANTS

Your dog is as smart as a two-year-old toddler – at least they are able to understand the same number of words and gestures – 250!

There are significant welfare benefits to desexing dogs when they are younger. Surgery is faster and easier because their anatomical structures are not fully developed (which means less tissue trauma), the surgery incision site is smaller, and bleeding is reduced and minimal. The smaller the dog the easier it is to prepare for surgery which means less time under general anaesthesia. The anaesthetic recovery times are also shorter.

Humans can identify a de-sexed male dog at a glance – no balls, but a female is a little harder to detect visually although a certain sturdiness in her appearance may become obvious as she gets older, not apparent in females who have not been spayed. I always check the left ear for the standard tattoo symbol indicating the animal's desexed status. RSPCA Australia encourages humane ear tattooing of dogs (and cats) while under anaesthesia. We do this routinely in practice to signify their desexed status and avoid accidental repetitive surgery.

But can dogs tell if their doggie mates have had the op? From observation it appears that dogs use their superior sense of smell to identify the state of another dog's sexual status; to dogs, a de-sexed adult male smells like a young intact male and an adult de-sexed female smells like a young female. Adult intact males rarely fight with de-sexed males, probably because they are not seen as competition; they mostly seem interested in finding a bitch on heat or a young female who has not been de-sexed with future mating in mind. Dogs can't seem to distinguish between a bitch who is between seasons and one who has been desexed so they sniff both for any sign of sexual readiness.

Why do I recommend desexing? Well, the obvious reason is that it will reduce the number of unwanted dogs; I have already mentioned how distressing it is to see so many healthy dogs euthanised. The second reason is the many health benefits, but before I talk about them it might be helpful to give a bit of an overview of a dog's reproductive life. Most male and female dogs mature to the point of being capable of sexual activity at about 6 to 12 months of age. Smaller dogs generally enter doggie puberty at an earlier age than larger dogs.

DESEXING THE FEMALE DOG

Before a bitch can be mated, she will have to come 'on heat' or go 'into season', known as oestrus. Female dogs usually reach sexual maturity at around six months of age. Some of the smaller breeds can have their first 'heat' cycle as early as four months. On the other hand, large and giant breeds can be up to two years old before they come into heat for the first time. On average a female will come into season about twice a year (or every six months), although it varies from dog to dog. When she's young it's quite normal for some variability in the time between cycles. Some females take 18 months to two years to develop a regular cycle.

In between seasons, a female is not sexually receptive to males and

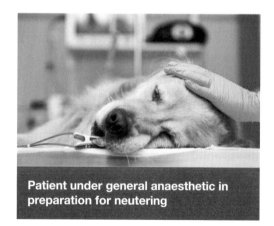

Patient under general anaesthetic in preparation for neutering

blood flow to her reproductive organs and hormone levels are at their lowest. When the bitch is about to come into heat, a massive release of hormones surges through her blood stream, stimulating the ovaries to mature and release eggs, and causing a dramatic increase in activity in the uterus and breast tissue, readying both for potential uterine implantation and milk production. This can affect the dog's temperament – they go a bit batty.

The season can last for three weeks and in the early stages she will bleed from her vulva – a messy, smelly business for her owner. During this time she will attract all the neighbourhood's intact male dogs that can pick up her scent from several kilometres away. If they are roaming about, they'll be there in a flash; if they're fenced in somewhere they'll destroy fences and dig tunnels to escape. You can keep your little lassie inside, but the boys will line up at your door eagerly wanting to present their credentials. During this stage she won't be very interested but a week or 10 days into her season she'll be just as keen as the waiting boys and at the most risk of becoming pregnant. No matter how much you try to keep her away from those panting suitors, a determined bitch often finds a way to get out – they're like teenagers.

After the heat is over, some bitches think they are pregnant and start lactating, regardless of whether or not they have been mated – this is known as a false pregnancy. The false pregnancy may be very mild and you may not notice anything, but the hormones associated with her heat have prepared her uterus and mammary tissue for pregnancy and lactation. Some dogs will have a full-on false pregnancy and start to make nests, stealing slippers or soft toys as substitute 'puppies'. They can also become aggressive and naturally all this behaviour can be a little distressing to both owners and the poor dog. Eventually the hormone levels wane and the mammary and reproductive tissues become less active, until they start their next reproductive cycle.

The same hormone surges that get a bitch's uterus and mammary tissue ready for potential pregnancy can have long-term damaging effects on those same tissues, especially if she does not fall pregnant. Because the uterus and ovaries are removed during desexing, desexed dogs will not get uterine cancer or ovarian cysts, however the rate of womb infections in older un-mated, non-desexed dogs is really quite high. It is a nasty, potentially fatal, condition called pyometra which literally means puss in the uterus. It is caused by an infection which travels up to the uterus via the vagina; it makes a dog very sick and surgery is risky.

We know that breast cancer is virtually unheard of in dogs that have been de-sexed before their first season as it removes the source of cancer-producing hormones. The sex hormone oestrogen can also predispose a dog to developing diabetes mellitus (sugar diabetes).

The downside of desexing female dogs is they can get fat, so you need to be careful with their diet. Obesity can also lead to diabetes. Another possible side effect is urinary incontinence which happens when the neck of the bladder weakens as they get older. But this can also happen in young dogs; my little Lab, Java, had this, as well as everything else! This condition is sometimes referred to as spay incontinence and is the result of a weakened urethral sphincter. Java was desexed prior to six months of age and just after she was one year old, I noticed she was dribbling urine while walking or lying down and there were wet spots on her bedding; she was also frequently licking her skin which was irritated by the leaking urine. She responded immediately to the medication – the majority of dogs do.

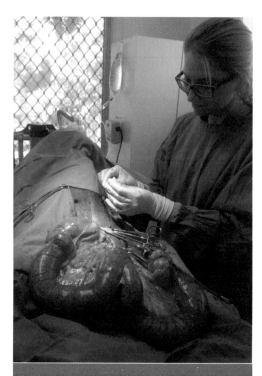

Here I am doing pyometra surgical procedure (pyometra literally means a pus-filled uterus). You can see the uterus ballooning from the pus in it. This poor dog was in a critical state but she recovered well after surgery. A disposal face mask is always used in surgery; on this day, the mask was itching my face so the nurses were giving me a moment's break from it while I replaced my needle.

Desexing is tougher on the female dog because it's major invasive surgery; several organs have to be manoeuvred to reach the uterus, so the incision is quite large. The length of time the operation takes will depend on the size of the dog – a small easy one may take 20 minutes. An hour denotes a degree of difficulty and two hours would be a very bad scenario indeed. The risks are higher in older dogs, especially obese ones but we still do this regularly. Some owners don't get their dogs de-sexed while they are puppies because they wanted to breed or they just didn't know that they had to.

Most bitches will be able to go home on the day of surgery, but they will need to rest to recover. Short toilet walks only for 10 to 14 days. At the post-operative check-up ask your vet when you can take her for longer walks. She will need to wear what we call a 'buster collar,' or sometimes an 'Elizabethan collar' the cone we put around their head to prevent her from licking the wound which could cause an infection. Contact your vet if the wound looks inflamed or weeping or if she appears to be unwell or in pain.

DESEXING THE MALE DOG

While male dogs don't have a reproductive cycle they do experience varying hormone levels, largely in response to the presence of a potential mate. When he sniffs out a bitch on heat a male dog will release more hormones to stimulate the production of more sperm. Once he's attracted to a female on heat, he will want to visit her before any other suitors and will use all his wiles to escape from any containment; a dog with love on his mind will throw caution to the wind and even put himself in danger; crossing roads can pose a significant risk of getting hit by a car.

Even if he cannot escape, the frustration of not being able to get out and mate can have consequences. The hormones that bombard his prostate can cause it to enlarge. This is called hypertrophy and although it's normally a benign condition cancers can occur in the prostate of the male dog. Prostatic hypertrophy appears to be more common in the sexually inactive male dog than in stud dogs that mate regularly. The male dog's principal hormone is testosterone and the prostate's constant exposure to this hormone can cause it to swell over time; this is called benign hyperplasia. An enlarged prostate can make it difficult for the dog to poo as it blocks his colon. A big prostate is also prone to infection, or prostatitis. De-sexed dogs do not get hyperplasia or prostatitis. Testicular cancer is thought to be caused by a complex mix of risk factors, some environmental and some genetic or hereditary. The danger of testicular cancer is its potential to spread to other parts of the dog's body.

Testosterone can affect the dog's temperament. One unwanted effect is increased aggression which puts the dog at higher risk of harming other dogs or being involved in fights, and less inclined to listen to their owners.

Early desexing in shelters has been widely accepted globally and has had a great result in controlling pet overpopulation, however new studies suggest that delaying castration for large breed male dogs is preferable. One reason for this is that removing the hormonal influence on the developing skeleton may have a negative impact on proper limb conformation, particularly in giant breeds. Early desexing of males may lead to increased risks of orthopaedic disease – such as hip dysplasia and cranial cruciate ligament disease – later in life. For this reason, many vets now recommend desexing male dogs only after they've reached musculoskeletal maturity, at about 12-18 months of age.

Another factor to consider is behaviour. Among most veterinarians it is generally accepted that early desexing of male dogs addresses behavioural problems such as roaming, mounting and aggression. But this might be more complicated then we first thought. In a recent study of 6,235 male dogs, Professor Paul McGreevy, Professor of Animal Behaviour and Animal Welfare Science, University of Sydney, assessed the effects on everyday behaviour of desexing male dogs and preventing them from going through puberty. This study suggested that dog behaviour matures naturally when sex hormones are allowed to have their effect. It's not all good news though, male dogs that were desexed later in life were associated with more indoor urine-marking and howling when left alone; but on the other hand, they were less likely to bark persistently and show signs of fear and anxiety. The current findings present a paradox. Early desexing may reduce the numbers of unwanted dogs at large, but it may increase the likelihood of problem behaviours making them more vulnerable to being surrendered to shelters. Yet another factor to consider in the decision-making process of when it's best to desex male dogs.

The surgical procedure is much simpler and quicker for male dogs because the vet does not have to enter into the abdominal cavity. We make a small nick above the scrotum to remove the testicles. If one, or occasionally both testicles are undescended — this is called cryptorchid and is detected at their puppy check — it's important that they are removed because they can become deformed in the abdomen and are prone to cancer.

The skin will take 7 to 10 days to heal for both speys and castrations although a castrated dog will often feel 100 per cent again in just 24-48 hours.

CHAPTER 5

Choosing the Right Dog

You've ploughed your way through the chapter on responsible dog ownership and all the other chapters on the things one needs to know about living with a dog; you've ticked all the boxes and now you want to proceed with selecting the right dog for you and your family. If you are adopting a rescue dog the choice might not be yours – the dog may choose you. Trust me, just one look may do it, especially if the dog has had a bit of a sad history and you're a sucker for a sob story.

If you are getting a puppy, well there is an enormous variety of breeds to choose from. Maybe you are replacing a beloved dog that died and want one that is 'just the same' or you're getting a friend for the dog you already have. Whatever your situation, there is a size, shape and personality to suit every conceivable taste and each will come with its own challenges and benefits.

While we may be drawn to the looks of a particular breed, its appearance should not be your only consideration. For instance, how trainable is it, how noisy, how good is it with children and something many people don't consider – what are the likely health issues the breed may have?

Dogs come in all sizes from shoebox to boxcar and in this chapter I go through the various sizes and the popularity of some of them. Believe it or not, size matters when you are choosing a dog. Small dogs don't necessarily mean less exercise and they can be at greater risk of an unwitting injury after being accidentally stepped on or tripped over. Large dogs need more room and their size can make some of the challenging dog behaviours such as jumping or straining on the lead even more problematic.

Size also impacts a dog's life expectancy so it might be an idea to match your chosen breed with your stage in life; a longer living breed might be better for a young family and smaller dogs tend to live longer than larger dogs. In fact, dogs who weigh less than nine kilograms have an average life span of 11 years and some breeds live even longer – Chihuahuas and little terriers live to be 16 years plus. The giant breeds have a shorter life span; Great Danes and Irish Wolfhounds often die at six or seven years of age. Dogs that weigh more than 40 kilograms generally have an eight- to ten-year life expectancy although many do live longer, and it often comes down to health.

Many people are totally unaware that dogs have an incredible number of the same illness and diseases that humans have plus a whole lot of canine-only ones. And while I'm not suggesting you select a breed on the basis of future health issues it should at least be a consideration. The RSPCA is trying to discourage the breeding of Brachycephalic dogs such as bull dogs and pugs. They are beautiful little animals, but their health problems are horrendous – ask any vet. I question the ethics around continuing to breed animals with very long list of inherited diseases. All breeds have particular diseases and conditions they are prone to and it's helpful to know in advance so you know what to look for and can seek help sooner rather than later. Many things can be successfully managed or completely resolved if caught early. In this chapter I have chosen 20 of the most popular purebred dogs in Australia and 10 popular cross and mixed breeds and list some of their positive and negative characteristics. I also and briefly outline possible health problems they might encounter and cover each of these conditions more fully in Chapter 10.

Getting a second dog

Once dogs were able to roam around the streets on their own sniffing and interacting with other dogs in the neighbourhood – there were fewer cars and no rules about being on a lead; today, the opportunity for dogs to socialise is in many cases greatly diminished and they are often left at home alone for long periods of time when their family is working or at school. Dogs are highly social animals and the decision about bringing another dog into the house is often about providing your pooch with some company for the daylight hours.

But how do you choose? And is it always a good idea to bring a second dog into the home? Picking a second dog in haste can lead to personality clashes between the old and the new member of the house. Sometimes it's an emergency situation when you have to take on a friend or relative's dog when they die or can no longer care for the dog; then you just have to make it work. Some people take their dog to the shelter in the hope that the dog will have some input into the choice but that doesn't always work either; it's a bit like a marriage based on initial impressions and there's no guarantee they'll co-exist happily down the track. There are a few tips to follow that will help increase your chances of a better match.

- **As a general rule don't go for female to female.** While it's not common for two dogs of any gender to fight if they live in the same household, but studies have shown that fighting dogs are more apt to both be bitches. Mixed gender sets or desexed male to male is more likely to work.

- **Activity similarity is more important than breed similarity.** Breed similarity helps because they will have similar behaviours and more likely to understand each other but when pairing dogs, their breed is only important as a marker for activity levels. It helps to have dogs with similar exercise capacities and who like to do similar things. Having one dog who loves a good run and one who just likes to have a 10-minute play fetching a ball or a Frisbee and then wants to sniff a bush or two before having a good lie down is going to present a few challenges.

- **Similar health status is more important than being of a similar age.** It's natural to suppose that the second dog should be around the same age as the first or to believe that bringing a puppy or younger dog into the house will pep-up an older dog. But I think that the decision should be more about the first dog's stamina; an older dog can get revitalised by a younger dog, but not if the older dog is unwell or slow with arthritis – in this case a frisky young dog would just stress it out.

How you introduce your new dog into the household will influence how your first dog takes to the new dog. It's common for the new dog to get lots of excited attention and while the new addition does need to some special attention in order to be integrated into the household, the old dog can feel kind of left out which could strain the canine relationship. Avoid this by giving priority to your first dog; let him know he's the number one dog by feeding him first, cuddling him first and giving him treats first. Make sure everyone in the family is on the same page about this rule.

Over time the two dogs will determine amongst themselves who has priority access to what's on offer. Food may be the priority for your first dog so you will always fill his bowl first while the newer dog may decide he rather have an ear rub or a favourite toy before eating. Over time you'll pick up what is more important to each dog by observing them. After about six months, in most cases, the new addition will be well integrated into your family and you will be able to relax about preferential treatments.

Large or giant dogs - more than 35 kilograms

While these very large canines can turn heads in the street they can also intimidate and may make people nervous about coming to your house – which for some dog owners is actually the point! Although most large breeds need a lot of space, some are quite low energy and make happy lounge lizards.

Great Dane males can grow up to 91kg at a healthy weight

A large strong dog will need an owner who is physically capable of handling it. They might make cute little puppies but think ahead to their adult or senior years; a large breed that develops arthritis will probably need help climbing stairs and getting in and out of the car.

Bigger dogs mean bigger everything – more hair, more drool and more poo. Cost is another consideration; the larger the dog the more it eats, the larger the doses of medications it needs and even the longer the surgical procedures, so almost all costs rise according to the dog's weight.

The top 10 biggest dog breeds in Australia that can easily weigh more than 35 kilograms are:

- Newfoundlands
- Bull Arabs
- Australian Shepherds
- Great Danes
- Alaskan Malamutes

- Rhodesian Ridgebacks
- Weimaraners
- Doberman Pinschers
- Rottweilers
- German Shepherds

Medium dogs - 13 to 35 kilograms

This is the 'Goldilocks' dog –it's great for people who like a larger dog but don't have the space for a giant breed and it's not as delicate as a small breed. So, it's just the right size, especially for people who like to go jogging, bushwalking and camping.

The top ten medium-sized dogs in Australia are:

- American Staffordshire Terriers
- Border Collies
- Bull Terriers
- Cocker Spaniels
- English Bulldogs
- Golden Retrievers
- Labrador Retrievers
- Poodles
- Staffordshire Bull Terriers
- Shiba Inus

Small and toy dogs - under 13 kilograms

Small dogs are perfect for apartment-dwellers or home bodies. Although there are some high energy small breeds that need a lot of physical and mental exercise, such as the Jack Russell Terrier, in general small dogs need less exercise. They also cost less to feed and because they can be easily picked up, they are quite portable.

If you are someone who likes to have more than one dog, two small dogs are easier to manage than two larger dogs. If you already have a large boisterous dog and are looking for a second dog, a small dog is a good option.

The top 10 small breeds are:

- Cavalier King Charles Spaniels
- Dachshunds

Australian Terriers are good apartment dwellers

- Australian Terriers
- Shih Tzus
- Pomeranians
- Beagles

- French Bulldogs
- Jack Russell Terriers
- Miniature Poodles
- Basset Hounds

The 20 most popular purebreds

I have put together some information about the 20 most popular purebreeds in Australia and with a bit of personal opinion thrown in. Each breed has its own health issues and I have listed the common ones for each breed here, but you'll find more detailed information in Chapters 9 and 10.

LABRADORS (LABRADOR RETRIEVERS OR LABS)

It's no wonder that the lovely Labrador always tops or comes near the top of the most popular breeds in Australia. They're popular because they are very loyal family dogs and very trainable. It's common for Lab puppies to go to families with small children – people Google 'family dog' and Labrador comes up so they get one. My darling Java was a chocolate Labrador – a very trendy breed at the time I got her. They also come in blonde and less commonly in black.

They start of as mad, energetic puppies – a bit like a toddler on amphetamines –they're very emotional and they chew everything and want to eat everything and they jump up everywhere. Their separation anxiety is traumatic – every time you leave the house they make you feel as if you're abandoning them forever. But don't fret, because in a few years they settle down to be the gentlest, kindest, most loyal family dogs you'll ever meet!

The more nuts they are as puppies the less time people tend to spend with them which can be a problem. But the family that puts in heaps of time with the little Lab are the ones that get the benefits. They need to have a good run at least twice a day.

The Lab is very food motivated, which is both good and bad. The good thing is that they'll do anything for food, so you can teach them to do anything; the bad side is they'll eat anything – and they'll eat all day. Consequently, about 90 per cent of Labradors are overweight and it's a constant battle to keep their weight down.

They are prone to joint problems later on in life – often canine hip dysplasia (CHD) – so the combination of loving food and having joint problems is not a good one. They're also predisposed to arthritis which doesn't go well with obesity either, and their lifespan is about 10-12 years.

STAFFORDSHIRE BULL TERRIERS

This breed, commonly known as the 'Staffy', has had a bit of bad press because they are often cross-bred with Pit bulls and their head structure is similar to that of a Pit bull, so people think they are a banned, restricted or dangerous breed. But the purebred Staffy is a usually a lovely natured dog and they are not banned in Australia.

The Staffy is referred to as the 'nanny dog' in the UK because it is good at looking after children and although most are gentle and well-behaved with children, some are a bit too enthusiastic for little kids. This breed is generally energetic and friendly, craves human companionship and has a tendency towards extreme separation anxiety; they feel the world even worse than Labradors. Man, do they have feelings! When they have to stay at the vet clinic and their owners leave, they're like… 'OMG, where did they go? When is my human coming back? How long do I have to be here?' When I have a Staffy in my clinic the nurses and I do our best to give these sooky bums utmost reassurance and love during their stay.

On the other hand, they're very loving so they're take love wherever they can get it. If you sit with them for a bit they'll forget their owner and it's 'You'll do!' They're gorgeous but you have to be prepared to be patient with their emotions.

Tenacious, and strong-willed, the Staffy does not usually seek a quarrel however if they haven't been properly socialised as a puppy, Staffys have a reputation for being dog aggressive and do not like to be challenged by strange dogs. Generally speaking, if a Staffy is aggressive I

Staffordshire Bull Terriers are energetic and friendly

have often found that it's not so much the breed but the environment they're in. This breed can live outdoors, although not in cold weather and they actually do better as an indoor pet and require a nice on-lead walk daily. Their coat needs minimal coat care.

Staffys are susceptible to health issues like canine hip dysplasia and occasionally cataracts, They tend to have a lot of itches and scratches, from things like demodectic mange (parasites that live in hair follicles) and flea allergy dermatitis. They get lumps and bumps, mast cell tumours on the skin, and can be susceptible to hemangiosarcoma and lymphoma. Staffys are also prone to rupture their cruciate ligaments, often requiring costly orthopaedic surgery, so it's a good idea to insure them. They have an average lifespan of 12-14 years.

GERMAN SHEPHERDS

This is a breed that I find difficult to read sometimes. They are big and commanding dogs. Once they have built a strong and loyal connection with their owner, they can become quite cautious with everybody else. When they come to the vet clinic they're usually wary of me and I'm never sure if everything's cool or if they're daring me to take one more step. They are happy to give you a warning if they want you to back off – and I do, swiftly!

I wouldn't recommend a German Shepherd as a first dog. I've known many families with German Shepherds and they absolutely love them but they're powerful dogs, and any powerful dog needs to be owned by responsible and experienced person. They rate very high on the trainability scale which is why they make good police dogs and guard dogs. They are used for a broad range of roles that require them to use their remarkable scent detection abilities, including accelerant detection, cadaver searching, explosives detection, narcotics detection, search and rescue operations, to name just a few. Their temperament traits include alertness, confidence, courage, curiosity, intelligence, loyalty and obedience. They come in a range of colour markings, but the majority have black body-markings and masks. These can vary from the classic saddle to an over-all blanket of black. The less common colour variations include the blue, pure-black or white, liver, and sable varieties.

Health issues with German Shepherds' include elbow dysplasia, which is similar to hip dysplasia, although not as common. It's caused by displacement in the elbow joint and the pain can make it difficult to walk and causes osteoarthritis, a degenerative disease of the elbow joint. They are also prone to a painful condition called perianal fistulas where the skin around the anal region forms smelly infected tracks in the tissue requiring long courses of antibiotics and anti-fungal treatments and sometimes surgery.

Megaesophagus, when the oesophagus loses strength and is unable to pass food properly, is another common condition in German Shepherds. One illness for which there is no cure is degenerative myelopathy, a genetic disorder which is frequently found in unethically bred German Shepherds. Haemophilia, a disease that affects the blood's ability to clot, is the result of years of inbreeding German Shepherds, and while not common it affects them more than any other dog breed. The median life span of a German Shepherd is between 10-12 years, but depends on their weight and health history.

FRENCH BULLDOGS

This has been the most popular and trendy dog in Australia for the last couple of years and is extremely popular in the United States. I love the Frenchie's stature – with their little legs and bat ears they remind me of an energetic little piglet. They're gorgeous and affectionate dogs which is why people love them. A Frenchies' short smooth coat can be brindle, fawn, white, black and brindle and white. They have soft, loose skin forming wrinkles around the head and shoulders.

Unfortunately, their shortened snout means it is one of those breeds with Brachycephalic Syndrome; this is a combination of an elongated soft palate, stenotic nares, and everted laryngeal saccules, which makes it difficult for them to breathe, particularly if they get stressed and over-heated. Believe it or not, this is a syndrome that has been bred into several breeds of dogs over a couple of hundred years by people desiring dogs with squashed faces.

Because of their short face, most Frenchies snort, snuffle, wheeze, grunt, and snore loudly. These sounds are endearing to some people; nerve-wracking to others, such as vets, who are constantly concerned about the breed's inherent respiratory difficulties. They also slobber and some drool, especially after eating and drinking. They are also known for their flatulence – this is caused by gulping air when they eat (and a diet of hard to digest food).

I always lecture owners about keeping their Frenchie out of the sun as much as possible, especially no running in the middle of the day in summer, and to never leave them in the car – which no dog owner should do anyway, regardless of the breed. You have to be particularly careful if the dog is black because they feel the heat more quickly. Having a squat frame means Frenchies aren't good swimmers so pool owners need to keep an eye on them. Some Frenchies are friendly with everyone, while others are politely reserved. They will bark to announce visitors but are otherwise quiet dogs.

Usually peaceful with other pets (though some will hunt small rodents), Frenchie males may bicker with other males. On the whole they are very sensitive little pooches; if you get cross with your French Bulldog he might go off and sulk.

They rate fairly low on the trainability scale and consequently are a bit challenging to be housebroken yet will remember what they learn, and will respond well to patient, positive reinforcement and encouragement using food motivation.

They're okay with children — although I think you have to work a bit harder to have a relationship with a Frenchy if you're a kid — but they usually get on well with other dogs and don't need much exercise which makes them good apartment dogs. And they aren't big barkers although they like to 'talk' using a complex system of squeaks and snuffles — the snuffling likely associated with their Brachycephalic Syndrome.

Along with respiratory disorders, Frenchies also suffer from spinal disorders, eye diseases, heart disease, and joint diseases. They have a life expectancy of 10-12 years.

French Bulldogs are popular and trendy

GOLDEN RETRIEVERS

These are delightful, loyal, trustworthy dogs. They're a tad calmer than Labradors but their temperaments are almost the same. This is a dog that loves everyone, especially children – walk a Golden Retriever down the street and everyone will want to pat him and he'll respond cheerfully. The breed was developed as a working retriever for hunters and this means he needs a high level of activity; he'll fetch a ball until your arm drops off! Try enlisting the neighbour's kids to play fetch with him because he'll play that game for hours — but don't overdo it for the first couple of years until he's fully matured.

This breed are not a home alone dog – leaving them at home can create separation anxiety, loneliness and boredom, driving them to barking, digging and general naughtiness. They're best suited to people who live active lives and enjoy long dog walks and or runs. Golden Retriever's also need mental stimulation so challenge their brain with puzzle toys; they're also highly trainable which is why they make good therapy and guide dogs.

The Golden Retriever has a dense, water-repellent double coat that comes in various shades of gold. They shed this coat heavily and require frequent brushing to keep the fur from flying – a Golden Retriever in the vet consulting room results in a fur bomb within seconds! Their grooming requires dedication and you'll be vacuuming non-stop if they're indoors.

Golden Retrievers have three high risk health problems – cancer, hip and elbow dysplasia and seizures. Partly due to their predisposition to cancer — namely mast cell tumours, lymphoma and hemangiosarcoma — they live to about nine or 10 years.

BORDER COLLIES

This is a gorgeous breed, but they must have space – and plenty of it. This clever and highly trainable breed were originally called sheepdogs because their job was herding cattle and sheep and they have a long history of physical and intellectual stimulation. That's why a farm is the best location for this breed! Collies make excellent working dogs and you can see them sitting looking around for something to chase. However, they are not good as a first dog and not high on the child friendly scale. But if they're getting their needs met and they're active and outdoors they can be a really wonderful pet, families included.

Border Collies need plenty of space

When I see a city-dweller with a Border Collie puppy, I really stress how important it is to become a runner and tell them to join the local running club because that will have to be their new life.

A house with just a small backyard won't be enough for this dog unless the owner is a triathlete and runs long distances every day. They are perfectly happy living indoors, in fact, they love to cosy up to their owners but only if they've expended a healthy amount of daily energy. Under-stimulated Collies are prone to destructive behaviour such as chewing, biting, barking and excessive digging.

This breed is prone to several health problems including canine epilepsy, which can sometimes be life-threatening. A common form of hereditary epilepsy in Border Collies is Idiopathic Epilepsy, the first signs and symptoms of which should occur within the first six months to five years of age. Other health issues include retinal atrophy (a slow progressive degenerative eye condition), congenital heart disorders, hypothyroidism (causing weight gain), cartilage and joint instability and hip dysplasia. The average age of death is 12 years.

CAVALIER KING CHARLES SPANIELS

This was my dog Sasha – the little love of my life when I was a child. Cute, gentle, very loyal and royal — from its heritage as the favourite dogs of King Charles the 2nd – the Cavalier is a toy version of a working spaniel. They have a medium-length slightly wavy silky coat which needs frequent brushing. The Cavalier is neither a digger nor a barker and fits the bill in many situations as an ideal house pet: equally good for older people and children; playful, affectionate and eager to please. He can split his time between the couch and walking the neighbourhood where he is friendly to other dogs, pets, and strangers; he does love a nice walk.

My Sasha was fit and adventurous; she adapted very well to living on a yacht and exploring the rainforests of Far North Queensland with me.

The Cavalier's major health concerns are a tendency to have heart problems, such as mitral valve insufficiency, a heart condition that affects almost all of them by ten years of age, and syringomyelia (cysts on the spinal cord). Because their snouts are still much shorter than they should be, they are also brachiocephalic but not as much as some of the other snub-nosed breeds. This breed lives 9-10 years.

No grown-ups were allowed when Sasha and I went off to do some exploring on our dinghy

ROTTWEILERS

The reputation of this breed as an aggressive dog makes many people wary. And to be honest, I am a bit wary of them too after my experience of being bitten on the hand by one while I was working in a veterinary clinic in London — a terrifying experience. The American Kennel Club refers to the Rottweiler, or Rotty, as a 'calm, confident, and courageous dog with a self-assured aloofness that does not lend itself to immediate and indiscriminate friendships'. Something I found out the hard way!

There is no doubt that this breed is a loyal, courageous, smart and known for its unwavering devotion to its owners, whom they will defend at all costs. That's most likely why Rottweiler people are Rottweiler people; such is their dedication they'll never go for another breed. Rottweilers are famous for their large, muscular build and unique coat colours and are certainly beautiful-looking animals. Originally bred as herding dogs, today's Rottweiler is often used as a guide dog, guard dog, police dog, and search and rescue dog.

They need to expend a lot of energy, so they need an owner that runs and spends a lot of time training them. These big, active dogs need at least one walk per day. Personally, I would not take the risk with young children around an unfamiliar Rottweiler although the breed does have a following with families that include young children.

The Rottweiler is a relatively disease-free breed but one of their most common health problems is hip dysplasia. They can also suffer from osteochondritis dissecans (a joint disorder), but the most common cause of early death in Rottweiler's is osteosarcoma or bone cancer. The Rottweiler is more susceptible than other breeds to parvovirus, which is why owners must adhere to the puppy vaccination program. Rottweilers are also prone to obesity which can lead

to other common health issues such as arthritis, breathing problems, heart failure, reproductive problems, diabetes, skin disease, and overheating.

The average lifespan of the Rottweiler is about 8-12 years, however females usually live a couple of years longer than males.

Rottweiler and her pup. A breed that does not make immediate friendships

AMERICAN STAFFORDSHIRE TERRIERS

This is the Pit bull and they're everywhere. There are obviously people who love them, but not always for the right reasons. They have an interesting history: the American Staffordshire Terrier and the Staffordshire Bull Terrier descended from the same lines originating in Britain. An old type of Bulldog was mixed with some terrier types, probably the English Smooth Terrier and the result was called the Bull Terrier, later to be called the Staffordshire Bull Terrier. After they arrived in America in 19th century they became known as the Pit Bull Terrier, or the American Pit Bull Terrier and later the Staffordshire Terrier which was eventually changed to the American Staffordshire Terrier. Confused? Me too.

This stocky, muscular dog evolved to have a sweet and trustworthy disposition around people. Owners describe their dogs as keenly aware of their surroundings, game for anything, and lovable family dogs, normally playful and friendly, even with strangers as long as the family is present. Nevertheless, I would be wary of recommending this dog to a family with small children. Being tenacious and fearless they need an outlet for their energy and a long daily walk on-lead or a vigorous game in the yard. They have a stiff, glossy coat that comes in many colours and patterns; coat care is minimal.

This breed likes mental and physical challenges and they are highly trainable. Unfortunately, this breed has sometimes appealed to people seeking to train them to fight and bring out their aggression rather than their loving abilities, which is why the breed ended up on the banned list in many countries. In the hands of the wrong owner who wants the dogs to look tougher, they have their ears cropped and their tails docked, often not by a vet and without anaesthetic. This is an absolute trauma for the dog because the tail is bone (so it's akin to removing a limb) and the ears are cartilage; no wonder they become aggressive, and for that I blame the owner. Ear cropping is illegal in Australia, so it's carried out in backyards; it is legal in the US where it is done by vets under anaesthetic.

White American Staffordshire Terriers can get skin cancer on their nose. Skin problems are very common, especially itchy allergies, cancers, and demodectic mange. Another serious health issue with this breed is hip and elbow dysplasia. Other growing concerns are hereditary eye diseases that can cause blindness, heart disease and thyroid disease. American Staffordshire Terriers can be born deaf, or partially deaf.

MINIATURE SCHNAUZERS

I rarely see the giant (full-size) or standard Schnauzers, but the Miniature Schnauzer is popular. My husband's parents have a Miniature Schnauzer named Sammy who is such a character, and having got to know him I have learned more about this breed in recent years.

This dog's popularity is due in no small part to their many desirable attributes – intelligence, affection, an extroverted temperament, and a personality that's twice as big as their size. They'll make you laugh when you look at that walrus moustache –and I have seen Schnauzers with some very weird haircuts – and their dark, sunken eyes covered by bushy eyebrows. His quivering enthusiasm will ensure you will never be bored when he's around and he'll be around you a lot, even following you to the bathroom.

Originally bred as a farm dog to keep barnyard vermin down, the Miniature Schnauzer's modern job has become that is of companion animal. He's a family-affectionate dog and can get a bit worried if left home alone during the day as anxiety can make him a bit destructive and lead to barking, whining and chewing. He's okay with children and usually friendly with other dogs and strangers. The same instincts that made him a good rat-catcher should caution any owner to watch him carefully around the family budgie! Despite his small stature, the Miniature Schnauzer is not a lazy lap dog; he's athletic and energetic and needs a bit more exercise than just a daily stroll around the block.

My in-laws take Sammy to the beach every day where he runs around in pure delight, barking like a lunatic and chasing people, children and dogs – like the true rat-catcher that he is! But with that done and dusted, he's more than happy to spend time sitting on the lap of George, my 80-year-old father-in-law as he rests in his armchair, both calm and content. He's a feisty little guy, protective of his family and territory. But the thing I love most about Sammy is the love he has for George. The love and closeness between this man and his dog is another example of how special this human-canine bond can be, especially for people in their senior years. Quiet the contrast to the raving rat catcher at the beach!

The Schnauzer is very trainable which is good because his natural instinct is to bark. The most common coat is salt and pepper black and silver, or just black. For many years it has been standard practice to crop the Miniature Schnauzer's ears because traditionally show winners have had cropped ears. However, many people in the dog show industry now frown on the practice which is now accepted as an unnecessary and often painful procedure for a cosmetic appearance. Unfortunately, tail-docking is standard procedure in many countries and is done when the puppy is about three or four days old.

Miniature Schnauzers don't shed a large amount of hair, they have a good health history and have a reasonably long lifespan of 12-14 years. However, they have a few canine health problems (some of which are fatal) and Miniature Schnauzers are more prone to them than the larger Schnauzers. They can be predisposed to eye conditions such as cataracts, which are often severe; progressive retinal atrophy, an inherited disease which can appear when the dog is quite young; and entropion, a painful condition which will require surgery. Other less common eye conditions include retinal dysplasia, glaucoma and lens luxation. This little pooch is more prone than other breeds to development very painful bladder or kidney stones at some point in their lifetime. If your dog has suffered from these, talk with your vet about a preventative diet to help keep stones from forming.

Pancreatitis, an inflammation of the pancreas is a common condition in Miniature Schnauzers. Other diseases sometimes found in Miniature Schnauzers are: canine hypothyroidism; Cushing's Disease, causing thirst, frequent urination and weight gain; heart disease (including mitral valve disease). Skin conditions include Comedo Syndrome which produces blackheads along the dog's back, and which is so common it is referred to as 'Schnauzer bumps'.

My father-in-law George and Sammy the dog – a beautiful bond

Like all small dogs, Miniature Schnauzers are very susceptible to periodontal disease in which food and plaque are trapped in their teeth, causing infection in the gums and the roots of the teeth. Dental disease should not be taken lightly in any breed, because as it can lead to even more serious problems. Ear infections, caused by allergies, bacteria and yeast are also common and can be very uncomfortable. The earlier you catch the infection the less pain your dog will suffer. For tips on cleaning teeth and ears see Chapter 8.

ENGLISH COCKER SPANIELS

A personal favourite! These dogs are ridiculously good looking, with soft and silky wavy coats, big puppy dog eyes and long floppy ears. Unless you know the breed it can be difficult to distinguish the English Cocker Spaniel from the American Cocker Spaniel; they are close cousins but two distinct breeds, the English Cocker is larger with a longer head.

These intelligent, loyal, life-loving dogs love to be trained. They are super faithful and want to spend every second with their owners – the sort of dog that wants to share your life from the time he wakes up to the time he goes to sleep at the foot of your bed. They are fantastic with kids and families; they love a playmate, love to fetch, swim, run and spin around. The English Cocker is alive with energy and will benefit from at least one brisk 30-minute walk a day.

Brushing and combing that beautiful coat should be done daily to minimise shedding and matting and to keep the coat looking its best. Any grooming should look as natural as possible, as if the coat simply grew that way.

This breed is prone to a number of health problems. Serious eye diseases, such as progressive retinal atrophy (PRA) and cataracts are the major concern, as they can progress to blindness. Other health-related problems include epilepsy, hereditary heart disease, canine hip dysplasia (CHD), kidney disease, hyperthyroidism and patellar luxation – dislocation of the dog's kneecap. Skin problems caused by itchy allergies and seborrhoea are also common, along with chronic ear infections. The particoloured dogs — dogs that have different colours in different areas or patches — are prone to deafness. English Cocker Spaniels live to between 12-15 years.

ENGLISH (BRITISH) BULLDOGS

Perfectly named, these are tough little guys – a brawny powerhouse whose characteristic crablike waddle exudes great strength, stability and vigour. They have a distinct appearance, with a large, spherical head and an extremely short muzzle, giving their face a flattened appearance. The English Bulldog's eyes are dark and set low and wide on the forehead. They have a thick-set, low-slung body, broad shoulders and chests and thick, sturdy legs. Basically, they are units – wide and muscular. And when they are owned by beefed-up gym junky blokes, I can't help smiling at the resemblance.

Yet in spite of their beefy appearance, the English Bulldog has the sweetest, most gentle disposition. Dependable and predictable, the Bulldog is a wonderful

English Bull dogs are tough little guys

family pet and usually loving to children. They are very people-oriented and actively solicit human attention. However, they have retained the courage that was originally bred into them for bull baiting, so they make fine watchdogs. Although they generally get along well with other family pets, English bulldogs can be aggressive to unfamiliar dogs.

English bulldogs take well to apartment living because they don't require a yard although they do need exercise to avoid obesity. It's also a breed that can easily overheat and suffer from breathing difficulties, particularly in hot weather – Brachycephalic Syndrome strikes again! They are loud breathers who tend to snore and wheeze, and many drool as well. They are moderate shedders and their short coats require little grooming although the wrinkles on the face should be wiped regularly to prevent skin infections.

Unfortunately, they are not the healthiest of dogs - the Bulldog's unique body and head structure makes him prone to various health problems, especially respiratory and joint difficulties. They can quickly become overweight if they don't get enough exercise and too much weight stresses their bodies. They commonly have skin allergies and demodectic mange and their screw tails can cause skin irritations around the anus. Eye problems include cherry eye, dry eye and entropion. Skeletal issues such as hip dysplasia and patella luxations are not uncommon. In other words, if you choose this breed, make sure you find a good vet and get pet insurance.

AUSTRALIAN SHEPHERDS

This is another gorgeous dog, affectionately named 'Aussie' – playful, loyal, smart and focussed. Australian Shepherds love to be active and to 'work', so if you're not putting them to work on a farm, teach them a few chores in the yard or give them a job as a Frisbee catcher or marathon runner. They are the perfect dog for outdoorsy owners — a couple of hour-long daily walks, jogs or hikes, plus some home training sessions will help to meet their need for activity. He can adapt to any environment as long as he's given a couple of hours of vigorous exercise every day. The Australian Shepherd is among the smartest of all breeds so it takes a lot of time and effort to keep him occupied to his satisfaction rather than bored and destructive. However, if you're ready to give him plenty of exercise and an outlet for his considerable intelligence, this dog can be right for you.

Australian Shepherds herd livestock by nipping at the animals' heels and without a flock to manage they may transfer this behaviour to children, other pets, and vehicles. Never let this sort of behaviour go uncorrected; instead redirect his behaviour towards demanding and interesting tasks or games that will provide him with the exercise and mental stimulation he needs. Australian Shepherds also make good search and rescue dogs, detection dogs and assistance and therapy dogs.

They are great with kids because they love to play. But remember he's a herding dog and they love to bark; he will bark to let you know that he sees or hears something out of the ordinary. The Australian Shepherd has a striking merle coat – dark blotches against a lighter background of the same colour but patterns vary – blue merle, red merle, black or red either with or without white markings. Avoid purchasing an Australian Shepherd who is primarily white because white is genetically linked to deafness and blindness in this breed.

The Australian Shepherd is prone to iris coloboma, nasal solar dermatitis, hypothyroidism, and canine hip dysplasia (CHD). It is also susceptible to cataracts, progressive retinal atrophy (PRA), lumbar sacral syndrome, collie eye anomaly (CEA), Persistent Pupillary Membrane (PPM), epilepsy, and patent duct arteriosus (PDA). To identify some of these issues early, a vet may recommend eye, hip, and thyroid exams for the dog, as well as DNA tests to confirm CEA. This dog can live to the ripe old age of 15.

The 'Aussie' – playful, loyal and smart

TOY POODLES

This breed is an incredibly smart dog with an upbeat personality, great for many people including families, the elderly and older children. The coat of a poodle is a blessing because it's one of the lightest-shedding, most hypoallergenic of all coated breeds — excellent for people who don't want to deal with dog fur all over their house or have allergies. Their coats can definitely be sculptured into some impressive poofed-up looks or they can be clipped to look like normal dogs; a short clip every four to six weeks keeps their curly coat practical and healthy. Poodles come in every colour under the sun (and I don't mean when they are dyed pink and blue for fun by the owners) – apricot, black, blue, brown, café-au-lait, cream, grey, red, silver, silver beige, and white. They can be particoloured or two toned.

Toy poodles have an upbeat personality

A good Toy Poodle is one of the most trainable of all breeds and cannot simply sit in the backyard and do nothing – they need mental stimulation to be happy. This is a clever dog that learns quickly and responds eagerly to positive training methods. They are miniature athletes and incredible performers who love to dance on their hind limbs – they thrive on attention and learning which makes them popular circus performers. While they sometimes attract prissy owners, they are themselves are robust little things and quite happy to play in the mud.

Most Toy Poodles make great watchdogs — they will bark sharply at the door and they tend to be reserved (though polite and non-aggressive) with strangers. They are peaceful and accepting of other dogs and cats although they can get upset if there's too much activity or conflict or roughhousing in the house — they prefer peace and harmony. For this reason they wouldn't be my first choice for a family with small children.

They do need daily exercise, as they are lively dogs and they also suffer from loneliness and separation anxiety if left alone too much. Poodles tend to learn the patterns of the day and can get flustered if you change their routines. They are sensitive dogs, sometimes hypersensitive so that if you touch them unexpectedly or startle them with a sudden loud sound, they tend to flinch.

When it comes to hospitalising and placing a drip in a dog, I would say this breed is the jumpiest. Knowing that they won't like the change of environment and disruption to their routine, the staff and I take extra care. We know they'll be experiencing some separation anxiety as they see their owner leave and they don't particularly like being poked and prodded by strangers. A gentle and conscientious veterinary team can have a Toy Poodle settled into its hospital bed, on a drip and resting within an hour or so.

Toy Poodles can live to be 15 years old, but they can suffer from a few health issues throughout their lives. Chronic problems include joint disorders (particularly patella luxations – a cute curly haired poodle usually equals unstable knees), eye diseases, disk disease, cardiac and bronchial diseases, progressive retinal atrophy, epilepsy, Addison's disease and collapsed trachea.

BOXERS

This is another distinct and beautiful looking specimen. Being large and muscular they might seem a little intimidating at first, but once you see their kind eyes, full of joy and mischief you realise how delightful and sweet these dogs are. Despite being a large breed, I think they are best as indoor dogs (you just have to get used to the snoring and the drooling). They are loyal pets that will fiercely guard their family and home against strangers. But a Boxer needs company and exercise; he can be destructive if left alone in the house. Boxers are ideal for people who want a canine companion with them most of the time or for larger busy families with homes that are often occupied by someone. They can do well in the country or in a city apartment as long as they have the opportunity to romp and expel energy. If you live in an urban area, regular walks are necessary.

I love Boxers because they are patient and calm as well as high-spirited, happy, and energetic. They are funny too - they often paw, cat-like, at their toys, food bowls, and even their owners. When they are excited, they 'kidney bean,' a little dance that involves twisting their bodies into a semi-circle, similar to the shape of a kidney bean, and then turning in circles. Boxers also make a unique sound, that I call a 'woo-woo', when they want something or are excited. Few Boxers bark excessively and if a Boxer barks there's usually a good reason.

They have regal, distinctly shaped square heads with an undershot jaw and blunt muzzle. The underbite (known as mandibular prognathism), can lead to a myriad of dental problems. They have a broad, deep chest and a relatively short, strong back. Boxers' ears fold over naturally, but traditionally their ears have been cropped to stand erect. Their tails are commonly docked when they are puppies but naturally are carried high. The Boxer's coat is short and sheds moderately. Boxers do not tolerate extreme weather temperatures, and care must be taken to prevent them from getting overheated. They also need protection from the cold since they are short-coated. Their coats, however, are very easy to care for and will be shiny and bright as long as they have a good diet, are bathed occasionally, and are given regular rubdowns with a grooming mitt.

Boxers are generally healthy, but like all breeds, they're prone to certain health conditions. They are especially prone to cancers – mast cell tumours, lymphoma, and brain tumours. White Boxers and Boxers with excessive white markings can be sunburned and may even develop skin cancer. Aortic stenosis/sub-aortic stenosis (AS/SAS) is one of the most common heart defects found in Boxers. Other common heart-related diseases include Boxer cardiomyopathy (BCM), also called Boxer Arrhythmic Cardiomyopathy (BAC), Familial Ventricular Arrhythmia (FVA) and Arrhythmogenic Right Ventricular Cardiomyopathy (ARVC). They also get Hip Dysplasia, hypothyroidism and Gastric dilation and volvulus (GDV). Like other larger dogs, Boxers are not particularly long-lived and their life expectancy ranges from about seven to ten years.

GERMAN SHORTHAIRED POINTERS

Another sporting dog, the German Shorthaired Pointer was breed for hunting and retrieving on both land and water, feathered game (e.g. ducks) being their favourite. Because of their hunting nature they may not be the best addition to the family if you have pet chickens or rabbits!

To my eyes, this one is also fabulously good looking – stylish and regal with stunning almond-shaped eyes. The German Shorthaired Pointer's idea of heaven is a day bushwalking and an evening curled up by its owner's side. This is an active dog that needs plenty of mental and physical challenges – at least an hour of exercise every day. German Shorthair Pointers are the wrong dog for elderly people or couch potato types, because chances

German short haired pointers – bred for hunting and retrieving

are he'll re-direct all that energy into destructive behaviours, like tearing up your furniture. They are great with children and love people, particularly those who embrace their needs for strenuous work and emotional connection. However, they do get nervous when left home alone as they really love companionship. This dog will be a devoted family pet, although at times he may be too overly boisterous for small children. They are a sensitive breed and responsive to gentle training. Some can whine or bark a lot. You won't need to spend any time grooming this dog as they have a short easy-care coat,

Like other dogs with deep chests (such as Weimaraners, Boxers and German Shepherds), these dogs are prone to GDV (Gastric dilation volvulus). Other common diseases seen in this breed are: hip dysplasia; Osteochondrosis Dissecans (OCD), a disease that affects cartilage and bone development in the joints; von Willebrand's Disease (vWD), an inherited bleeding disorder; entropion, an inward rolling of the eyelid; pannus, an immune system condition that occurs as a result of UV light damage to the side of the cornea; and lymphedema, abnormal fluid retention. This breed has a lifespan of 12-14 years.

AUSTRALIAN CATTLE DOGS

One of the sturdiest dogs you'll come across – the Australian Cattle Dog is as tough as nails. He has several other common names – Blue Heeler, Red Heeler, Australian Heeler and Queensland Heeler, but officially he's the Australian Cattle Dog. The heeler tag comes from the fact that these dogs were bred to herd cattle by nipping at their heels. I was bitten by my neighbour's Blue Heeler when I was about six, I remember it clear as day. His instinct is to nip cattle, sheep, children, pets, cars, anything that moves. This tendency to bite must be properly directed with socialisation and training when he's a puppy.

Like all working dogs, they thrive on exactly that – having a job. He's a high-energy working dog, not a couch potato. But his energy must be directed, or he'll become bored and will resort to entertaining himself, usually by doing something you consider naughty, like digging up your garden. The Cattle Dog's best and, if not managed appropriately, worst quality is its protectiveness. This dog usually attaches himself closely to one person and bonds less closely with others, which is why they are sometimes known as the Velcro dog due to their serious attachment to this chosen person. They will protect their family above all else and as a consequence are wary of outsiders and sometimes act aggressively to intruders, such as the little girl next door who may wander naïvely into the yard.

Besides their herding work, the Australian Cattle Dog does well at canine sports and obedience trials. Another part of his instinct is his strong prey drive. He's fascinated by cats and other small animals. If the dog is raised from puppyhood with other pets, including cats, he can be trusted to live peacefully with them in his home. However, he's likely to consider those outside his household to be fair game. This breed can live in a secure shelter outdoors, but they also like to be in the house with the family, however they are not suited to apartment life or anything that restricts their movement. Occasional combing and brushing will encourage hair turnover.

The Australian Cattle Dog's work has involved handling high temperatures, rough terrain, and long distances making him both highly tolerant of pain and intensely focused. He'll keep working even when he's injured so owners must pay careful attention to make sure he stops working or competing if he gets hurt.

Some of this dogs' major health concerns are progressive retinal atrophy (PRA), canine hip dysplasia (CHD), elbow dysplasia, deafness, and Osteochondrosis Dissecans (OCD). A few diseases occasionally seen in this breed are lens luxation, cataracts, von Willebrand's Disease (vWD), and Persistent Pupillary Membrane (PPM). My advice is to get your vet to regularly test his eyes, hips, elbows, and ears. Australian Cattle Dogs have a lifespan of about 10-13 years.

WEST HIGHLAND WHITE TERRIERS

This wee white dog is straight from Scotland! Affectionately called a Westie, he's a happy and friendly little chap to everyone – although it should be noted, not with small pets. They were originally bred for hunting and ratting and owners say they still do this, so probably not a great option if you're a rat owner or breeder. They are stocky dogs, compact and short and I'm always surprised when I pick them up to put them up on the consultation table because although they are small, they are quite weighty.

They have a double coat; a wiry straight outer coat with a somewhat soft white undercoat. This double coat fills out their faces giving them a beautiful rounded face appearance but also protects them from the element. They have strong teeth and jaws.

Westies are intelligent dogs with temperaments varying from dog to dog, some being very playful with kids and affectionate with their owners while others prefer solitude and can be quite stubborn and don't tolerate rough play. I've known a couple of Westies to be rather food and toy possessive, so socialisation and training is important in puppyhood. They enjoy regular exercise or playtime in the yard. They are barkers and they like digging, so expect some backyard excavations. Their coat needs combing two or three times weekly and professional grooming every few months. In some part of their body, such as paws and around the mouth, it may be difficult to keep their coat white.

Major health concerns with Westies are: globoid cell leukodystrophy, Legg–Perthes Disease, Craniomandibular Osteopathy (CMO) and skin diseases – I have treated a many westies for skin allergies! They are also prone to Keratoconjunctivitis Sicca (KCS), patella luxations, cataract, and copper toxicoses. They have a life span of 12-14 years.

BULL TERRIERS

I'm surprised this breed is on the popular list as I don't see that many of them in my surgery. It's a distinctive looking dog due to its long egg-shaped head (also sometimes called the Bull Terrier Roman nose) with a flat top and small dark close-set eyes; the body is broad and the back short and strong. Originally bred as a fighting dog, the Bull Terrier nowadays make wonderful companions as pets, but due to their inherent fighting instinct are banded in some countries (not Australia) and in some States in the USA.

If you get a Bull Terrier it's important to know what they were originally bred for; early socialisation and training is absolutely essential, as they can be aggressive toward other dogs, animals, and people they don't know. While they have a friendly, feisty and extroverted personality and make loyal family dogs, they can also be possessive and jealous. Because of these traits and their need for constant stimulation and exercise, sadly a lot of these dogs end up in shelters.

Training can be tricky because they can be chewers, barkers, tail chasers and, to be frank, nutcases. So you'll need to be committed to training and socialisation – these dogs are not happy if left alone most

Bull terriers need early socialisation

94

of the day. Bull terriers must be exercised daily in a fenced-in yard or with walks on leash and should not be permitted to run free, even if trained and socialised. Because of their stocky build they can easily become obese, so care must be taken not to overfeed.

They are not ideal for families with babies and toddlers who might find them a bit too rough and boisterous, but they are great family dogs with older kids who can keep up with their tireless and fun-loving boundless energy. The Bull Terrier's coat is short and dense and an average shedder. It comes in white, black, brindle, red, fawn or tri-coloured.

Because they are prone to some genetic diseases, is essential that you get your Bull Terrier from a reputable breeder – one who tests their breeding dogs to make sure they don't have anything that they might pass onto the puppies and who also breeds for sound temperaments.

They commonly suffer from patella luxation, and are also prone to heart complications, allergies and compulsive behaviours. More serious conditions include kidney failure and deafness. I encourage owners to get their vet to run tests for cardiac, thyroid, hearing and kidney function to clear them of these common problems. Their lifespan is about 10-12 years.

Crossbreeds – the designer dog

The new kids on the dog block are the crossbreeds, sometimes referred to as designer dogs or hybrids because the most popular of modern crossbreeds only became known mid 20th century. A crossbred dog is a cross between two (or sometimes more) known breeds, and is usually distinguished from a mixed-breed dog, which has ancestry from many sources, much of which may not be known.

While we may think the popular crossbreeds we see today are a new trend, don't forget that our established pure breeds were created by crossbreeding for centuries. All dogs were originally crossbreeds and mutts until breeds were uniformly defined and documented in the 19th century as they started to be selectively reproduced according to breed standards in various countries. Even then dogs continued to be mixed across breeds to create the perfect herding dog, hunting dog, sled dog or whatever job needed to be done. Later on, crossbreeding was also used by the upper classes, for preferences in looks. So, crossing dogs with different characteristics to try to create something better than each of the individuals is nothing new; it's been going on since the very first dog decided that hanging out around humans seemed like a win-win situation.

Today's crossbreeds are popular, due to the belief that they have increased vigour without the dog losing any of its attractiveness. Hybrid vigour (strong, healthy genes) occurs when new blood is brought in from outside the usual breeding circle. This is the opposite of inbreeding, which can cause purebred dogs to suffer from a multitude of inherited diseases. Planned crossbreeding between purebred dogs of different breeds to create 'designer dogs' can produce puppies worth far more than their purebred parents, due to a high demand.

However, bringing a crossbreed into your life is a bit like living with a mystery parcel – you can never be sure what's inside. People often assume that a crossbreed will combine the best of two or more breeds, but genetics doesn't always work that way and it's not something a breeder can always control. Crossbred puppies can look very different even if they are from the same litter. When you invest in that cute puppy, bear in mind that it might not be all that was promised — not necessarily healthier than a purebred or even hypoallergenic.

There is no scientific evidence that any breed or crossbreed is more or less allergenic than any other dog. Some people with allergies may react less severely to particular dogs, but no reputable breeder will guarantee that their dogs are hypoallergenic – meaning that they can supposedly be tolerated by people who have allergies to dogs. Allergies are actually caused not by a particular dog coat type but by dander, which are the dead skin cells that are shed by all dogs and people.

There is a general misconception that hybrid vigour automatically applies to crossbreeds however, if the genetic pool remains the same over time, the offspring won't have hybrid vigour. However, if a purebred breeder brings in a dog from an unrelated line, those puppies will have hybrid vigour, even though they're purebred.

Many of the really tiny crossbreeds, or 'teacup dogs', can suffer from serious health conditions like fragile bones and improper bone development. Many teacup dogs will have soft spots on their skulls even when they are full grown.

If you want the temperament that the hybrid is meant to provide, get a puppy from a responsible breeder who has taken care in selecting the parents. Hybrid vigour can produce a superb animal, but poor parent selection can result in the worst traits of both breeds with none of the good ones.

The 10 most popular crossbreeds

COCKAPOOS

A cross of Cocker Spaniel and Poodle, the happy and affectionate Cockapoo is the original 'designer dog'. Cockapoos are bright-eyed, scruffy-coated puppies that grow into dogs that retain a puppy-dog sweetness. They love families, children (especially older ones), other dogs, and even cats. The Cockapoo's size, colour, coat type, temperament, activity level, and health risks will vary depending on what traits an individual puppy has inherited.

Because Poodles have a reputation for being hypoallergenic, Cockapoos are sometimes promoted as being hypoallergenic and as they produce low amounts of dander and shed less, they are usually good for people with allergies. Cockapoos are an easy size, being small enough to cuddle and big enough to romp with bigger dogs. They have an infectious zest for life – These little guys are just plain happy to be alive. They have the intelligence and spirit of the Poodle with the sturdiness and field spirit of the Cocker.

The Cockapoo is not known to be a barker. Some, however, will bark when they see someone approaching their house, or when they're left alone for long periods at a time. Give him daily brushing and get his hair trimmed and clipped occasionally. This is an indoors dog so he will adjust to apartment life. The Cockapoo is easy to train with positive reinforcement; he needs early socialisation to expose him to many different people, sounds and sights to grow into a well-rounded pooch. They have a moderate energy level but still need daily exercise – at least 20 minutes per day – and a variety of activities. The Cockapoos like to hang out with the family and can suffer from separation anxiety when left alone for too long.

Cockapoos – the original designer dog

I have listed a few health issues to be aware of when considering this breed: cataracts, Patellar Luxation (a common problem in small dogs), hip dysplasia, skin allergies, and ear infections. Not every Cockapoo will get any or all of these diseases, but it's important to keep them in mind. The lifespan of a Cockapoo is 13-16 years.

MALTIPOOS

This one part Maltese and one part Poodle, is another fun-loving and affectionate-natured little dog. It's a living, breathing, barking incarnation of cuteness – a small, clever, playful pooch that stays puppy-like well into its senior years making the Maltipoo one of the more popular crossbreeds in Australia. A well-bred, well-raised Maltipoo should be friendly, people oriented, and easy to train — and just a little bit of a mischief-maker. Be warned, however, that a Maltipoo from an irresponsible or inexperienced breeder can be a mess of the combined genetic problems of his ancestors, without the benefit of the kind of health and temperament testing done by good breeders. That can mean a snappy, noisy tyrant of a dog, nearly impossible to housetrain and with a wide variety of costly health problems.

A Maltipoo may inherit some of the genetic conditions common to the Maltese and Poodle such as mitral valve prolapse, which is also known as Left-sided congestive heart (see Chapter 10). Other conditions include the brain disease, necrotising meningoencephalitis (found in the Maltese), orthopaedic problems, progressive retinal atrophy eye and epilepsy from Toy Poodles. Maltipoos can also suffer from the neurological condition 'white dog shaker syndrome'. They have a lifespan of 10-15 years.

White Maltese poodle is affectionately named 'Maltipoo'

LABRADOODLES

The Labradoodle is a Labrador Retriever and Poodle hybrid; an intelligent, friendly, and affectionate mix and one of my personal favourites. They come in three sizes: miniature (7-13 kilos – mixed with Toy Poodles), medium (13-20 kilos), and standard (20-45+ kilos – mixed with Standard Poodles) but because they are a crossbreed their traits are not fixed, so there is no guarantee that the Labradoodle puppy you buy will fall into the desired weight range. They will also have different coat types – wiry, woolly, wavy, curly, or fleece-like. The colour of the coat also varies, including cream, gold, red, black, chocolate, brindle and multi-patterned. Contrary to belief, some Labradoodles do shed, though far less and with less odour than a Labrador Retriever. Their coat should be brushed and shampooed regularly.

Labradoodles have a moderate to high activity level and they need a good walk or active playtime each day. They are athletic enough to participate in dog sports and generally the larger the Labradoodle the greater the exercise requirements. Both of the breeds used to create Labradoodles tend to be smart and learn quickly. Like Labs they are amazing fun-loving loyal family dogs and good with children; like Poodles, they are very smart and can be protective of their people. Labradoodles can make good watchdogs and therapy dogs and get along well with other animals. Not surprisingly, considering their mix, Labradoodles love the water and can be exceptional swimmers. They can be cautious or shy with strangers and may also be prone to restlessness or loneliness if left along for too long.

This breed may suffer from genetic health issues commonly seen in its parent breeds so if possible, it would be a good idea to find out as much as you can about the history of your Labradoodle's parents to determine any prevalent health concerns. Its ears and eyes need to be checked often, as these have common hereditary problems. Other health issues the Labradoodle is prone to include, but is not limited to hip dysplasia, Addison's disease, and eye disorders such as progressive retinal atrophy. They live to be about 12-14 years.

Labradoodles are friendly and cheerful

GOLDENDOODLES

This pooch results from breeding a Poodle (commonly a standard or sometimes a miniature) with a Golden Retriever. They are intelligent, friendly, and affectionate and have many of the same characteristics as the Labradoodle. They come in the same three sizes as the Labradoodle, however there is no guarantee that your puppy will fall into the desired weight range.

Goldendoodles have been bred primarily to be family pets, although they can also make terrific service dogs and as such make a wonderful addition to almost any home. They usually have the kind, friendly, trainable, people-oriented disposition of their Golden Retriever ancestors, blended with the natural intelligence and low-shedding coat of the Poodle. They need a good walk or active playtime each day. Both of the breeds used to create Goldendoodles tend to be smart and learn quickly.

First-generation Goldendoodles are highly variable in appearance and coat. Multi-generation Goldendoodles (where both parents are Goldendoodles) are much more consistent in type. If well socialised from puppyhood, Goldendoodles usually are great with children, adults, strangers and other pets. This breed has a personality and temperament that is intelligent, level-headed and cheerful. Due to their relaxed, outgoing personalities, Goldendoodles also make excellent companions for people with disabilities.

While crossbreeding can introduce hybrid vigour, Goldendoodles are still at risk of developing some of the problems seen in their parent breeds. I have listed a few of the more common diseases: atopic dermatitis, epilepsy, patellar luxation, Cranial Cruciate Ligament Rupture and hip dysplasia, which is a very common cause of hind-limb lameness in Goldendoodles, especially as they get older. Middle-aged Goldendoodles sometimes suffer from degeneration of retinal nerve cells and Von Willebrand Disease. The Goldendoodle lives between 10-15 years.

MALTESE SHIH TZUS

A crossbreed without a 'poo' or 'doodle' in sight! A cross between a Maltese and Shih Tzu the Maltese Shih Tzu is a small, loveable fluff ball. Classed as a toy breed and sometimes known as a Malshi, this little guy is affectionate and playful and one of the most popular crossbreeds in Australia. It is also highly adaptable, fitting in with a variety of different lifestyles from young city-dweller to quieter suburbanite. They don't need much exercise – a 30-minute walk each day is fine.

Because there is no breeding standard for the Maltese Shih Tzu they tend to vary slightly in their appearance. Once matured, the Maltese Shih Tzu measures up to 30 centimetres tall and a bit over five kilos in weight. They usually do not have the bulging eyes and snubby nose of the Shih Tzu but a short muzzle and round head. Their soft coat which comes in white, black and brown combinations does not shed a lot but they still need grooming.

Sweet loving and loyal, the Maltese Shih Tzu has a temperament generally more placid and tolerant than its Maltese heritage. It also has a reputation for being confident and outgoing and for being highly tolerant of kids of all ages and will happily play along with all family members determined to please everyone. However, discipline should be established during training and must be maintained, especially during initial training for the home. This little dog will tolerate other pets, but early socialisation at puppy stage will be necessary.

Maltese shih tzu puppy – a lovable fluff ball

Although breeders have made attempts to screen out the Malshi's genetic health problems, unfortunately this doesn't always happen, and some health issues and diseases are still present. Here's a brief run-down on the health problems your little dog may be predisposed to. Both parent breeds, the Maltese and the Shih Tzu, are genetically predisposed to Brachycephalic Respiratory Syndrome, the respiratory condition commonly seen in dogs with a short nose and flattened face shape. White Shaker Syndrome is prevalent in many small dogs, and not just white ones. The dog's whole body will shake unexpectedly and is caused by an idiopathic inflammation in the brain. Sometimes owners may mistake the shaking for their dog just being cold. But if the tremors persist, then you should contact your local vet. Patellar Luxation is a common orthopaedic problem in many dogs and is a condition common in small and toy breeds, this one included. This little bloke has a lifespan of 12-14 years.

PUGGLES

A Beagle/Pug cross sounds like an odd mix but it has produced a little pooch with sweet looks and a fun-loving personality. While both breeds are short-coated, small, cute and popular, that's about all they have in common. In theory, the Pug influence is meant to temper the Beagle's independent ways and offset his tendency to be an escape artist and a roamer with the Pug's love of home and family. On the upside, Puggles are people-friendly, enthusiastic and an easy to train little mates. On the downside, they're stubborn, selectively deaf and can be a bit stand-offish and uncooperative. Unfortunately, the worst thing about this particular crossbreed is that it's a top money-maker for puppy mills and backyard breeders.

Puggles have a fun-loving personality

A well-bred Puggle should have the best character traits of the Pug and Beagle, and be a robust, healthy little dog with a playful spirit, a sense of humour and a desire to please. He will also be a little greedy guts – both the Beagle and the Pug are notorious for wanting to eat until they pop, as well as for a devious ability to steal food from right under your nose so obesity is a problem. The Puggle's size, colour, coat type, temperament, activity level, and health risks will vary depending on what traits of the two breeds an individual puppy has inherited from his parents. One important thing to know is that Puggles often turn out to be larger than people expect, so you might get a slightly larger dog than the portable seven kilogram model you were expecting.

Puggles are companion dogs – they love their family and need to live in the house, never outdoors. Their activity level is low to moderate and they love walks and indoor play, however as with all dogs little kids need to be supervised when playing with him as they might accidentally hurt him or vice versa!

Some Puggles may snore and snort if they inherit a Pug trait, the result of their Brachycephalic features. Pugs are prone to respiratory problems and to overheating during exercise. To get an idea of the health issues Puggles might be prone to, it's a good idea to investigate the Pug's genetic background. Some problems that might come from the Pugs' genes include flat faces that cause their eyes to protrude from overly shallow sockets which means they are more likely to damage the surface of their eyes and to pick up eye infections.

Unfortunately breeding for the Pug's jaunty screw-tail has also come with a price – deformed spinal bones which can cause painful back problems.

By comparison Beagles seem blessed with robust good health. However, they can suffer hip dysplasia and canine epilepsy. Mixing the two breeds has toned down some of the Pug features and the Puggle is likely to fare better health wise than a purebred Pug. If the Puggle's weight is kept in check, they can live up to 15 years.

SCHNOODLES

Cross a Miniature Poodle with a Miniature Schnauzer and you get a lap dog, a family dog, a therapy dog, or a performance dog. Crossbreeding with a Standard Poodle or Standard Schnauzer will produce a Schnoodle in various sizes and may make a difference in his personality – from feistiness and dominance to a more soft temperament. Whatever the size he's a real cutie combining the intelligence of both parent breeds plus the boldness and loyalty of the Schnauzer and the fun-loving friendliness of the Poodle. The Schnoodle is smart and learns quickly. He likes to be active and loves a brisk walk or even a jog. And play – he really loves to play. But beware of his tendency to dig – some just love a good old dig in the garden.

A Schnoodle is a companion dog – he needs to live in the house and hang out with his people. He can get separation anxiety if left alone for long periods of time and he has a low boredom threshold. Smaller Schnoodles can live happily in apartments but the larger ones need a yard with a fence. He's a barker, sometimes too much – a trait that should be nipped in the bud during training when he's a puppy.

He has fine bones with quite long legs in proportion to the body. The head and face are generally less refined than in the Poodle, and the body is lean and strong – a reflection of the Schnoodle's athleticism. He has a high-maintenance coat somewhere between the rough and wiry Schnauzer's and the soft and curly Poodle's. The coat can be many different colours, including grey, brown, apricot, black, white and sable.

Schnoodles come in a variety of sizes

The Schnoodle has inherited some health issues from its parent breeds. They include: Addison's disease, a hormone deficiency arising from autoimmune damage to the adrenal glands; cataracts – congenital and early onset cataracts are relatively common in the Schnoodle; Diabetes Mellitus – another hormone deficiency caused by damage to the cells in the pancreas; epilepsy and progressive retinal atrophy which are common in many breeds. The Schnoodle has a life of expectancy of 15 years.

PEEKAPOOS

Probably the cutest breed name out, this little dog is a cross between a Pekingese and a Miniature (or Toy) Poodle and one of the oldest designer mixed breeds dating back to the 1950s. It was bred with the intention of creating a companion dog that was low shedding. It can vary in appearance and its soft, wavy, easy to care for coat comes in a range of distinct colours and pattern combinations of silver, white, cream, apricot, red, chocolate or black. All truly beautiful.

It has an interesting temperament – from the Pekinese side it is friendly and affectionate, and it gets intelligence and hypoallergenic genes from the Poodle. The Peekaboo (or its other permutations – the Pekepoo, Peke-a-Poo, Peke a Poo, or Pekapoo) is a lapdog, with the heart of watch dog. While cuddling up on your lap he will always be alert; the approach of someone to the house brings out his protective instincts.

This clever little dog is a bundle of energy and great for families with an active lifestyle. They like a lot of human interaction to work their brains and burn off energy – as puppies they are aggressive chewers and need teething toys to keep them occupied. Although loving with their family, they can be a little intolerant of rough house play and therefore aren't always the best choice for kids. However, they are easy to train and your Peekapoo should be socialised as early as

Peekapoos come in a range of colour and pattern combinations

possible to get him get used to children and to prevent any major barking and nipping issues.

Unfortunately, the health of the Pekingese parent may have been passed on to the puppy – I'm talking about the Pekingese being a Brachycephalic breed which could make the energetic Peekapoo unable to burn off its energy properly. The Peekapoo is prone to collapsing trachea, which is a disease that comes from the Poodle heritage and is a progressive, irreversible disease of the trachea. Other diseases include: tooth overcrowding – common in toy and designer breeds; keratoconjunctivitis sicca (also known as 'dry eye'), the impaired ability to produce tear film; Patella Luxation which occurs when the patella (kneecap) slips out of its normal position, very common in Toy Poodles or anything mixed with it; progressive retinal atrophy, another inherited condition which can result in blindness; and von Willebrand's disease, an inherited bleeding disorder which is common in Poodles. A Peekapoo has a lifespan of between 13-15 years.

YORKIPOOS

A cross between a Yorkshire Terrier (Yorkie) and a Miniature Poodle, the Yorkipoo is particularly suited to apartment life. The two breeds were crossed to combine the intelligence, trainability, and reduced-shedding coat of the Poodle with the bright, bold nature of the Yorkshire Terrier. Yorkipoos tend to be friendly, people-oriented and easy to train. They're impossibly cute as puppies, with their bright little eyes, brassy attitude and playfulness. It will be love at first sight but a word of caution – make sure you choose your Yorkipoo from a responsible source or you could end up with the genetic traits of this pooches' ancestors and get a snappy, barking little dictator and a lot of costly health problems.

Yorkipoos are usually little dogs, and although a well-bred one will probably be okay with children and other dogs, you just have to be careful that he isn't hurt by rough play. His Yorki ancestry might give him 'little man syndrome', making him feisty enough to challenge dogs much bigger than himself, so you'll need to keep him on a lead when around large dogs.

The Yorkipoo comes in many different colours and patterns taking on either the blue and gold of the Yorkie to the many solid colours of the Poodle to a colour plus white, or particolour. This is most definitely an indoors dog – he'll want to be around you and the family. But being a house dog doesn't mean he's lazy; he's is an active dog that requires exercise on a regular basis – this might be walking, chasing a ball, and even swimming – yes, he got the swimming gene from his

Poodle side. The amount of energy-burning activity he requires will probably depend on the parent genes your Yorkipoo favours.

The Yorkipoo is at some risk of all the conditions of its parents' breeds although several are seen more than others and the conditions that afflict the smaller breeds are the most likely. These include two joint disorders to which both the Yorkshire Terrier and Poodle are prone – Patellar luxation and Legg-Calve-Perthes Disease, which involves spontaneous degeneration of the head on the femur bone. A Yorkipoo can live from 12-15 years.

GOLDADORS

This dog — which sounds like something out of Harry Potter — is also known as a Golden Labrador, a hybrid of two of the most popular dogs in Australia – the Golden Retriever and the Labrador. This makes it a wonderful family pet as well as being suitable as a service dog, guide dog, assistance dog and tolerant working dog, for which they were originally bred. The Goldador is a breeze to train because he just wants to make you happy and eat his treat – he gets on with other animals and kids. Whether playing, working or relaxing, your Goldador's favourite place will be at your side. Their affectionate behaviour and loyalty is why they are truly 'man's best friend' and they don't like being left alone for long periods of time.

He's a large, athletic dog best suited to a house with a big backyard, although with enough exercise, they can adapt to apartments. Goldadors need a fair amount of exercise –of about 30 minutes of physical activity – walking or playing – daily. He needs guidance and structure in his life, so once you've set up a routine, stick with it. Their versatility and easy-going attitude are just two of the many things people love them for! He's ideal for the first-time dog owner.

The Goldador has a good health record but some concerns include arthritis in the hip and elbow joints, and eye issues. This breed has an average lifespan of 10-15 years.

Mixed breeds, mutts and mongrels

A mixed-breed dog, sometimes referred to as a mongrel or a mutt, is a dog that does not belong to one officially recognised breed. As most of the mixed breeds are not the result of intentional breeding, their existence is a true testament to nature. Without any input – some might say interference — from humans, the mixed breed defies description. These non-pedigree canines come from chance liaisons between many different breeds over many years making it difficult to detect their original ancestor without DNA testing (which is available nowadays at most vet clinics and fun to do). Available in all sizes, shapes, colours, and patterns, he might have a long snout or a short nose. He may display prick ears or floppy ones. He could have a stubby tail, spindly legs, a giant spot over his left eye – or all three. The mixed breed is gloriously, wonderfully someone else's design.

As the ultimate family dog, the mixed breed excels where the purebred lacks. Drawing from a broader, more diverse gene pool, his intensity is softer than his pedigreed cousins, and his drives and compulsions mercifully muted. The mutt's loyalty, warmth, and deep desire to please, however, remain as fiercely intact as any dog you could choose to create.

Among the mutts are some of the most popular dogs in Australia and include the following interesting mixes: Staffy x Kelpie; Kelpie x Border Collie; Bull Arab x Staffy; Maltese x Shih Tzu; Border Collie x Kelpie; Mastiff x Staffy; Boxer x Staffy; Jack Russell x Pug; Labrador x Rottweiler; and German Shepherd x Rottweiler.

Getting rid of inherited disorders

About 20 per cent of dog breeds are known to have breed-specific conformational issues that can lead to health disorders; some breeds have visible exaggerations that cause pain and discomfort. 'Conformation' refers to the expected shape, size and coat of a particular breed. For thousands of years, dogs have been bred for their usefulness and, more frequently over the past couple of hundred years, for appearance. Breed standards have been developed in an endeavour to tackle inherited disorders.

However, in 2009-2010, research by Professor Paul McGreevy, helped show that while some of the inherited disorders were related to breed standards, others were not. In other words, even if there were no breed standards and dogs were bred solely for health and welfare, many inherited disorders would still occur. In fact, the vast majority of inherited disorders have nothing to do with conformation and all inherited disorders (and all desirable inherited traits) are the result of random mutations in DNA that occur in all species.

As a result of this discovery, Professor McGreevy who was then working at the Royal Veterinary College London, helped establish a not for profit research project VetCompass UK. In 2019 he became chair of VetCompass Australia, launched by the University of Sydney.

By involving all seven Australian Veterinary schools, VetCompass Australia is able to collect clinical records from hundreds of vets across Australia for researchers to investigate. Analysis of these records will enable researchers to see the trends in the prevalence of inherited and acquired disease, identify treatments and help vets and breeders improve the quality of the lives of dogs.

VetCompass Australia has joined a global research project that is providing an ever-increasing number of DNA tests for known canine inherited disorders, enabling (in many cases) elimination of the disorder. The disorders are tracked and monitored over time to record how commonly they are seen with the assistance of hundreds of participating vets around Australia. The vets report what dogs are being treated for and what treatments actually work. Any clusters of new disorders emerging will sound alarm bells on the VetCompass real time database.

Example of a mixed breed

The information collected by VetCompass and MyBreedData — a Finland-based website that collects the results of genetic analysis from a huge number of dogs to identify mutations known to cause particular inherited disorders — will provide a foundation for research into ways to control inherited disorders within breeds. It also has the potential to reveal the extent to which hybrid vigour exists in dogs. Evidence from other species suggests that hybrid vigour in dogs could be present to a limited extent in traits relating to their health and wellbeing. The greater the genetic difference between two breeds, the greater the hybrid vigour can be expected in the first-generation offspring of the two breeds. However, breeding beyond first generation cross breeds reduces hybrid vigour and may produce unpredictable outcomes.

CHAPTER 6

Food, Food, Glorious Food

What's a good diet?

Most dogs have very enthusiastic appetites and although I've met quite a few dogs that we have trouble finding the right food for because they are so finicky, even picky eaters have to eat. And it seems like a simple and obvious premise – what a dog eats will determine its health. But what is a good diet for a dog? There are a number of potential diets and vets are increasingly asked if dogs should be fed human diets such as Paleo, vegan or organic. Many vegetarians are very insistent that their dog would do very well on a vegetarian diet and it's often hard to convince some people otherwise – it's not uncommon for them to quote something they've read on Google and let's face it, a lot of misinformation can be found on the internet.

However, although today's domestic dog is largely a carnivore that eats some plant-based food, dogs being omnivores is nothing new. Dogs' diets have included high fibre/vegetable content since the early wild dogs whose ancestors were omnivores. Prior to domestication, wild dogs hunted and ate the gut contents of herbivore animals which contained lots of grass and roughage; they are known to eat grass and plant matter in the wild as well.

Dogs have adapted to commercially processed foods very well through domestication. When deciding what to feed your dog it's important to make an informed decision – all dogs are individuals and what might be suitable for your neighbour's dog might be inappropriate for your pooch. If you are getting a rescue dog, you won't necessarily know what sort of diet he had in his previous life. You can get some guidance from the shelter as to what they have been feeding him; other than that the best person to ask about the right diet for your new dog is your own vet. However, I'd like to share some general advice.

First, it's important that your dog's diet is complete and balanced for his stage in life – from the time he's a puppy to when he's reached old age as well as taking into consideration any medical issues along the way and owners of certain breeds need to be aware of selecting the right diet to avoid certain health conditions. And take it from me, it is entirely acceptable to feed your dog a pure kibble diet. Or you can mix their diet up with some cooked or raw meat, fish, vegetables and rice. And of course, some healthy reward treats.

The raw meat debate

There is a passionate debate about raw meat versus commercial kibble and canned food and there are many myths to support whichever side you are on. One myth is that vets don't know anything about nutrition, which is one way of saying they don't agree with their advice. Not true. It was not the most exciting subject when I was at vet school, but it was an important one because nutrition is a major component in the treatment of many medical conditions.

Another myth is that vets make money from selling commercial kibble; this is not true either. The salary of a vet remains the same no matter how much food they sell; where commission is offered it is often sacrificed to keep costs comparable with that of pet stores whether or not the food is a prescription diet. Another misconception is that pet food companies invite vets to presentation dinners to woo them into stocking their product. It's true that vets get the occasional free dinner but it's usually to focus on newer products for various health issues and why their product is superior to their rival's.

Those on the raw diet bandwagon list a range of benefits after they start their dog on one. I have seen some of these benefits myself. Let's examine them:

- **Better coat.** Raw meat is often higher in fat and protein which may contribute to coat quality.

- **Decreased allergic symptoms.** Without any grain in the diet one potential allergy is eliminated. However, pets can have allergies to meat proteins as well.

- **Highly digestible.** Raw food has a lower fibre content making it easier to digest; this in turn results in less poo.

- **Longer life.** This is a bit speculative as there are no long-term studies of dogs on a raw food versus those on a commercial food diet. However, if it's true it may have something to do with the attitude of the dog's owner. People highly invested in their pet's nutrition (whatever its composition) tend towards certain behaviours that are good for the overall health of the animal. Everything they do benefits the dog – regular exercise, vaccines and flea and worming kept up to date, consistent teeth brushing, no over-feeding and any problems promptly addressed by consulting the vet.

One of the main reasons why most vets are not enthusiastic about raw meat diets is the bacteria found in uncooked meat, such as Salmonella. Most healthy dogs will not be affected by the effects of Salmonella if exposed to it; the primary concern is that it can be found in their faeces. Apart from the Salmonella risk in the daily preparation and handling of the food there is also the risk of contamination from other pathogens. Research into 35 frozen raw meat products from eight different brands of dog food in the Netherlands — a country where more than half the dog owners are thought to feed their dogs raw meat or a partly raw meat diet —revealed some unpleasant surprises. After thawing the meat, scientists at Utrecht University found 23 of the products contained a type of E. coli that can cause renal failure in humans and 80 percent across seven brands contained antibiotic resistant E. coli . Species of listeria were found in more than half the products; Salmonella was found in 20 per cent of the products and a species of Sarcocystis in 23 per cent and Toxoplasma gondii in six per cent.

Many parasites are rendered harmless by freezing but it only renders a fraction of bacteria harmless although most are killed with high temperatures/cooking. So, prior to the application of heat, bacteria pose a risk of cross-contamination with human food during home kitchen preparation. From a public health perspective, I find it rather concerning that multi-drug resistant bacteria is turning up in our animals' food source. The dogs most at risk of exposure to any nasty pathogens will be puppies, old dogs and those with compromised immune systems.

If you do want to feed your dog a raw meat diet you should make sure your food hygiene is first class as the risk of either you or your dog getting a food-borne bacterial infection such as Campylobacter or Salmonella is going to be higher. Store the food properly and make sure the eating areas and dog bowls are clean. Some raw diets will not be appropriately balanced for your dog's stage of life or medical conditions so it's a good idea to have your vet formulate the diet for you.

BARF – which stands for 'Biologically Appropriate Raw Feeding' — is the name of one brand of frozen raw product that contains human grade meat. But the same problem remains in terms of potential contamination with bacteria, whether it's human grade or not. Humans that eat raw meat every day are also at risk, but majority of our diet is cooked, making the risk of ingesting pathogens significantly reduced. If you or I ate rare hamburgers, raw eggs or raw oysters on a daily basis, we too would be at high risk of food poisoning from pathogens like Salmonella, E. coli, shigella, staphylococcus and listeria. And the risk of pathogens in raw meat remains regardless of what animal it came from, beef or kangaroo. Most of the bacteria found in raw meat diets can survive freezing.

You can vary the raw diet with a small amount of cooked lean meat such as boiled chicken or low-fat beef cuts, but if you are sharing your own food with the dog, avoid cooked bones or toxic substances such as onion sauces on the meat. High fat meats such as found in a big dose of fatty chicken skin, pork, bacon or lamb chops, can cause pancreatitis in dogs. As an occasional treat you can give your dog tinned sardines or tuna, or tinned salmon in spring water, but always check for fish bones first.

Raw grated carrots, boiled pumpkin or sweet potatoes will add fibre to your dog's diet. Sometimes I recommend owners to get some psyllium husks from the local pharmacy; but you should only do that if your vet advises it as it can cause bloating and tummy cramps or even allergic reactions in some dogs.

Wet and dry commercial food

Having dealt with the beef about raw meat, what problems do people see with commercial dog food? The main problem with kibble or dry food seems to be aflatoxin and mycotoxin contamination. Over the years there have been incidences of toxin contamination in some popular dog food brands which have caused illness and even death of dogs. Mass produced food is a challenge and sometimes not even the best quality control can avoid contamination. Commonly it's the brand with low quality food and lower quality control that has the higher the risk of contamination. So cheaper is definitely not better.

Dry kibble is the most convenient type of food, for storage and for feeding. Various brands have different formulations for the various ages and health conditions of the dog – puppy, oral health, renal, hypoallergenic, urinary, senior, etc. Many owners like to be able to the leave kibbles in their dog's bowl for him to graze at leisure over the day.

THE PROS AND CONS OF WET FOOD

Always ensure your dog is well hydrated by making sure his water bowl is filled up at all times with clean water and changed daily. He needs to be able to help himself whenever he wants to. But never let him drink from the bird bath; birds carry pathogens causing diseases such as chlamydiosis, salmonellosis and cryptosporidiosis that can affect both dogs and humans.

However, not all dogs drink as much water as they should, and so wet foods can be a good source of hydration. Certain health issues can make wet foods a better choice – for instance, older dogs that have lost some of their olfactory senses may be more inclined to eat wet foods that have a richer scent and flavour. Wet foods are a good option for dogs with missing teeth, poorly aligned jaws, or smaller mouths and is a good alternative when your dog is unwell and lacking in appetite or if he cannot smell as well. A wet diet will assure he gets the proteins, vitamins, and minerals he needs. I don't recommend wet food daily for dogs unless they medically need it – if, for instance, they are dehydrated, inappetent, geriatric or they have a dental problem such as no teeth or for 24-48 hours after a dental procedure. The reason I'm not in favour of a regular wet food diet is because they get hooked on the awful stuff; it's much more palatable than dry food but dogs were inherently designed to chew with every meal – without this action their teeth suffer.

Dental disease is actually a huge problem with wet food particularly in toy or small breeds (lap dogs), a market heavily targeted by the manufacturers; owners of these breeds tend to pamper them more with wet food and they become finicky eaters. But regardless of the size of the dog, if wet food is their main diet it will negatively impact their teeth and they will need extra dental care. Another drawback is that once it has been opened, wet food has lost its shelf life. It will need to be covered and refrigerated and used quickly before it goes off.

Wet food is not always as economical as kibble and in most cases is more expensive (depending on quality) and needs to be bought in smaller quantities or individual packs. Because premium dog food is so jam-packed with nutrients your dog may need less of it therefore making it more economical because you feed the dog much less volume. Another advantage is because the nutrients are readily available for the body to use, there's less poo to clean up. Hooray! The volume of a dog's stool is directly related to the amount of indigestible ingredients in the food. Some level of indigestible fibre from healthy sources is good, since fibre helps clean the digestive tract, stabilise blood sugar and maintain good weight – but too many 'fillers' used in cheap low-quality brands means health problems later and big bulky stools. Lots of owners, especially of big dogs, are very relieved when they swap from a poor-quality diet to a high-quality diet because the faeces are now smaller and healthier. It's a win, win!

READING INGREDIENT LABELS

Reading ingredient labels is complicated and depends on ratios, formulations and the pet food manufacturers 'guaranteed analysis' which is their requirement to list the guaranteed maximum or minimum percentages of particular nutrients. Generally, the more expensive products formulated by veterinary nutritionists — such as the premium veterinary-endorsed products sold in vet clinics or pet stores – are the best. While there are exceptions, I am cautious of supermarket brands as they are generally rubbish.

Here are some important things to consider when reading pet food labels.

● Read the Nutritional Adequacy statement. This indicates whether the product is 'complete and balanced' to meet nutrient guidelines established by the globally recognised US body, the Association of American Feed Control Officials (AAFCO) when fed as a sole source of nutrition. Some foods are not 'complete and balanced' and are intended for supplemental feeding only. Unless otherwise specified by your vet, rotating among several 'complete and balanced' foods is recommended to provide your dog with nutritional variety.

● At a minimum the dog food brand should be a member of the PFIAA (Pet Food Industry Association of Australia Inc) to ensure the food packaged in accordance with the Australian Standard 5812. This means that all Australian pet owners can have confidence that the information provided on the label is in fact true. The PFIAA represents the prepared pet food industry in Australia and along with State and Federal Government departments, the Australian Veterinary Association and the RSPCA developed the Australian Standard AS5812 for pet food labelling. However, AS5812 approval (95 per cent of dog food on Australian shelves have this endorsement) does not mean it is superior food, only that the claims on the packaging are true.

● Take note of the ingredient list. Ingredients must be listed in descending order according to their weight, with the ingredient weighing the most listed at the top. When it comes to ingredient lists, be careful of 'ingredient splitting' or 'fractioning' to make it appear that there is less of an ingredient in a product. For example, 'corn' could be split into 'ground corn', 'corn meal' and 'corn gluten'.

- Meat meal used to make pet food contains meat by-products. If the ingredient is listed as 'chicken' or 'beef', it is likely to include parts of the body like hearts, tongue and oesophagus. But no need to freak out; while these ingredients sound pretty disgusting to us, your dog would probably disagree, and they are a healthy source of protein.

- The product name can also give you an idea of how much meat is actually contained in the dog food, for example dog foods with the meat name in the title such as 'Salmon & Tuna Dog Food' or 'Beef for Dogs' will contain more meat than a product that says 'with'. For example, 'Doggie Dinner with Chicken' will contain much less chicken compared to a product that says, 'Chicken for Dogs'. And finally, if it says 'flavoured', leave it on the shelf. It will contain only tiny amounts of the meat, for example, 'Beef-flavoured Dog Food' – thanks but no thanks.

How much food does your dog need?

How much food your dog needs will largely depend on his size, breed and age, as well as how regularly you exercise him. You don't want to overfeed or underfeed him. When assessing your dog's size and weight, it's more important to look at his body shape than at his weight. You want your dog to be lean, which means you should be able to feel his ribs when you run your fingers firmly over his side and see a defined waist. If this isn't possible, it's diet time. Obesity in dogs is linked to decreased longevity and diseases such as osteoarthritis, and while it is not totally preventable as it happens in most dogs, it is significantly worsened by obesity. If you're not sure, ask your vet to assess your dog's diet and nutrition, and the condition of its body and overall health.

Overweight Bulldog; physical activity would be very difficult for a dog of this size and respiratory anatomy

Ask your local vet or vet nurse to determine where your pooch is on a body condition score chart, and where he needs to be. Veterinary nursing staff are a wonderful source of nutritional information about getting your dog to their ideal weight. Popping in for regular weigh-ins (and charting the weight changes over time) at the vet surgery is free of charge and can keep you on track with your doggies' weight loss goals. Some clinics even run 'The Biggest Loser' competitions!

Any change in your dog's diet should be done gradually over a few days unless directed otherwise by your vet; change too quickly may cause a gastrointestinal upset and possibly diarrhoea and vomiting. Some diets may be contraindicated to certain medical conditions.

Diet in relation to age

8–16 WEEKS

This is the age when most puppies will arrive in their new home and it's important to not make immediate dietary changes as you might inadvertently cause a stomach upset. Find out from the breeder what they have been feeding your pup and it's best to continue with this if possible. Change to the diet you wish to feed them in small incremental stages over a few weeks until you are feeding your pup your preferred diet completely.

The best food for a puppy at this age is a good quality commercial kibble designed to ensure the puppy gets all the nutrients he needs to grow and

---

TRANSITIONING YOUR DOG TO A NEW DIET

If you need to change your dog's diet your vet can advise you on the best way to transition your dog to the new diet. My advice is to do it gradually over five days, so they are less likely to notice the change. You can apply this method to any scenario where you need to change a dog's diet.

- Day 1. Mix 20 percent of the new food with 80 percent of the old.
- Day 2. Mix 40 percent of the new food with 60 percent of the old.
- Day 3. Mix 60 percent of the new food with 40 percent of the old.
- Day 4. Mix 80 percent of the new food with 20 percent of the old.
- Day 5. Feed 100 percent of the new food.

---

develop. You can add cooked meats and vegetables or rice if you wish; however, if they are on a good quality puppy diet this isn't necessary, the main diet needs to be the commercially balanced kibble. I don't recommend a raw diet for very young pups because their immune system is not yet developed to cope with the bacteria load but more even importantly the fact that it's very difficult to balance a raw diet for growing puppies.

Puppies have a high nutritional demand and their tiny tummies can't go for long without food. Feeding a puppy is a bit like demand feeding a human baby – small meals regularly.

The number of feedings a day depends on your pup's age: two to three months old – four meals a day; three to six months – three meals a day; 6 to 12 months (and up to 24 months for the largest breeds) – two meals a day.

OVER 16 WEEKS

At about 16-weeks or a little earlier, you can introduce some chew toys. Permanent teeth start erupting at this age, so a chew toy will encourage him to chew on something other than your shoes or table leg. One hide chew or puzzle toy that you hide kibble in a week is generally enough for a puppy. At this stage your puppy may become possessive over its food when he's eating and may growl or snap if you attempt to take the food away. It's a good idea to discourage children from getting too close to the puppy when he's eating. Food guarding can be prevented by handfeeding the little pup in the early stages. For more on possessive behaviours see Chapter 12.

When introducing a new food to your puppy, watch for any signs of illness such as a bloated tummy, vomiting or diarrhoea. Dogs are the same as humans when it comes to food intolerance and allergies; sometimes a certain food may simply not agree with the puppy. Sometimes people assume something is a food allergy and it actually turn out to be an unrelated condition or parasite. So, keep notes of what you fed your pup if you get a reaction or illness and take this with you when you consult your vet. Writing down notes is valuable as it documents a possible connection – but sometimes I find the food is not the true culprit in the end.

As your pup gets older, you can gradually reduce the number of feeds to twice per day but it is important not to overfeed or underfeed, so be sure to get advice on the correct amount of food to feed your dog. The amount of food per meal depends on the brand of food, your puppy's age, size, breed and activity levels, so get your vet's advice about the correct quantities.

ADULT DOGS

Small or medium breed dogs are generally considered to have reached adulthood from the age of 12 months, while larger breeds take a little longer not really becoming adults until 18–24 months. By the time a dog reaches adult dog status he should be having a meal of high-quality commercial dog food either once or twice a day, making sure it's appropriate for his life stage and health status. Small to medium-sized dogs transition from puppy to adult food at 12 months, whereas large and giant breeds should transition to adult food between 18-24 months.

Stick to the same feeding guidelines as outlined for other age groups, ensuring the diet you choose is complete and balanced – I'm advocating kibble, but you can mix it up by adding meat (cooked or raw), and vegetables or fish for variety. Many owners ask me for my favourite home-cooked dog food recipes. Cooking for your dog is a feel-good thing to do – humans nurture through preparing and cooking meals for those they love, so I can understand why people want to do this. But my advice is to keep home-cooked meals as a treat; the occasional stew-type meals with lots of vegetables, lean meat (no bones or chicken skin) and rice is a delicious once a week meal for dogs. The problem is, it is very difficult to make complete and balanced home-cooked meals and these soft foods are bad news for dogs' teeth. For that reason, they are best as a loving addition to their diet, rather than their staple source of nutrition. Most importantly, you don't want an overweight dog so don't over feed.

SENIOR DOGS

When your dog reaches old age – which, depending on the breed, can be anything from five to eight years and beyond – you will need to monitor his health carefully. Many older dogs have chronic health issues such as arthritis, diabetes, kidney disease, cancer and dementia all of which require special veterinary attention to assist in their treatment. And remember overweight dogs age much faster than lean dogs. Old dogs are usually fine with dried food unless it is just after a dental procedure or if they have no teeth. A fair number of small dogs end up in later life with few or no teeth because they have been fed wet food since puppyhood which rotted the teeth and they all had to be extracted. Adding to the problem is that many of these little dogs also have over-crowded teeth.

The majority of geriatric dogs have lower energy requirements but often have high protein requirements; higher quality protein in premium senior dog foods helps to maintain their body weight and muscle mass without putting too much strain on the kidneys. An important thing to remember is that dogs need more water as they age. The body's ability to maintain a healthy water balance decreases with old age so always provide plenty of water. I recommend owners provide several water bowls because one invariably gets knocked over — actually this happens at all stages of a dog's life! Be guided by your vet about your dear old dog's special dietary needs, as they can differ from dog to dog. One of the most common senior dog foods I prescribe are ones that contain glucosamine and chondroitin supplements for those old achy joints. But a little reminder here: all the supplements in the world won't help your old dog if he is obese – so reducing the calorie intake should be the first goal if your dog is on the heavy side.

The smelly fart problem

Stinky dog farts are normal for most dogs but excessive farting or a change in the amount of farts your dog does may signal food allergies or some sort of gastrointestinal upset. Some of those silent but deadly ones can catch you by surprise – phewy and be an embarrassing social problem! Dog farts can also be linked to dogs ingesting high-fat snacks, especially if they are getting human table scraps. Although occasional people foods are acceptable snacks for dogs, fatty foods and large amounts of human foods aren't a good idea. Your dog's farts might also be related to him eating too quickly. If you notice your dog is gassy after gobbling his food you might try feeding him smaller meals more regularly or use a slow feeder to encourage your dog to eat more slowly.

Some dogs do fart more than others and it usually goes that the bigger the dog the bigger the gas problem; English Bulldogs, French Bulldogs, Pugs and Boxers in particular are known for their farts. This is because the Brachycephalic breeds are short muzzled and breathe through their mouths more than their noses, swallowing more air and becoming prone to pass more wind as a result. Food guzzlers such as Labradors also gulp air along with their food, which can also lead to excessive farting.

Every dog needs a highly digestible diet. Grain-free dog food diets are great for some dogs, but include foods such as peas, soybeans and sweet potatoes which may produce flatulence because the bacteria in your dog's gut causes them to ferment. Just like you, your dog's gastrointestinal tract is teeming with bacteria, both good and bad. Along with a diet change I advise a dog probiotic.

Probiotics contain millions of good bacteria that can help maintain a healthy balanced gut flora and aid digestion. If a dog has bad wind and loose poo or diarrhoea fairly often, it could be a sign of a gastrointestinal condition such as inflammatory bowel disease (IBD).

If you are feeding your dog a high-grain kibble and you're also giving him freeze-dried-fruit dog treats, dehydrated vegetable treats or table scraps, you may want to switch him to something more digestible such as homemade boiled chicken and rice; this is good as a temporary diet for an upset tummy or you can get complete and balanced chicken and rice commercial diets which are available in both wet and dry formulations for the long-term. You could experiment a little until you find the combination of foods that cuts down the flatulence problem.

Farting could also mean that your dog is not getting enough exercise; if he's still emitting super-smelly air after a diet change, increase his exercise – longer walks, more intense games of fetching balls or find an off-lead place where he can run around for a while. Exercise helps dog gas work its way out more gradually instead of building up.

If your dog starts farting a lot and exhibiting other symptoms of gastrointestinal upset, such as loss of appetite, vomiting, diarrhoea, or a distended or uncomfortable abdomen, it's important to check it out with your vet pronto.

Does your dog's stomach gurgle?

If you have ever mistaken a dog's stomach gurgling for a normal dog growl, you're not alone. Your dog's gurgling tummy will most likely be completely normal, but it shouldn't be totally ignored as it can indicate a real medical issue. The correct name for stomach gurgling in dogs is borborygmus (pronounced bor-bor-rig-mus) and it happens when the fluid or gas passing throughout the animal's intestines becomes very loud, signifying anything from trapped wind – a bit uncomfortable – to a twisted stomach i.e. gastric dilation volvulus (GDV) – extremely serious. Intestinal parasites and other conditions of the gut such as haemorrhagic gastroenteritis (HGE) , can also cause stomach grumbles. Stomach gurgling after recent surgery may be indicative of the intestines moving about again after anaesthesia.

Stomach gurgling may also mean the dog has swallowed a foreign body or something that doesn't agree with him, so try to rule out any unusual or toxic items in the house the dog may have munched on such as toys, underwear, chocolate, raisins or rat bait. (See Chapter 7 for a list of foods your dog should never eat.) However, the most common reason for your dog's stomach gurgling is likely to be that something has upset his stomach; table scraps or changes in diet can cause the production of more gas; the intestines are trying to move food along to get it out as fast as possible. Try to stop the dog from scavenging or feeding it food from your table or feeding it cheaper food because it's near to the expiry date.

What to do about a picky eater

You feed your dog tasty and nutritious food, and yet he only sniffs and licks at it. It's time for the next meal, but the previous meal still isn't finished.

Many people think their dogs want or need variety. I can debunk that theory; the truth is a dog will happily eat the same food every day its entire life! Your dog is descended from opportunistic hunters that were accustomed to eating what they could get when they could get it.

In my experience the cause of a dog's finicky eating can usually be laid squarely at the feet of its owner. The number one most obvious reason is that they are feeding it table scraps or too many treats. This not only increases the risk of obesity (and around 40 per cent of dogs are overweight) but can encourage finicky behaviour. Your dog avoids eating in hope of getting more exciting food than what's in the bowl. To avoid this, stop feeding your dog from the table and limit the number of treats. Remember that dogs have different nutritional needs to us, so what we eat isn't necessarily balanced for them.

When your dog was a puppy, did you try offering him several different foods to determine what he liked best? If the answer is yes, you may have encouraged him to hold out for something better. Whether it comes in the form of treats, bones or leftovers from your plate, they simply want to eat something better. They aren't starving, so they're more than happy to hold out and see what's to come. If you're still opening multiple cans of food and trying to coax your precious pooch into eating something every meal, your dog has trained you instead of you training your dog to eat the food that's available to him.

Of course, you need to rule out any underlying health issue. For instance, some cancer patients (initially) show no signs of illness but go off their food (they might still eat delicious table scraps but aren't interested in anything else). While other symptoms appear later sometimes the first clue to illness is something as simple as being off their food. If the dog is a finicky eater start with a vet check and a urine examination and complete canine blood profile to check they're in good general health and there is no underlying medical reason for this behaviour. To know for sure if your dog's picky eating is a habit or an underlying health issue, work with your vet and record his dietary habits, such as writing down all the food he ate over a 48-hour period, including treats and any human food.

When you have a rescue dog, especially an older dog, it's unlikely you will know what his diet was in his previous life and picky eating was the last of your concerns when you got him home. Start the transition slowly, remembering rescue dogs are experiencing a change of pack/leaders, environment, rules and possibly diet. With time, you can teach an old dog new tricks but in the beginning be compassionate in minimising change. So, if you've ended up with a picky eater due to the way he was raised, it's not too late to turn that behaviour around. Once he's settled into the family and new home then it's a good time to tackle the diet change. You may feel mean during the process, but it's important to remember that it's just like taking him to the vet or giving him a bath. He may not like it, but it's for his own good.

However, when a dog that was a good eater suddenly changes to be a bad eater can signal a bigger problem. Other signs include weight loss, vomiting, sluggishness, diarrhoea and upset stomach. When these symptoms combine, it's important to take your pet to the vet right away to identify a possible underlying medical cause and avoid dehydration.

Believe it or not, picky eaters are actually quite common in the canine community. Any breed of dog can turn into a picky eater.

TIPS TO REMEDY PICKY EATING
- First and foremost, stop feeding your dog scraps from your plate.
- Teach your dog that no options exist. What's available is what's available.
- If your dog hasn't eaten his food in 30 minutes, take it away.
- When it's time for his next meal, again put a fresh serve of the same food down for him and take it away in 30 minutes, whether it is eaten or not.
- After a couple of days, he may start looking for extra treats. Don't give in! Your dog isn't starving. If he's hungry, he will eat. A healthy well-hydrated dog can

survive two to three days without food! Although if your dog is a puppy, senior or has medical condition this tough approach isn't appropriate.

Oh yes, you may have to endure his sad pleading eyes during this process, but this is an effective way to eliminate finicky eating behaviour. If you find that these tips aren't working, have a chat to your vet to see what else could be wrong. If the vet recommends a change of food, be sure to change it gradually. You should start by combining a little of the new food with the old food, gradually increasing the amount of new food as you reduce the amount of old food. This will be helpful in getting your dog accustomed to the new food and avoid a hunger strike. If you're switching from wet to dry food, try mixing in a small amount of warm water with the dry food, 15 minutes before serving. Owning a dog can have its ups and downs. On one day, everything looks great and he's wolfing down his new food enthusiastically. The next day, he's turning up his nose and you have to go through the whole diet change business again. Keep smiling. Through all the changes, one thing remains the same — your dog loves you and would thank you if he could for all the loving care you're giving them.

Feeding a large breed dog

Owning a large breed dog comes with matching responsibilities, especially when it comes to food. A long, healthy, active life starts with good nutrition. Feeding a properly formulated, high-quality diet is one of the most important things you can do to keep your dog healthy and prevent disease. There are a few things you need to know about large dog nutrition to help you choose the best food for your dog from the time he's a puppy until the time he's a dear old senior.

I advise feeding your large breed dog a complete and balanced commercial diet which includes the wide range of nutrients your dog needs. A high-quality dog food combines sources of protein, fibre, carbohydrates, vitamins, and minerals in a manner that is easily digested. Large dog nutrition is similar to small and medium dog nutrition, with a few important exceptions. Large breed puppies require special diets to avoid certain health risks, and large breed adult dogs require careful monitoring for signs of orthopaedic disease, obesity, and bloat. Each of these diseases are heavily influenced by nutrition. It's a good idea to talk to your vet if you are considering a home-cooked diet or alternative feeding regime for your dog to get some tips on balancing your dog's nutritional needs.

Large and giant breed puppies grow faster and over a longer period of time than smaller dogs. A dog born weighing less than a kilogram can grow to 68 kilograms in the first 18 months of its life. This rapid growth rate means that large breed puppies are very sensitive to nutrient and caloric intake – imbalances, deficiencies or excesses all negatively impact your large breed puppy's health. Excessive growth has been linked to developmental orthopaedic disease (DOD), which covers a range of conditions including hypertrophic osteodystrophy, osteochondrosis, retained ulnar cartilage core, panosteitis, hip and elbow dysplasia. Overnutrition plays a major role in excessive growth, which is why it is important to feed your large breed puppy a diet specially formulated for large breeds. These diets should be lower in fat, have good calcium content, an appropriate calcium and phosphorus ratio and provide high quality protein.

How much you feed your puppy also matters and I discourage free feeding because it has also been linked to DOD. Instead, feed your puppy several smaller meals throughout the day and monitor his weight to make sure it stays within a healthy range. Once he reaches adulthood, it is time to find yet another food. This transitional period is a good time to talk to your vet about the best food for large breeds. There are three conditions that are influenced by your dog's nutrition that affect large breed adult dogs:

1 **Orthopaedic disease.** Large and giant breed dogs are more prone to developing musculoskeletal and orthopaedic disorders like hip dysplasia, arthritis, and osteochondrosis. These diseases are linked to excessive growth, hereditary factors, exercise and nutrition. There is not much you can do about hereditary factors, but you do have control over growth rate, exercise and nutrition. Feeding your puppy an appropriate large breed puppy diet decreases the dog's risk of developing DOD. Once he is an adult, it is up to you to monitor diet and exercise to make sure he maintains a healthy weight. A good quality diet with the proper balance of nutrients for large breed dogs helps prevent joints and bones from various conditions such as lesions and arthritic growths as mentioned above. Many large breed adult formulas include the joint supplement glucosamine to further improve orthopaedic health.

2 **Obesity.** Obesity is particularly dangerous for large breed dogs, as it increases their risk of developing orthopaedic diseases as they get older. Extra weight stresses their joints, muscles and bones, which can lead to serious conditions that affect their quality of life and mobility. Obesity has also

been linked to other serious health conditions, including type 2 diabetes, kidney disease, and high blood pressure.

3 **Bloat.** Known in the veterinary community as gastric dilation and volvulus (GDV), bloat is a very serious and often fatal condition that affects large and giant breed dogs. It's a condition caused by the rapid accumulation of gas in the stomach which have no way of escaping and can be fatal in just a few hours. Prevention is the best option and some steps to reduce the risk of bloat include:

- Instead of one large, heavy meal, feed several smaller meals a day to prevent rapid eating;

- Feed from floor level (not a raised feeder);

- Avoid foods with high-fat contents (foods with oil and fat in the first four ingredients on the label);

- Feed large kibble foods and

- Avoid strenuous exercise one to two hours after eating.

Because dog food designed for senior dogs is relatively new talk to your vet about the best food for large breed seniors. Adult formulas, all life-stage formulas, and senior formulas can all be appropriate foods for senior dogs. Senior dogs often develop other health problems that require a vet's attention and maintenance, so sometimes a prescription diet is the best dog food option for large breed seniors, as these veterinary-approved foods are specifically formulated to address your dog's needs.

CHAPTER 7

Bones

and

Other

Dietary

Issues

To give a dog a bone

Dogs and bones seem like a natural match, promoting clean teeth, aiding nutrition, rewarding good behaviour and providing mental stimulation. But not all bones are good for dogs. It might be tempting to give in to the dog longingly eyeing off the left-over bones and uneaten fatty bits on your dinner plate. Both are dangerous for dogs – the fat trimmed from meat (both cooked and uncooked) can cause pancreatitis or gastritis, and cooked bones should never be given to your dog. Cooked bones can become sharp and brittle and when they break off can cause serious and life threatening damage to your dog's gastrointestinal tract.

Raw bones are generally better but if you are going to give your dog a bone you should not just toss him any old bone. Even with raw bones I recommend you monitor his chewing activity. Round bones are not completely safe because they can cause a range of problems that I outline below. Raw bones can also bring Salmonella into the house, especially if the bones are left lying around for lengthy periods of time. This can be particularly dangerous for any dog or human who has a compromised immune system due to ill health. Raw chicken necks, made of soft cartilaginous rings (you can get them from the butcher) are considered a bone, rather than a chew, and are good for smaller dogs.

Or not... Many veterinary specialists are now advising against bones completely and some vets are actively discouraging raw bones due to bone related illnesses and deaths they commonly see in practice. While I believe that for most of the time it is safe to feed your dog large raw meaty bones under close supervision, I acknowledge that they can cause life threatening illnesses and of course unwanted vet bills. Here are a few reasons why you should think twice about giving your dog a bone.

- **Broken teeth.** Bigger breeds have immense jaw strength; German Shepherds, American Pit Bull Terriers and Rottweilers can exert an average of 145kg of pressure on a bone but even small dogs have very strong jaws with enough bite strength to work down a bone. Many dogs, both small and large are aggressive chewers and will try and break the bone in order to eat it (and get to that delicious bone marrow) and this can easily chip or fracture a tooth.

- **Mouth, tongue and jaw injuries.** Bone fragments can pierce the tongue and can get easily wedged in between the upper molars on the hard palate. Round marrow bones can get looped around your dog's lower jaw, a frightening and painful experience for your dog that usually requires sedation in order to saw the bone in half the release it.

- **Bones can get stuck.** There are many places fragments of bone can get stuck if swallowed. The oesophagus: a greedy dog may try and swallow a bone that is too big to pass easily into the stomach. The trachea: your dog can accidentally inhale a small piece of bone or may aspirate it while trying to gag if it got stuck in the oesophagus. This is an emergency – you will need to get your pet to a vet immediately. The stomach: even if it went down okay, the bone may still be too big to pass out of the stomach and into the intestines. Your dog will show signs of vomiting and pain and will need surgery to remove it. The intestines: a bone stuck in the intestines can cause blockage and again require expensive surgery to remove it before it damages, or worse, perforates the bowel wall.

- **Peritonitis** This is a painful, life threatening bacterial infection of the abdomen caused by tiny bone fragments piercing holes in your dog's stomach or intestinal wall which allows all the digestive contents, loaded with bacteria, to seep into the abdominal cavity.

- **Constipation** Your dog may have difficulty passing the sharp bone fragments and partially digested bone 'gravel'. Calcium in the bones can also cause his stool to be hard and dry and uncomfortable to pass.

- **Severe bleeding from the rectum.** This can happen when a sharp bone fragment causes rectal trauma on its way out.

The rawhide option

All dogs need to chew. It's a natural instinct and they can spend hours chewing every day. Chewing can provide stimulation and help relieve anxiety. Rawhide chews have become a popular treat for dogs as an alternative to bones. But having given you the bad news about bones, are there any drawbacks to giving your dog rawhide treats? Are there other alternatives that work just as well? Rawhide treats come from the inner layer of cow or horse hides. During manufacturing, the hides are cleaned and cut or ground and then pressed into chewable dog treats of different shapes and sizes. To make them tastier for dogs, some manufacturers rawhide treats have been flavoured with beef, chicken, or liver. If you have a puppy, treats like rawhide bones can be a great substitute for your leather shoes and anything else he might fancy chewing.

Because chewing also keeps dogs' jaws strong, teeth clean, and consequently keeps breath a bit fresher, dogs that chew regularly on rawhides and other bones or toys have less plaque and tartar build-up on teeth. That's not to say there are no risks with chewing rawhide, although given the amount of rawhide a dog might consume in a year, the risks are minimal. Still, risks should not be ignored.

The most common risk associated with chewing rawhide treats include:

- **Contamination.** Rawhide chews can contain trace amounts of toxic chemicals and like other pet food, are open to possible contamination from Salmonella or E. coli.

- **Digestive irritation.** This is possible if a dog is sensitive or allergic to rawhide or other substances used in their manufacture and signs of this may include diarrhoea and vomiting.

- **Choking or blockages.** Rawhide bones and other edible chews can pose a choking and blockage risk. In fact, this is a much bigger risk than contamination or digestive irritation. If your dog swallows large pieces of rawhide, the rawhide can get stuck in the oesophagus or other parts of the digestive tract. Abdominal surgery may be needed to remove it from the stomach or intestines. If it isn't resolved, a blockage can lead to death.

Chewing on rawhide bones provides stimulation and can relieve anxiety

OTHER ALTERNATIVES

Dogs don't need fancy flavours, additives, preservatives, artificial colours or added sugar in their chewy treats. Labels on products should be easy to read. First, you need to decide if you want natural dog chews or fake vegetable compressed sticks. If you choose natural animal-based dog treats then you need to work out if you are buying them just for long chewing or to provide some nutrition. Wet commercial dog food is usually grain based and soft and gets stuck between the teeth; that, along with any added sugar, is going to rot your dog's teeth. Wet dog food does not actually do anything positive for a dog's jaw or gums and will lead to gum disease.

However, there are some excellent dry dental dog foods, such as larger, more robust kibble that ensures the chewing action; this chewing action breaks down the bacteria laden plaque and tartar at the gum line and which reduces the risk of periodontal disease. This is why a natural long chewing dog treat can clean the teeth and clean the gums. If it doesn't have a heap of sugar added and isn't so hard that the dog gives up or breaks a tooth, it's a good option for your dog.

We know dental chews can improve breath and create happy, healthy teeth but unfortunately not every brand or type of dental chew is good for your dog. Take a walk through your local pet food barn or let your fingers do the walking online and you'll be bombarded with dozens of exotic-sounding chewy treats from pig snouts to kangaroo knee tendons. Many commercial dental chews do not take into account the intestinal health of your dog when putting together their formula. Some brands that are promoted as good for dental health and give dogs nice-smelling breath, have notoriously harmed pets causing vomiting, diarrhoea, dangerous internal blockages, even death.

How can you tell if a dental chew is going to cause trouble? One thing you can do is soak it in a bowl of water; normal dog treats and even rawhide chews will soften considerably or dissolve after 24 hours. If it doesn't break up in water after a couple of days, it probably won't break up in your dog's intestines either, even though the dog's stomach/intestinal fluid is packed with hydrochloric acid and digestive enzymes. Any non-dissolving chew is dangerous if your dog decides to swallow it, and what dog doesn't try to swallow a treat? It may be made of plant fibre, but it can have the same effect as eating plastic, which is something no responsible pet owner would allow. Chew toys made of nylon, such as rope toys can also pose a risk if swallowed because they will not dissolve in the stomach.

You also need to think about is the size of the chews in proportion to the size of your dog; be sure to get the appropriate size chew or they won't do any chewing at all and gulp it down in one go. There are some chewy snacks made of hardened Himalayan yak cheese which many dogs are partial to; it is tough and requires a lot of chewing to soften. It has a porous fibrous structure which scrapes plaque off a dog's teeth.

Pork products such as pig's ears and pig ear strips provide long chewing for many dogs, but are relatively high in fat and don't provide a great deal of good protein. One of the most popular chewables is Bullysticks – also known as bully chews or bull willies – 'yummo' …for the dog that is! Jerkys come in all flavours – beef, roo, chicken and duck; beef and roo are by far the hardest, but if you want something even harder you could try your dog on roo tendons or beef tendons. Cow hooves are good for larger dogs. Fish skins are low in fat; shark cartilage and fish tails are better option for smaller dogs because they actually chew them, whereas bigger dogs swallow them whole. All these things are safe and fabulous most of the time and then a vet will see a bowel obstruction, or a chew caught in the upper air way, or a bout of pancreatitis from a fatty chew – and start advising against it.

What your dog should never eat

Dogs are dogs and there are some foods that people enjoy which are dangerous for dogs. It's important to familiarise yourself with the most common ones.

Stone fruit. Peaches, apricots and any other fruit with a hard-centralised pit should be kept away from your dog. The flesh is not the problem, it's the pit which contains cyanide, also dangerous for humans.

Chocolate. Dogs may love the smell, the taste and the texture of chocolate but it's toxic for them. Chocolate contains a substance called theobromine, which is found in cacao seeds (the contents of the beans that provide the basis for chocolate products). Theobromine toxicity can cause vomiting and diarrhoea, panting, excessive thirst and urination, hyperactivity, abnormal heart rhythm, tremors, seizures and even death. Darker chocolate has a higher level of theobromine and consequently more dangerous than milk chocolate which has a lower level. Baking chocolate contains the highest levels so no chocolate-based cakes or biscuits for your dog either.

Sasha got into our pantry one day when I was at school and devoured a bag of dark chocolate chips. I remember finding her surrounded by chocolaty vomit when I got home from school and we rushed her to the afterhours veterinary centre. Thankfully she recovered, but I remember the vet saying it was touch and go as she developed a severe heart arrhythmia from the toxin.

Onions, garlic and chives. Onions are extremely toxic to dogs; oxidative damage to their red blood cells causes the cells to rupture leading to anaemia. We see this most at the good old Aussie sausage-sizzle; after the barbecue is all finished, people innocently give the dogs the left-over tray of cooked onions.

Citrus. The citric acid found in the stems, leaves, peels, fruit and seeds of citrus plants – grapefruit, lemon, lime and orange – contain varying amounts of citric acid which can cause irritation and possibly even central nervous system depression if ingested in significant amounts. Small doses of the fruit are not likely to present problems beyond minor stomach upset.

Milk and dairy products. Dairy is not good for any dog, ever. Despite those cute scenes of kids sharing their ice cream with a puppy, this is definite no-no.

Raw yeast dough. While a small piece of bread is pretty harmless for your dog, raw dough is another definite no-no. As the yeast rises in the dog's digestive system, it can cause a painful gas, which is has the potential to rupture its stomach or cause gastric dilation and volvulus (GDV). For more on gastric dilation and volvulus (GDV) see Chapter 10.

Fatty foods. Maintaining a healthy weight for your dog rules out feeding him sweet and fatty foods. Another problem with fatty foods — especially fatty bacon, sausages and bone marrow – is that they can lead to illnesses such as pancreatitis. For more on pancreatitis see Chapter 10.

Salty foods. While salt is an essential component to your dog's diet by helping muscle and nerve function, dogs with chronic disease such as kidney, heart or liver problems need to watch their salt consumption.

Xylitol. This sugar substitute found in chewing gum, confectionary, certain baked goods, some peanut butters and other 'sugar-free' items, is safe for humans but extremely toxic to dogs. Worryingly, with increased xylitol sweetened products now on the market, xylitol toxicosis in dogs is becoming more common. Even small amounts, such as a few pieces of chewing gum, can cause low blood sugar, seizures, liver failure and even death. Most owners are aware of the dangers of chocolate for dogs, but few are aware of the risks of xylitol.

Coffee and caffeine. Pets are more sensitive to the effects of caffeine than we are. Like chocolate, coffee contains theobromine, which is found in cacao seeds the fruit of the plant used to make coffee. The ingestion of even moderate amounts of coffee grounds, tea bags or one or two caffeine-based diet pills can cause death in small dogs or cats.

Pizza. If your dog is lactose-intolerant or sensitive to wheat steer clear of pizza. It has minimal nutritional value for dogs anyway and the meats on pizza are usually highly processed and high in sodium.

Alcohol. Never give your dog alcohol, either as a drink or in food products containing alcohol. It can cause vomiting, diarrhoea, decreased coordination, central nervous system depression, difficulty breathing, tremors, abnormal blood acidity, coma and even death. If you suspect someone else has given your dog an alcoholic drink get him to the vet quick smart. Giving drugs and alcohol to dogs is classed as animal abuse.

Grapes and raisins. We don't actually know the toxic substance in grapes and raisins but we do know that they can cause kidney failure in dogs, which is pretty serious. Until more information is known about the toxic substance, I suggest you don't feed your dog grapes and raisins.

Macadamia nuts. These nuts are yummy to humans but they can cause weakness, depression, vomiting, tremors and hyperthermia in dogs. These signs usually appear within 12 hours of eating and can last approximately 12 to 48 hours.

Coconut products and coconut oil. When ingested in small amounts, coconut and coconut-based products are not likely to cause serious harm to your dog. However, because the flesh and milk of fresh coconuts contain oils that may upset your dog's stomach or give him diarrhoea my advice is to avoid offering them to him. Coconut water is high in potassium and should not be given to your pet.

Marijuana. When a human smokes or eats food infused with marijuana they usually know what they're doing. If a dog eats marijuana it does not. Dogs can get 'high' but it does not mean that it's okay or that they find the effects of marijuana enjoyable. First, it's important to understand the difference between what is known in Australia as 'medicinal marijuana' which is used to relieve pain and the stuff you buy on the street or grow that makes you high. The medicinal variety is made from cannabidiol (CBD) oil culled from the marijuana plant and contains little or no amounts of tetrahydrocannabinol (THC) – the psychoactive ingredient that gives you a high.

If a dog eats marijuana, it's rarely fatal but they can become very sick. The effects include ataxia (an uncoordinated 'drunken' walk), incontinence and hypersensitivity to touch and noise. I don't advise giving the dog any medications or getting him to vomit. THC is a depressant which can suppress the gag reflex and the dog may not be able to expel the vomit properly and food could become aspirated into the lungs. Instead get the dog to the vet because there is no way of knowing how the animal will be affected.

Be upfront with a vet if you suspect they've had exposure to drugs; even if they are illegal the vet's primary concern will be the dog's welfare and the more information you can give the faster they can make a diagnosis and provide appropriate treatments. Recovery is normally 12 to 24 hours; if symptoms persist it's probably not marijuana. If the dog has tucked into a bag of hash cookies he could get a huge hit of other things that are bad for him such as chocolate, sugar, butter and fat. Edible marijuana will take longer to leave a dog's system since the THC dose is for adult humans and highly concentrated.

OTHER NASTIES TO WATCH

Giving your dog toxic food is not the only thing you have to be careful about. They're such busy bodies and often get themselves into trouble while foraging, sniffing and chewing. Dogs are usually exposed to potentially toxic household products and medications accidentally. But sometimes well-intentioned owners unknowingly give their dogs harmful products and medications. Here are a few to be aware of and any of the symptoms described need an urgent visit to the vet:

Cane toads. As revolting as these are, it may be tempting for a curious dog to sample one with a lick, particularly when a toad's favourite spot to unwind is in dog water bowls — and they do eat dog food! Your dog might also be tempted to take a bite of roadkill, particularly if you live in Queensland and across the top end of Australia where they breed in epidemic proportions. Cane toads can kill a dog within 15 minutes of a dog biting or licking it. Cane toad poison consists in large part of bufadienolides, a steroid that is a type of cardiac glycoside. Perhaps the most obvious signs that a dog has been affected is drooling, shaking, and the colour of their gums which will be strangely bright red, because the toad toxin is such an irritant. The signs can then move to seizures, abnormal heart rhythm, collapse and breathing difficulties.

However, while the onset of symptoms is quick, the toxin is rapidly absorbed through the mucous membranes of your dog's mouth. If you suspect your dog has mouthed a cane toad, apply immediate first aid; the toxin can still be removed because it's so sticky. First thing to do is to grab a damp cloth and use it to wipe the tongue and gums thoroughly removing any residual venom. Because the venom is pretty sticky, you have to rub firmly around all his mouth. Rinse the cloth in the sink between wipes and keep wiping; You could have the hose on a very low pressure and hold it across the mouth to rinse it, but do not point it into the back of the mouth because it can create even bigger problems to deal with such as bloat or aspiration pneumonia. You need to do this as well as the wiping technique though because it's so sticky. Continue this for about ten minutes and take the dog to the vet immediately because there may still be heart and neurological issues to deal with.

Ibuprofen. Ibuprofen, a non-steroidal anti-inflammatory drug with analgesic, anti-inflammatory, and antipyretic effects is available in a variety of strengths over the counter at pharmacies. It has a narrow margin of safety for dogs and acute toxicoses is common, but the real effect will depend on the amount the dog has swallowed and the age of your dog – it is more serious in older dogs. It can affect the central nervous system and cause gastrointestinal problems and abdominal pain, vomiting, diarrhoea, renal failure and even coma. However, if you get your dog to the vet immediately so the vet can induce vomiting most dogs are expected to recover.

Ant and roach baits. The product names and container names may vary, but most ant and roach baits use an attractant such as a sweetening agent and bread. These baits once contained compounds that were highly toxic to dogs such as lead arsenate but the insecticides in ant and roach baits today are much less toxic. Because of the lower concentration of the insecticide and the small size of the bait, serious toxicoses are unlikely; however, if the dog swallows the plastic or metal part of the container there is a risk of obstruction which is life-threatening.

Rodent baits. The most commonly used rodenticides in the world contain anticoagulants. Eating rodent bait that contains anticoagulant can cause coagulopathy, the inability of blood to clot normally. This usually sets in after about two to four days (depending on the type of anticoagulant contained in the bait), after the dog has swallowed the bait, possibly sooner in younger dogs. Coagulopathy is very serious and the dog may require a blood transfusion. A positive prognosis cannot be guaranteed and may depend on the bleeding site. Sasha did the chocolate toxicity and Java did the rodenticide toxicity! Both survived, but only just.

When I was at vet school I used to take Java with me when I was studying in the common room – we were not supposed to take dogs there but I took her anyway. There was a rat problem in the common room and the janitor had put down Ratsak which unbeknown to me, Java ate. I knew she was unwell and when I saw blood in her urine I thought she had a urinary tract infection. I had a lecture in the teaching hospital that day and I raced in with Java and handed in a note for my lecturer: 'My dog was just admitted, her name is Java and she has haematuria (which means blood in urine) and I think she has a bladder infection. Can you please see her asap? Thank you, Claire Stevens.' So he told his class that they were going to practice cystocentesis, which is taking a urine sample by inserting a needle into Java's bladder.

Because I was a vet student he assumed I was right and it was a bladder infection and because he was my lecturer I assumed he knew what he was doing. In his defence, there were no other signs of bleeding and without further blood tests to check the platelets and clotting he couldn't have known what was really going on. He inserted a needle into her bladder and she started to bleed profusely from her urinary tract; Ratsak stops the blood from clotting but neither of us knew she had eaten it. The first transfusion practically poured out of her because she was losing so much blood – thankfully they gave me that one for free. It was a good class because the vet students learnt a lot that day (and so did I) – that is, always get a complete history, ask the owner lots of questions), do a full physical examination and perform all necessary diagnostics.

After being in practice for more than a decade, I came to understand that the nature of medicine is uncertain, even after doing all the right things, you can still get the diagnosis and treatment plan wrong. Java was in hospital for weeks and it cost me everything I'd saved for a planned trip to Africa. But she lived. Lessons learned – chocolate and rat poison have always been kept well out of reach of my dogs ever since.

Acetaminophen. This drug is toxic to dogs and it's available as tablets, capsules, or liquids, either alone or combined with other compounds such as opioids, aspirin, caffeine, and antihistamines. Acetaminophen toxicoses is serious, often causing irreversible liver damage. The first clinical signs people notice area laboured breathing, a swollen face, neck and limbs, grey-brown gums and vomiting. Recovery will depend on how much your dog has swallowed and how quickly you get him to the vet.

Pseudoephedrine-containing cold medications. Many cold medications contain pseudoephedrine, a drug structurally similar to amphetamines and no longer sold as over-the-counter medication in Australia. Pseudoephedrine can stimulate the dog's cardiovascular and the central nervous systems. Even a small amount can be life-threatening; the most common symptoms include agitation, hyperactivity, panting, hyperthermia, hypertension, tachycardia (irregular and fast heartbeat) and head bobbing. This is a medical emergency and the dog will need to get to a vet as soon as possible.

Thyroid hormones. Natural and synthetic derivatives of thyroid hormones are used to treat hypothyroidism in both animals and people. A dog that has a massive overdose of the drug L-thyroxine can develop thyrotoxicosis which commonly causes hyperactivity and tachycardia; however, dogs have shown a huge resistance to developing thyrotoxicosis. Signs that the dog has had a mild overdose may be so minor they can be missed.

Bleach. Most household bleaches are mild to moderate irritants and are not associated with a marked degree of tissue destruction. Household bleaches can cause skin or eye irritation, mild oral or oesophageal burns, or gastrointestinal irritation. Inhaling bleach can cause respiratory irritation, coughing, and bronchospasm. More serious damage can occur when bleach is mixed with ammonia-containing agents, forming chloramine and chlorine gases. Inhaling these gases can lead to a chemical pneumonitis. In this case you need to take the dog to the vet because treating corrosive damage may require pain medications, antibiotics, and nutritional support.

If the dog's skin has been exposed to bleach, stand him in a tub or bath and wash him over with mild dishwashing liquid. If he has swallowed bleach, dilution is effective if it is given early so give him milk or water. Making the dog vomit is not recommended due to the irritating properties of household bleach and the corrosive effects of commercial bleach.

Fertiliser. Fertiliser formulations come in liquid, granular and solid combinations and additives may include herbicides, insecticides, fungicides, iron, copper, or zinc. Because fertilizers are usually a combination of ingredients, several toxic outcomes are possible. In general, a dog's body does not easily absorb these ingredients and most toxicity will be related to gastrointestinal irritation; vomiting, hyper-salivation, diarrhoea, and lethargy are common in dogs after swallowing fertilisers, especially the product containing high percentages of phosphorus and potassium compounds. In most cases these signs are self-limiting and resolve within 12-24 hours.

Antifreeze. This is an additive put into a car's cooling system to either lower the water's freezing point so it won't freeze or to raise the boiling point of the engine's coolant to prevent overheating. So antifreeze (which contains toxic ethylene glycol) is good for cars in challenging climates but bad for dogs anywhere. In fact, it's so dangerous that if you even suspect that your dog has ingested antifreeze get him to the vet as fast as possible and take the packaging with you so the vet knows what the ingredients are. The prognosis will depend on how quickly he gets medical help.

Antifreeze poisoning is fast and serious and within about 30 minutes dogs will be lethargic, uncoordinated, will probably urinate and drink excessively and may vomit. The vet's priority when treating antifreeze poisoning is to prevent the dog's body from metabolizing the ethylene glycol, the fast-acting and possibly fatal component. If your dog is taken to the vet within the first one to two hours of antifreeze exposure and providing the dog isn't suffering from any neurological impairment, your vet will probably attempt to induce vomiting.

Strange as it might sound, the antidote commonly used to treat antifreeze poisonings is ethanol, also known as vodka! The vodka is delivered intravenously, meaning the patient must be hospitalised because… well, he's going to be sloshed (on top of everything else!) But if the vodka is administered in time, treatment is usually successful. The alcohol dosage for a medium-sized dog is equivalent to approximately eight shots of vodka every four to six hours and so it's no surprise we see the consequences of alcohol intoxication. Pets need to be monitored during this alcohol infusion for obvious medical reasons (and to ensure they don't bark up the wrong tree). It puts a whole new spin on the term, 'hair of the dog'.

One of the biggest problems with antifreeze is that dogs are often attracted to the sweetness in the chemicals. It is odourless but clean up any spills, leaks or drips to prevent your dog from exploring the fluid with a lick – even a lick can be dangerous. Keep antifreeze stored away from your dog and take extra special care around inquisitive and destructive dogs or young puppies who are more likely to be curious and explore areas where they could come into contact with chemicals –that includes brake and transmission fluid.

Hydrocarbons. You can find hydrocarbons in numerous products, including paints, varnishes, engine cleaners, furniture polish, lighter fluid, lamp oils, paint removers and fuel oil. Vomiting, diarrhoea and mild to moderate eye irritation are common symptoms in dogs that have swallowed hydrocarbons. Acute, but prolonged skin exposure to some hydrocarbons can result in dermal burns and, occasionally, systemic effects. Low-viscosity, highly volatile hydrocarbons (those found in kerosene, gasoline, liquid furniture polish) can cause breathing problems such as pulmonary damage, transient central nervous system depression or excitement, hypoxia, inflammation, and, potentially, pneumonia.

The risk of pulmonary aspiration (where food, drink or contents from the stomach enter the air ways) rules out making a dog vomit who has swallowed products containing hydrocarbons. If the dog's skin has been exposed, bathe him with a mild liquid dishwashing detergent. Flush his eyes copiously with saline in cases of eye exposure.

Please note that while I have offered some first aid advice in this chapter, I still recommend you call or visit your local vet in all cases as some cases are more severe than others and need medical treatments such as antidotes, intravenous fluid therapy and dressings.

CHAPTER 8

Keeping your Dog Clean and Trim

Cleaning your dog's teeth

Not taking care of your dog's teeth can actually reduce his lifespan. Up to 80 per cent of dogs have periodontal disease by the time they are three years of age. Periodontal disease is a progressive disease of the supporting tissues surrounding teeth and the main cause of early tooth loss. It starts when bacteria and food particles combine to form plaque on the teeth and within a matter of days, minerals in the saliva have bonded with the plaque to form tartar, a hard substance that adheres to the teeth. The bacteria work their way under the gum and cause gingivitis, which is an inflammation of the gums. Once under the gums, bacteria destroy the supporting tissue around the tooth and this can lead to your dog losing his teeth. This condition is known as periodontitis. Gingivitis and periodontitis make up the changes that are referred to as periodontal disease. The bacteria associated with periodontal disease can also travel in the bloodstream to infect the heart, kidneys and liver.

It's important to catch dental disease in the early stages so you need to inspect your dog's mouth regularly for tartar which may appear as a brownish-gold build-up on the teeth, close to the gum line. Gingivitis may appear as redness or bleeding along the gum line. Other signs of dental disease include bad breath, drooling, pawing at the mouth, difficulty chewing and loose or missing teeth. If you notice any of these signs in your pet, make an appointment with your vet as the only way to effectively remove tartar from a dog's teeth and prevent the progression of periodontal disease is to get a dental scale and polish at the vet clinic.

With a vet clean and follow-up care, gingivitis is reversible. Periodontal disease is not reversible, but regular at-home dental care can lengthen intervals between vet cleanings (which for many dogs need to be done annually) and slow down the progression of the condition.

Many dogs quite like having their teeth brushed. Apart from the sensation and the flavours of the doggie toothpaste (beef, poultry, seafood), they mostly like the attention they are getting from you. All that attention makes them very happy. Nevertheless, some dogs are not comfortable at all about having a toothbrush poking around inside their mouth. And it can be hard to get a dog accustomed to that on a daily basis. With that in mind the earlier you get your dog used to the process the easier it will be, so start when they are a puppy. This, of course may be harder with an older rescue dog which may have never had its teeth cleaned. In that case I suggest you take it slowly and train your dog in the habit of teeth brushing over time.

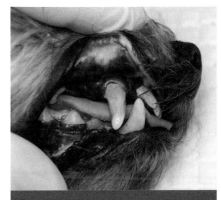

Grade 3 dental disease in a dog. Vets will give your dog a grade of dental disease based on a dental grading scale of grade 0 to grade 4. I recommend a professional dental cleaning and evaluation under anaesthesia for any pet receiving a grade 2 or higher.

These are the steps I advise owners to take before they sink their teeth into the job, always remembering to stay calm, cool and patiently loving. Once your dog gets used to the process it comes down to about one minute a day of brushing for your dog to have better dental health for the rest of its life.

1 **Before you brush.** Select an area of the house where you'll be doing future brushing. Get your dog to sit — on a tabletop if the dog is small breed — and then just rub his muzzle, lift his lip and simply look at his teeth. Give lots of loving praise and reward with a treat.

2 **Introduce the toothpaste.** Start by just putting some toothpaste on your finger and rub it around your dog's mouth while holding the toothbrush in the other hand. Once they are tolerating that, bring the toothbrush up near his face. If you go slow, he will see it coming and understand that it's not going to hurt him. You can also try putting a dab of paste on a favourite treat and then put it on top of the brush so he can get used to the bristles by his mouth. Again, follow up immediately with praise and a treat, even if you already put a treat on the brush — it's his lucky day!

3 **Brush lightly.** Begin by slipping the toothbrush between one of your dog's cheeks and teeth and move it back and forth, or with a circular motion from

back to front. It's not important to be brushing correctly – you've both still got your training wheels on. A few seconds is plenty at first try, followed with the usual praise and reward. If that goes well try the same thing on the other side of your dog's mouth, including the praise-and-reward part.

4 **How long?** Aim for no more than a minute for the whole mouth – front, sides, and back, both outsides and insides of the teeth, if possible. Eventually, you won't have to give a treat each time. Move through steps 1-3 slowly, this process might take two weeks or longer for some more sensitive or older dogs.

5 **Which toothpaste?** Never use human toothpaste, baking soda, or hydrogen peroxide, as they are all unsafe for dogs to swallow. Use the special doggie toothpaste which you can get at your local pet supplies outlet or vet clinic.

While daily brushing is great, your vet may also recommend a back-up treatment – a plaque prevention product that you apply to your dog's teeth and gums on a weekly basis. The product adheres to the surface of the teeth, creating a barrier that prevents plaque from forming. Several dental diets and treats can also help keep plaque and tartar to a minimum. These diets tend to have larger kibbles to provide abrasive action against the tooth surface when chewed or may contain ingredients that help prevent tartar mineralisation; some vets sell them as prescription products.

Trimming your dog's nails

Many owners get a bit nervous about trimming their dog's nails because if done incorrectly it can cause their dog pain, so they prefer not to do it or to pay someone else to do it. But trimming a dog's nails is not something that should be ignored because if they become too long, the quick (blood vessel and nerve ending inside the nail) gets longer, making it even more difficult to cut the dogs nails in the future, and in severe cases they can actually affect a dog's posture and joints by physically making the dog's gait uneven and cause it to limp.

A successful trim really comes down to the comfort of the dog and the technique used by the trimmer, either   you, your vet, or your groomer if you choose not to do it yourself because of the pain and bleeding that it may cause. If you're hesitant about trimming your dog's nails safely at home, let's start with a few basic facts about dog nails.

COMPOSITION

The dog nail is composed of layers. The strong outer 'shell', the part we actually see, is a protective coating. Inside this is a soft inner layer known as the quick. This layer, which contains blood vessels and nerves, begins at the base of the nail, and ends near the curve. If you cut the quick it could cause your dog to yelp plaintively and will also cause bleeding so it's important that you know precisely where that inner layer is situated.

The quick is easy to see if the dog has light-coloured nails – it's a pinkish-coloured segment near the base of the nail. Dark or black nails usually conceal the quick so see if you can find someone who has a dog with light-coloured nails (e.g. white-coated dogs) so you can get a better idea of where it's positioned but keep in mind that some dogs quicks are longer than others because it depends on their age and how frequently the owners have clipped their nails. Once you've located the quick, if possible, avoid trimming closer than two to three millimetres away.

Ideally, the nails should be short enough so that they do not touch the ground when the dog is standing on a firm, level surface, but they should be long enough to aid the dog when climbing up a hill or digging. If you don't trim your dog's nails on a regular basis, the quick grows with the nail. In some cases, when the nails are extra long, the quick may lengthen so much that it reaches the tip of the nail. When this happens, you won't be able to trim much of the nail without cutting through the quick. In this case, it's usually best to do a few at time because it can be a bit sore. Ask your vet or dog groomer to show you how to gradually trim the nail to encourage the quick to recede. Otherwise, you risk hurting your pet.

The secret to keeping your dog's nail tips short is to give frequent, gradual nail trims, or to make sure they get adequate activity on a regular basis. Each time you trim the nail a little bit more every week, the quick should gradually recede further up into the nail bed. Usually within seven days of trimming a small portion of an overgrown nail, the quick should have receded enough to allow you to trim off another little bit of nail again.

Guillotine nail clippers clipping white transparent nails. These are the easiest to clip because you can clearly see the nail and avoid the pink quick.

The ultimate goal of gradual nail trims is to have the quick recede more and more so you can allow your dog the luxury of healthier, shorter and stronger nails. Generally, dog nails are trimmed via three methods:

1 Trimming/cutting with a tool

2 Natural abrasion

3 Manual abrasion/grinding

If you are having a go yourself for the first time, ask your vet or a dog groomer to show you how much you can cut if you are trying for the first time and have them watch you. If you don't feel comfortable trimming your dog's nails and want to get those quicks to recede fast, you can ask your vet for help. Sometimes vets need to sedate or anesthetise a dog so the nails can be trimmed well back. If we expose the quick (which we often do because the quicks are so long) we then either dab with a styptic powder or cauterize the inner blood vessel to reduce bleeding.

TOOLS

Check out the available tools for home trimming at your local pet store. Some people prefer clippers; others like grinders. Choose whatever you think is going to make you and your dog feel most at ease. Grinders can provide extra control and smoothness but some dogs are freaked out by the buzzing noise. Clippers are available in two varieties: scissor and guillotine. The first is self-explanatory; guillotine clippers have a hole in the middle through which the dog's nail pokes. When you squeeze the handle, a blade snicks up to cut the nail.

PREPARATION

Good preparation and practice will ensure that you trim your dog's nails safely and successfully. Don't rush in; it's a good idea to experiment a bit so you can decide which trimming tool you prefer. But before you start, you need to get your dog accustomed to having his paws held. Some dogs don't like foot contact so simply hold each paw in your hand daily, touching the nails for a few seconds. The moment you let the paw go, reward the dog with heaps of praise and a tiny treat.

After doing this for a few weeks, put your chosen trimming tool on the floor with a few tasty treats on top. Let your dog sniff the tool and eat the treats while you praise him. If your chosen method is a grinder, switch it on for a couple of seconds and give your dog a treat. Do this for two to three weeks, or until your pooch seems completely at ease.

Once you're ready to try an actual trim, keep some favourite (preferably low-calorie) training treats nearby plus some cotton balls and a small jar of styptic powder for patting around the nail tip to stop any bleeding. Bleeding is common in dogs with black-coloured nails because it is difficult to identify where the quick lies. Find a comfy well-lit spot and get your dog in a relaxed position, either standing or lounging on the floor. Take a deep breath and calmly begin.

Clipper method

1 Hold the clipper in your dominant hand.

2 Hold your dog's paw firmly in your other hand - thumb on the foot pad, fingers at the top of the foot, near the nail bed.

3 Begin at the very tip — especially if your dog has dark nails.

4 Only trim about one to two millimetres at a time, gradually moving toward the quick.

5 Examine the cross-section of your dog's nail each time you cut.

6 When you start seeing a tan-coloured oval, you're nearing the quick so stop cutting.

Grinder method

1 Hold the grinder in your dominant hand with the dog's paw firmly in your other hand.

2 Gently touch the grinder to the tip of your dog's nail and silently count to two.

3 Remove the grinder for a few seconds; praise your pooch; repeat.

4 Continue until you start to see the tan-coloured oval … then stop.

Tips

- Go very slowly offering lots of praise and treats.
- Never trim when you're rushed.
- You don't have to do all four paws at once.
- If your dog starts sending out stress signals such as yawning or squirming, take a break.

Lap dogs, handbag dogs and coach potato dogs have the most troubles with overgrown nails because they are not getting the natural manual abrasion from climbing, walking and running around outside. On the other hand, active and adventurous dogs, the kind you see running each morning with their equally athletic owners, usually have healthy short nails, with receded quicks and don't have to have them trimmed at all – another reason to get outside and get moving with your furry friend.

Cleaning your dog's ears

Dog's ears can build up wax and other bits of gunk and they need regular cleaning to prevent ear infections. But don't overdo it; if your dog is scratching his ears or if the skin inside looks red and irritated, he'll need to see the vet. Cleaning his ears, with a mild veterinary approved ear cleaner may clean out the gunk but ultimately the source of the problem, usually an infection or underlying allergy, will need to be treated. If a dog has a nasty ear infection and you clean the ears it will just sting the poor pup like hell; so it's better to get the vet to diagnose the cause and provide suitable treatment before cleaning at home. Also, it gives the vet an opportunity to have a look down the ear and make sure the eardrum isn't ruptured before anything gets squirted down there. It's very important that any ear infections get treated promptly as untreated infections can have serious consequences. For more information on ear infections see Chapter 10.

HEALTHY EARS

Cleaning for general maintenance is encouraged for healthy ears; if the ears are infected a vet will still recommend regular cleaning but only after making sure the ear drum is intact and any underlying issue is being treated. Your vet may clean your dog's ears, you can take him to a professional dog groomer or you can also do the job yourself at home, which may be less stressful for your dog. Dogs generally are not too keen on having their ears cleaned so you'll have to work with him. It's important to associate ear-cleaning with something positive; a bag of reward treats will usually help most dogs co-operate with the process.

Before you try cleaning your dog's ears yourself, it's a good idea to get him used to having his ears handled by gently playing with them and practice holding his ears open to peer into them. You can even gently rub the inside of his ear with your finger. If your dog is used to having his ears touched, cleaning will be much less stressful when you need to do it.

You will need a gentle ear rinse and cotton balls – never use cotton buds because, just as with human ears, they can damage the ear. If you don't use rubber gloves make sure you wash your hands thoroughly, before and after.

The most important 'tool' is the ear rinse; you'll need a product that contains no antibiotics, no steroids (unless prescribed by your vet), and no alcohol or toxic ingredients of any kind. I am wary of home remedies with owners pouring acid down a dog's ear without knowing if the ear drum is ruptured – something that can cause irreparable damage. Some of these home remedies include vinegar which if not watered down adequately can be very painful and irritating. And while vinegar might aid cleaning it's not an effective treatment for bacterial or yeast infections.

Before you start make sure you have everything you need within reach – the last thing you want having to get up halfway through the cleaning process to get something you forgot. Do that and you may have to wrestle your reluctant pooch back into position and possibly even have to start again. Some dogs are better sitting up for ear cleaning while others may prefer to lie down, head on the ground; experiment to see which works best for you and your dog.

Dogs' ears are sensitive and to clean them without causing harm, start on the outside and work your way in – but only until you start to feel resistance. It's important to be cautious; if you try to push further in, you could damage the eardrum. Stop and immediately if his ears start to bleed at all and contact your vet.

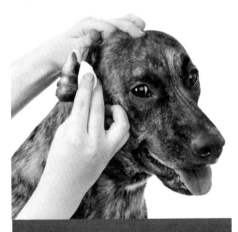

A calm dog having ears wiped out with cotton wool. Dogs that have had regular ear cleaning since puppyhood usually find ear cleaning relaxing and enjoyable.

Soak the cotton ball with ear rinse and gently wipe the part of the ear that you can easily see, the outer flap. Give him a treat. Then wet a new cotton ball to clean the inner ear, squishing it a bit so that the solution drips into the crevasses of the ear. Continue wiping with cotton balls until they come out clean, rewarding him with a treat or two throughout the process. if the cotton balls or gauze are especially dirty or a bit smelly consult your vet to see if everything is okay. Finally, wipe the ears out with dry cotton balls. And don't forget to give your dog heaps of praise when you've finished.

Brushing your dog's coat

How lovely it is to see a well-groomed pooch, his coat smooth and shiny or his long hair flowing in the breeze as he trots along happily beside his proud owner. Dogs love to be pampered and brushed and I have set out a few grooming tips to help you keep your dog's coat healthy.

- First, start brushing your pup when he is young, even if he doesn't need it. In this way he'll get used to being groomed and start to love it, especially if you hand out yummy treats afterwards so he associates it with happy things. Having said that, remember what I said earlier about being careful not to overuse treats, because they soon stop working for them and might start to pack on the pounds; dogs love friendly praise and cuddles too and often that's enough.

- If your dog is a medium-haired or long-haired breed you will know that some areas matt easier than others, such as behind the ears and legs, in the armpits, on his underbelly and where his collar or lead halter rubs. To stop matting before it starts use a detangling cream or spray to prevent fur from clumping up. Use this before your dog jumps into a river, lake or the sea to make the after-swim brushing easier. Be careful to only use products specifically made for dogs.

- See your vet if your dog's coat is severely matted or hasn't been cared for in a while because it's important your pooch does not have any skin irritations.

- The next time you use a professional groomer, have a chat with them about best way to brush your dog at home and what kind of brush to use as the best brush depends on your dog's coat type. The better brush work you do at home the easier her job is.

- Remember that the hair that grows between the pads in your dog's paws can get matted too. Keep it short with dog clippers at home. Paw pads are sensitive (ouch!) and clippers are better than scissors.

- Last, but not least, it's important to remember that a good diet (especially those containing fish oils, omega 3 and 6 fatty acids) helps your dog have a healthy coat that's less likely to get tangled. See Chapter 6 for information about the composition of a good diet.

CHAPTER 9

Systems, Vital Signs and Cancer

As I mentioned in an earlier chapter, dogs have most of the common human diseases plus a range of special canine ones. Before I take your through the common doggie ailments and treatments, I thought I'd briefly outline the body's anatomy and physiology as it applies to humans and their dogs.

The anatomy & physiology of your dog

Both human and dog bodies are divided into different 11 or 12 systems depending how you categorise them.

CIRCULATORY OR CARDIOVASCULAR SYSTEM

This is the system of the heart and blood vessels. The heart's job is to pump blood around the body and the vessels take it to all different body parts and muscles. Blood contains the nutrients and oxygen that our cells need to function. The circulatory system also picks up the waste and brings it back to the liver and kidneys which are the two most important organs in the process of eliminating waste. It also works to equalise temperatures; when we're hot we get flushed because all the blood comes to the outside of our body and when we're cold it wants to preserve what's most important – our core and our organs, so it moves to the centre of the body.

DIGESTIVE SYSTEM

This system includes the mouth, the teeth, salivary glands, the oesophagus (the tube that goes down to the stomach), the stomach, intestines and the pancreas, which produces a lot of digestive enzymes (I mentioned earlier that dogs that eat fatty foods sometimes get pancreatitis). The liver and the gall bladder also belong to this system. Its job is to digest food, absorb all the nutrients and then eliminate solid waste through faeces. An interesting fact about the digestive system is that it's chemical, mechanical and physical. The chemicals are our gastric acids and digestive enzymes which break down the food; the mechanical is the chomping of food our teeth do; and the physical is the physical movements of the stomach (called peristalsis) and the contractions of the digestive tract (or the intestines) as it moves the food along. So our food gets digested chemically, physically and mechanically.

ENDOCRINE SYSTEM

This involves several hormone-producing glands around the body. Hormones are sort of messengers that send chemical communications through our bloodstream to various organs. Endocrine glands include the thyroid, which is responsible for hyperthyroidism and hypothyroidism (both of which affect dogs, especially the latter); the parathyroid gland, which is the gland next to the thyroid; the adrenal glands, which are responsible for Addison's and Cushing's diseases both really common in dogs; and part of the pancreas, which produces some hormones, like insulin.

INTEGUMENTARY SYSTEM

This is the skin, or skin and fur in the case of dogs, plus the nails, toenails, sweat glands, and exocrine glands, which are any glands producing exterior body substances such as sweat. The importance of skin cannot be over-estimated. It keeps us together and protects all our organs and muscles. And a dog's fur insulates it against heat loss and keeps it warm. Dogs don't sweat all that much through their skin but through their nose and their paws which is why they sometimes have little moist foot pads when they're hot. Unlike humans, who control our temperature through sweating, dogs control theirs through panting.

MUSCULOSKELETAL SYSTEM

This is the bones, muscles and joints. We see a lot of arthritis in dogs and lots of hip dysplasia and cruciate ligament disease – football players rupture their cruciates all the time, so do dogs. It's really common and usually happens when a dog is bolting around and makes a sharp turn, the force of which ruptures the little ligament.

NERVOUS SYSTEM

This is the system that processes information through nerves. It also includes the brain and the spinal cord. Our reflexes all come via our nervous system. It's the system that is affected by the neurotoxin of a tick bite.

RENAL SYSTEM

This includes the kidneys, the ureters, the bladder and the urethra. When sometimes joined with the reproductive system it called the urogenital system. The kidney's job is to filter our blood and extract the urine and the waste, eliminating it as urine through the urethra.

REPRODUCTIVE SYSTEM

This refers to the sex organs and producing offspring.

RESPIRATORY SYSTEM

This includes the nose, mouth, trachea, lungs and smaller airwaves i.e. bronchi and bronchioles. It's responsible for inhaling oxygen and exhaling carbon dioxide. The respiratory system plays an important role in the dog's temperature regulation.

HAEMATOPOIETIC SYSTEM

This system produces the cellular components of blood including bone marrow, thymus, lymph nodes and spleen. The most important role of this system is production of three important cells made in the bone marrow – white blood cells (part of our immune system which attacks invaders and fights infection), red blood cells (the part of our blood that carries the oxygen), and platelets (important for clotting). If a dog doesn't have enough platelets (also known as thrombocytes) they have bleeding problems, such as immune mediated thrombocytopaenia (see Chapter 10 for more information).

LYMPHATIC SYSTEM

This is a network of lymphatic vessels, that carry a clear fluid called lymph. The lymphatic system a big part of the immune system that helps to fight disease. It defends the body against pathogens such as viruses and bacteria. Without it, we would all be dead.

IMMUNE SYSTEM

This is a really important system so I'm going to delve into it a little deeper. The overall function of the immune system is to protect the body by preventing infections and recognising foreign material, such as the abnormal growth of cancer cells. It has a vast network of cells and tissues that are always on the hunt for invaders. It can distinguish between normal, healthy cells and unhealthy cells by recognizing a variety of 'danger' cues called danger-associated molecular patterns (DAMPs). Cells may be unhealthy because of infection or because of cellular damage caused by non-infectious agents like sunburn or cancer. Infectious microbes such as viruses and bacteria release another set of signals recognised by the immune system called pathogen-associated molecular patterns (PAMPs).

Both DAMPs and PAMPs trigger the immune system to act a bit like an army; once the signal is triggered, the immune system responds and attacks the invaders. Pretty cool, right? The immune system has to be functioning appropriately because it has to distinguish between self and foreign. When an immune response is activated when there isn't a real threat or is not turned off once the danger passes, different problems arise, such as allergic reactions and autoimmune disease.

The immune system is complex with numerous cell types that either circulate throughout the body or live in a particular tissue. Each cell type plays a unique role, with different ways of recognising problems, communicating with other cells, and performing their functions. By understanding all the details behind this network, researchers may optimise immune responses to confront specific issues, ranging from infections to cancer.

One autoimmune response is inflammatory bowel disease, when your own immune system is attacking the bowel. Dogs get this too although not as commonly as humans. The common diseases dogs get when the immune system is in overdrive are immune-mediated haemolytic anaemia (when the body attacks its red blood cells) and immune-mediated thrombocytopaenia (when it attacks its thrombocytes, which leads to clotting problems).

Allergies are another example. Dogs can be exposed to a mite or a flea's saliva and the immune system goes nuts to protect it. But in this case the immune system is actually creating more harm than good. Then there is immunocompromise – which is the opposite to overdrive. This is when the immune system is impaired, and we definitely see that as a result of chemotherapy, but you also see it in age as well. Other conditions like leukaemia are caused when a body is immune-compromised because it doesn't have enough white blood cells, an important part of the immune system.

DETECTING VITAL SIGNS

Veterinary staff get a lot of information about the state of a dog's general health by measuring three simple things – their temperature, their respiratory rate and their heart rate. We call these 'vital signs' or a 'TPR' — temperature, pulse and respiration. Vet nurses often check these vital signs along with the patient's weight, capillary refill time and colour of their gums before the vet starts the consultation. Taking note of these signs is so second nature to vets and vet nurses that most will have it done in a couple minutes without the owner even noticing. Even my receptionist can detect minor abnormal breathing patterns in dogs from just peering over the front desk and counting their respiratory rate. It is an everyday procedure and we've all mastered the art.

Body Temperature. In general, a dog's body temperature is higher than a human's. A dog's normal body temperature range is 38-39.2 C. Much to the owners' embarrassment (or entertainment) a dog's body temperature is normally measured rectally. Naturally I'm quite desensitised to the practice of rectal examinations. Once, a little boy accompanying his mum and dog for a consultation got the shock of his life when I inserted the thermometer into the dog's bottom. The young boy fell back into his chair laughing hysterically, 'Mum, she put that thing in Georgie's bum hole! That's so disgusting!' It was a funny reminder that a trip to the vet can be a bit weird for the unsuspecting.

Respiratory Rate. Respiratory rate is the number of breaths per minute. Normal respiratory rates are assessed when the dog is resting. The standard respiratory rate for dogs is officially 10-34 breaths per minute unless panting, but I often find it is between 18-24rpm (respiration per minute). A dog that is in pain, having heart or respiratory problems, suffering from heatstroke, or simply excited, will usually have increased respiratory rates. It is important to gauge the overall situation and condition of the animal when assessing their respiratory rate.

Heart Rate. The standard heart rate in dogs depends on their size. Resting heart rates (or pulse) for a small dog is 90-120 beats per minute (bpm), for a medium dog 70-110 bpm and a large dog 60-90bpm. Larger dogs have slower rates than small dogs, and dogs that are in good physical shape will have lower heart rates than dogs of similar age and size that are not physically fit, just like humans. Puppies typically have higher heart rates; up to 180 beats per minute is normal for dogs up to one year of age.

You can learn how to measure these parameters at home; just ask your vet or vet nurse to teach you (especially if you're a breeder). It can be useful for monitoring your dog's health and it will mean you'll know what is 'normal' for your pet.

Dogs get cancer too

Cancer is relatively common in dogs. If your vet says the word 'cancer' or 'tumour' when talking to you about your precious pooch, it's likely to sound quite frightening. However, many tumours turn out to be benign and can be treated successfully.

All cancers arise from damage to genes. Some specific cancer-producing genes have been inherited and the cancer arises from a direct genetic cause; but in other individual dogs or breeds the genetic link is less easy to trace. But whatever the genetic predisposition, the cancer is triggered by the growth of abnormal cells which have tricked the immune system into leaving them alone. Having by-passed the body's natural defences, the cancer cells then multiply rapidly to form a tumour.

Tumours are divided into two categories: malignant (cancerous) and benign (non-cancerous. Malignant tumours may also spread via the bloodstream or lymphatic fluid to other parts of the body. Benign tumours usually grow slowly and don't spread. Tumours in dogs are commonly found in their skin, mammary tissue, bones, the lymphatic system, spleen and liver.

Malignant tumours are classified according to where they originate. Carcinomas grow in the tissues that line the surfaces of a dog's organs; sarcomas form in the tissues of muscles, blood vessels and bones; and lymphomas arise in the tissues of the lymph system. How immediate the threat of a malignant tumour is depends on where it is, the rate of growth and whether it has spread to other organs. When making a diagnosis your vet will take into account your dog's age, his medical history and breed. It is usually necessary to carry out a number of tests to determine if the growth is benign or malignant.

Imaging tests – x-rays and ultrasound – are used to detect internal cancers. A more detail image can be gained from magnetic resonance imaging (MRI) but it's expensive. If a tumour is found it is impossible to make a correct diagnosis without tissue sampling which is done with a biopsy – removing a small piece of abnormal tissue or a fine needle aspiration to remove some cells to examine under a microscope. Benign tumours are usually harmless and may need no treatment unless they are very large and pressing on surrounding organs or causing pain or discomfort, in which case they may need to be surgically removed. Hormone-secreting tumours are also usually removed as they can disturb the dog's hormone balance.

TREATMENT

Surgery. The most effective method of treating a malignant tumour is to remove it along with a margin of healthy tissue around it. If the cancer is in the mammary glands the vet will probably want to also remove the lymph nodes from that side of the body to stop it from spreading.

Radiotherapy. If it has not been possible to remove the tumour completely or if the mass is inoperable, radiotherapy may be used. It is particularly effective for localised radiation-sensitive tumours such as soft tissue sarcomas, mouth and nasal cavity tumours and mast cell tumours. Radiotherapy is generally carried out in specialist veterinary centres.

Chemotherapy. Certain types of cancer respond well to chemotherapy which is when the dog is given anticancer drugs to kill the rapidly multiplying cells. Fortunately, most dogs tolerate chemotherapy much better than humans; only about ten per cent of dogs require hospitalisation due to chemotherapy-related side effects. My primary goal in using these drugs is to provide the pet with a good quality of life for as long as possible, so if side-effects are cropping up, the specialist and I will work together to alter the treatment plan.

Immunotherapy. Immunotherapy drugs help your immune system work harder or make it easier for it to find and get rid of cancer cells. Several immunotherapy drugs have been approved to fight cancer in human medicine and hundreds more are being tested in clinical trials. Although immunotherapy is not yet widely available in veterinary medicine, early results are promising.

Palliative care. The aim of palliative care is to preserve the quality of life, even if it means a shorter life. Like most vets, I feel it is not ethically sustainable for an animal to suffer during treatment, so in some cases the best thing is not to try to cure the cancer if it means putting the dog through potentially painful treatments, but to use pain relief and anti-inflammatories to enhance the dog's physical and emotional wellbeing. In certain types of cancer, the corticosteroid drug prednisolone has enhanced the quality of a dog's life and even increased its life expectancy.

Among the breeds at most risk of dying from cancer are Rottweiler, Afghan Hound, Standard Poodle, Staffordshire Bull Terrier, Boxer, Golden Retriever and Weimaraner. Those breeds at least risk include Border Collie, West Highland White Terrier, Yorkshire Terrier and Cocker Spaniel.

The most common cancers in dogs

There are many different types of cancer that effect dogs and the older the dog the greater the risk of developing most types of the disease. This is because cells have had more time to develop genetic damage and the dog's natural defences have become less efficient with age. The following are the ten main cancers I see in practice.

LYMPHOMAS

This is a blood borne cancer of white blood cells called lymphocytes and it develops in the lymphatic tissue. This tissue is mainly situated in the lymph nodes but is also found elsewhere including bone marrow, liver, spleen, the intestines and the skin. Dogs most commonly present with enlarged external lymph nodes. Although only one node may be enlarged in most dogs the disease is usually widespread by the time it is diagnosed. Lymphoma is the most chemotherapy responsive tumour we treat, especially in smaller dogs.

MAST CELL TUMOURS

These tumours, also known as mastocytomas, are made up of immune cells (called a mast cells) which are found throughout the body. This means the disease can develop in any organ system although these tumours are more frequently found on the skin. Older dogs are more prone to develop this cancer, however they are also found in younger dogs, notably Boxers, Labradors and Golden Retrievers.

The biggest predictor of the aggressiveness of a mast cell tumour originating on the skin is something vets call the 'histological grade' which is determined through biopsy. The most commonly used grading system is called the '3 Tier Patnaik Scale' which designates tumours by grade. Grade 1 tumours are usually no big deal, they are benign and are generally considered cured following surgery. Grade 3 tumours on the other hand are malignant, which means they can recur following surgery, spreading to regional lymph nodes and internal organs, which can be fatal. The grade 2 tumours fall somewhere in between, and these ones can be difficult to predict – some behave more like grade 1 and others go on to be more aggressive and spread like a grade 3. Low grade cancerous tumours are surgically removed; a variety of treatments – chemotherapy, radiotherapy and immunotherapy – may be used on more aggressive tumours. When mast cell tumours develop on internal organs the prognosis is poor.

OSTEOSARCOMA

This is the most common primary bone cancer in dogs and mostly occurs in the long bones of the legs of large and giant breeds; less commonly in the jaw or ribs. It can spread to other parts of the body. This type of tumour is often found in mature dogs who suddenly become lame with no history of an injury to the affected leg. It is a painful condition, usually diagnosed with an x-ray and amputation of the limb is necessary to provide relief. Dogs handle amputation well and the younger the dog and smaller the breed the better the chance of it recovering mobility. Amputation alone is the best way to relieve the pain, but without chemotherapy only 10 per cent survive a year and there are no long-term survivors. If you use chemotherapy 50 per cent survive the next 12 months and 30 per cent are long term survivors, so the two are usually used in combination. Limp-sparing surgery and palliative radiation is the best option in situations where the dog has other chronic illnesses and problems making amputation a non-viable option.

LIPOMAS

This is a benign tumour of excess fatty tissue, more common in older, overweight female dogs. Lipomas are painless and can grow on any part of the body. They usually grow slowly but can grow very large. Lipomas have a characteristic round fatty appearance but like all tumours, diagnosis can only be confirmed with a biopsy or fine needle aspirate. If the growth interferes with the dog's ability to walk (e.g. along a limb) it can be surgically removed. Surgery is also recommended when the lipoma is growing between muscle tissue, called intramuscular lipomas; complete removal is challenging due to their location, but radiotherapy can be used as a back-up or when the tumours are too large to be removed. Lipomas can also grow within the chest cavity, compressing vital organs and becoming extremely uncomfortable for the dog.

ORAL MELANOMA

This is one of the most common oral cancers in dogs and a serious form of skin cancer; it often grows rapidly and spreads locally and to other areas of the body. Breeds with darker pigmented gums and tongues are in the high-risk category. Complete removal of this tumour is difficult, and the best outcome may be an aggressive initial operation by a specialist vet surgeon. Because of its propensity to spread, pre-surgical testing of lymph nodes and chest x-rays will be necessary.

Following surgery, radiotherapy may be given at the surgical site and any other areas where the cancer has spread. Radiation therapy is often used to treat malignant melanomas larger than 2cm in diameter and the melanoma vaccine may also help.

ANAL GLAND ADENOCARCINOMA

Dogs have glands at the opening of their anus that release a foul-smelling substance when they defecate. Tumours of these glands are not common but when they do occur they can be extremely aggressive which is one of the reasons we vets perform regular rectal examinations on our doggie patients. Anal sac adenocarcinomas secrete a hormone that tricks an affected dog's body into thinking their blood calcium level is low causing massive absorption of calcium from their diet, bones and kidneys. This can raise the dog's blood calcium levels and occurs in 25 per cent of patients causing nausea, weakness and heart problems.

Anal sac tumours can spread to the lymph nodes in the pelvic region, then to the lungs, liver, spleen and even bone. If possible, surgical removal of the anal sac tumour is recommended, usually followed by chemotherapy – the smaller the tumour the more positive the outcome.

MAMMARY TUMOURS

Tumours of the reproductive organs are common in female dogs over six years old and the most frequent are in the mammary glands. Un-desexed females are more at risk due to the hormone influence on mammary tissue. There's an even split between benign and malignant mammary tumours and about half who develop the malignant type will die from the condition.

Most mammary tumours are painless; they are often multiple mobile masses situated near one or more of the bitches ten or twelve teats. Some bitches develop a painful, inflammatory form of breast cancer, often in the glands nearest to the groin.

The condition's risk to the dog will be assessed with a biopsy of the tumour. Many primary mammary tumours can be treated with surgery alone although some will be treated with chemotherapy as well to prevent or delay reoccurrence and/or spread.

LUNG TUMOURS (PRIMARY AND SECONDARY)

Lung cancer occurs mainly in older dogs and is often diagnosed incidentally when the dog is screened during its annual vet health check or during x-rays which were taken to examine something else. The incidence of primary lung cancer in dogs is relatively rare when compared to the rate in humans, no doubt because dogs don't smoke! However, secondary lung cancers, spreading from either bone tumours or from other soft tissue is relatively common.

Whenever a malignant tumour is diagnosed somewhere in the body, the chest is usually x-rayed to see if the cancer has spread to the lungs or lymph nodes. If the cancer has spread to the lungs, the prognosis is poor (survival is usually only about two months) and the vet might suggest palliative care or euthanasia. If there is only one tumour and the vet has identified its location clearly with a CT scan, they will probably suggest surgery to remove the portion of the lung containing the tumour.

THYROID CARCINOMA

This is another cancer more frequently found in older dogs. It may be felt as a lump on the dog's neck while petting it or by the vet during a routine check. Some thyroid tumours actively secrete thyroid hormone which causes the dog to become hyperthyroid, losing weight, becoming hyperactive, panting and showing signs of being generally unwell. The tumour can be surgically removed – requiring great care due to the very vascular nature of the tumour – and radiotherapy can be used to treat a tumour that can't be completely removed. Chemotherapy is often recommended to delay or prevent spread.

HEMANGIOSARCOMA

This is a soft tissue cancer. Benign haemangisarcomas develop in the lining of blood vessels and occur most commonly in the spleen; malignant haemangisarcomas may appear in the spleen, heart liver and skin. When the spleen is affected the dog usually won't show any sign of illness until the tumour ruptures and they bleed internally. This is life-threatening and requires emergency surgery to remove the spleen. The prognosis for dogs with haemangisarcomas depends on the location of the primary tumour and can range from a few months to two years. Treatment involves a combination of surgery, radiotherapy and chemotherapy.

CHAPTER 10

Common Diseases and Medical Conditions

I f you love your dog, its health will be uppermost in your mind as you enjoy your lives together. Good care includes understanding not only his psychological needs but also his health issues. No-one wants to see their dog in pain or suffering so knowing the types of medical problems that he might face during his life may help you cope when he gets sick and to know when to consult your vet – and how fast you need to put your skates on.

In this chapter I have outlined various health issues and some of the more common diseases your dog might encounter, along with a couple of the rarer ones he is unlikely to. This is by no means an exhaustive list; dogs are prone to simply hundreds of ailments, both serious and mild so I have selected the ones I have most commonly encountered as a vet. For a more comprehensive compendium of medical conditions in dogs I have listed some good reference material at the back of this book.

Orthopaedic (musculoskeletal) conditions

OSTEOARTHRITIS

The term 'arthritis' simply means an inflammation of the joint and is used to describe a variety of painful conditions that can develop in any joint of your dog. There are many types of joint disease, both inherited and degenerative, but the most common is the degenerative osteoarthritis. Degenerative joint disease (DJD) is a 'wear and tear' disease process that happens as a consequence of anything that causes bones to rub against each and results in arthritis. Degenerative joint disease (DJD) will affect about one in five dogs during their lifetime and larger breeds are more likely to develop it than smaller dogs. DJD occurs when the joint cartilage is unable to stay healthy or repair itself after an injury.

The first signs of DJD are often subtle; your dog may slow down walking up stairs and struggle to get into the car or is not so excited to run to his food bowl; with time symptoms of stiffness and lameness become more obvious. If it gets really severe to the point when they can't even get up to go to the toilet and become incontinent in their bed, then you have to question the dog's quality of life and you might have a difficult decision to make about euthanasia.

The vet will diagnose the severity of the arthritis by flexing, extending and rotating the joint to assess its range of motion and the degree of pain. X-rays may show a narrowing of the joint spaces, new bone formations called osteophytes, or calcium deposits in the joint cavity.

The aim of treatment is to control the pain which is done with the vet's non-steroidal anti-inflammatory drug of choice, improving mobility with gentle exercise and weight control. In some cases of severe DJD, surgical fusion of the affected joints such as hock and elbow or other surgical procedures may relieve the pain.

HIP DYSPLASIA

The hip is a ball and socket joint: the ball is the top of the femur (thighbone) and the deep, cartilage-lined socket (acetabulum) is located within the pelvis. If the fit is not right — such as slight misalignment and the femoral head is loose — the cartilage of the femoral head rubs against the socket. Eventually the cartilage wears out causing what we call hip dysplasia. This becomes apparent when the dog shows signs of muscle wastage, lameness, an abnormal gait and pain which comes from the resulting arthritis, also known as osteoarthritis.

Hip dysplasia is more common in large, fast growing breeds such as German Shepherds, Labradors, Golden Retrievers and Rottweilers. A vet will diagnose hip dysplasia by breed history and by feeling the hip joint for laxity and x-rays are used to determine its severity. It can usually be managed by controlling the dog's weight, moderate exercise, joint supplements, a series of cartilage protective injections and pain medication such as non-steroidal anti-inflammatory drugs (NSAIDs). However, in more severe cases, surgical intervention, such as a pelvic osteotomy, femoral head ostectomy or a total hip replacement may be necessary, particularly when pain and restricted movement is severe.

ELBOW DYSPLASIA

Another condition seen in large breeds such as German Shepherds, Labradors, Golden Retrievers and Rottweilers, it is a combination of various elbow conditions involving developmental abnormalities, especially to the growth of cartilage. The primary problem seen is usually related to osteochondritis dissecans (OCD) which starts during the puppy's growth and results in the separation of a flap of cartilage from the joint surface, described in more detail below. Other common contributors to elbow dysplasia are anatomical abnormalities such as un-united anconeal process and a fragmented medial coronoid process.

As you can see, these conditions are quite a mouthful and can be difficult to understand. If your dog is diagnosed with elbow dysplasia, ask your vet to explain the abnormalities by showing you the x-rays and a model of the elbow joint. The condition is diagnosed with an x-ray and managed with weight control, gentle exercise, and analgesics to control the pain. Surgery is sometimes recommended to repair the damaged bones.

OSTEOCHONDROSIS DISSECANS (OCD)

This is a bone disorder which starts when a puppy is growing and bits of developing cartilage flake off into the joints; this is caused by a defect in the calcification of the growth plates near the ends of the long bones. The raw parts of the bone may become inflamed while the bits of cartilage floating in the joint fluid inhibit smooth joint function. OCD occurs more frequently in the shoulder joints but is also found in the elbows and hocks of fast-growing heavy breed dogs that have been fed a high energy diet.

OCD is diagnosed with x-rays and possibly an arthroscopy for the larger joints. Sometimes rest is all the dog needs, but other dogs may need to have the floating bits of cartilage surgically removed.

PATELLA LUXATION

The patella is the kneecap and it moves up and down within a bony groove when the knee is flexed and extended. Some dogs have an abnormality which causes the kneecap to slip in and out of the groove when the knee moves. There are two types of luxation: medial – when the patella shifts towards the inside of the knee and lateral when it shifts towards the outside, but this is less common. Medial patella is common in toy and miniature breeds, such as Chihuahuas, Pomeranians and Miniature Poodles. The usual symptom is non-weight bearing lameness when the dog has a skipping gait when walking or running. A vet can diagnose this by feeling the patella move in and out of the groove while manipulating it. Depending on the severity of the condition, it can be managed with non-steroidal anti-inflammatory medication, physical therapy or surgery to repair the conformation defects in the knee. With appropriate treatment the outcome is generally good.

RUPTURED CRUCIATE

Dogs are always pulling ligaments and straining muscles when they're running about having a ball, so the musculoskeletal system is something vets treat a lot. There are two cruciate ligaments that stabilise each knee joint. Spontaneous rupture or tearing of the of the cranial (anterior) cruciate ligament is relatively common especially in obese and older dogs. Some dogs are more prone to this injury than others. I see it frequently in Staffies, Rottweilers and Labradors, because when they run around with great gusto they place huge amounts of force on this little ligament and sure enough they bust their cruciate! A dog that does lots of fetching, ball chasing and bolting is more prone but I've also seen it in little lap dogs that have done it running around the house.

The most common symptom is sudden lameness. Diagnosis is made by x-ray and a physical examination. If it's a complete rupture it requires surgery. If it's a partial tear, a course of an anti-inflammatory and rest (i.e. no running) may be sufficient; however, the partial tears often end up tearing completely anyway so most dogs will end up having orthopaedic surgery. And as if this news is not bad enough, at least half of the dogs that have a cruciate ligament problem in one knee will likely have the same problem in the other knee at some point in their life.

INTERVERTEBRAL DISC DISEASE (IVDD)

Intervertebral disc disease is a condition where the cushioning discs between the vertebrae (the shock absorbers of the spinal column) either rupture or herniate (Hansen Type 1) or bulge (Hansen Type 2) into the spinal cord space. In some dogs, usually larger breeds, the fibrous exterior might remain intact but the disk may still slip or bulge (Type 2). A suddenly ruptured disk is painful for the dog and he may lose muscle function on one or both sides of his body. When the spinal cord nerves are compressed, the nerve impulses are not able to transmit their signals to various parts of the body. Severe damage can cause paralysis and loss of bladder and bowel control.

In Type I, common in the smaller breeds, the outer layer of the disc develops calcification enabling it to break down easier. Any forceful impact such as jumping and landing can cause one or more discs to burst and the inner material to press on the spinal cord. With Type 2, the discs become hardened and fibrous over a long period of time and the jelly-like centre bulges out (it doesn't rupture like type 1) and compresses the spinal cord. This is more similar to the human version of disc disease. Type 2 generally has less severe signs and symptoms.

Symptoms of IVDD may include:

- Unwillingness to jump
- Rear leg lameness
- Yelping in pain
- Anxious behaviour
- Muscle spasms over back or neck
- Hunched back or neck with tense muscles

In severe cases complete paralysis of the hindlimbs and incontinence the vet will base a diagnosis on the dog's history, breed and symptoms. Plain X-rays can show the decreased spaces between the discs so can assist in the diagnosis. But contrast x-rays or even better magnetic resonance imaging (MRI) or computed tomography (CT) scans will show the extent of the compression on the spinal cord. Sometimes to our surprise we find that there is actually no evidence of IVDD or pressure on the spinal cord at all, in which case we start investigating other possible diagnosis such as spinal shock (usually associated with trauma), fibrocartilaginous embolism or degenerative myelopathy.

The recommended treatment for IVDD is based on the stage or severity of the condition, and it's important to be aware that the condition can progress from mild, moderate to severe in just hours to days. Dogs with the milder form of the disease are usually treated with anti-inflammatories, pain relief and strict rest. In the more severe cases, or where the condition is deteriorating, surgery may be required. In advanced cases the sooner the surgery is done the better the chance of recovery. The most common spinal surgery performed in the dog is for intervertebral disc disease.

IVDD is an age-related, degenerative condition. However certain 'at-risk' dogs — called chondrodystrophic breeds (and their crosses)— can suffer disc problems from when they are young adult dogs. Chondrodystrophic breeds are those with long backs and short legs, such as the Dachshund, Beagle, Shih Tzu and Basset Hound, are more prone to ruptured discs because their anatomy causes the spine to flex and puts pressure on the discs. Most dogs with degenerative disc disease are middle-aged, from three to seven years old. There is likely a genetic predisposition to this disease. Certain breeds, especially the Dachshund, Poodle, Pekinese, Lhasa Apso, German Shepherd, Doberman and Cocker Spaniel have a high incidence of IVDD .

Hormonal diseases

ADDISON'S DISEASE

Also called hypoadrenocorticism, Addison's disease is caused by an under active adrenal gland and is more difficult to diagnose than Cushing's disease (see below) because the clinical signs tend to come and go. Female dogs between the ages of two and seven are the most prone to the condition and the breeds in which I most commonly diagnose Addison's disease are Standard Poodles, West Highland Terriers and Great Danes. The most common symptoms are loss of appetite, lethargy and depression.

Addison's disease is usually diagnosed during what we call an 'Addisonian crisis'. This is where the dog experiences a life-threatening episode of shock and collapse. It's a very frightening acute medical emergency requiring immediate hospitalisation and intensive therapy to manage the symptoms. Blood will be checked for levels of electrolytes in the blood serum as it's common to find low levels of chloride and sodium and high levels of potassium. A method of diagnosis is to use a hormone stimulation test. Dogs with Addison's are treated with corticosteroid supplements.

CUSHING'S DISEASE

This condition, also known as hyperadrenocortism, is the over-activity of one or both adrenal glands causing the production of too much cortisol. Symptoms of Cushing's can include increased thirst and increased urination, increased appetite, development of a pot belly, panting, muscle weakness, hair loss and susceptibility to skin and bladder infections. Some of these symptoms can take years to develop and vary from dog to dog. The breeds prone to develop this disease include Beagle, Boxer, Dachshund, German Shepherd, Labrador, terriers and poodles, both miniature and standard. About half the dogs that develop Cushing's are found to have small tumours on the pituitary gland. Some may have a tumour on the adrenal gland itself.

Blood tests will show changes to white cells and increased liver enzyme activity and there may also be too much sugar in the blood; x-rays or ultrasound show liver enlargement in most affected dogs. Pituitary-dependent Cushing's is treated with drugs to suppress pituitary over-activity. If the condition is caused by a tumour on the adrenal gland, the vet may recommend surgery to remove it or may prescribe drugs to suppress over-activity of the adrenal glands.

DIABETES

There are two types of diabetes in dogs. Type 1 (also known as sugar diabetes or diabetes mellitus) is when the blood lacks enough insulin, whereas type 2 (insulin resistant diabetes) occurs when there is too much insulin in the blood but the cells don't respond to it. Type 2 diabetes can sometimes be reversed with weight loss, diet and exercise, but Type 1 is not reversible and needs to be managed with insulin for life.

It is not completely clear why some dogs develop diabetes; some may be more genetically prone to the condition. It is known however, that being overweight can increase the risk and this may be because obesity causes cells in the dog's body to become more resistant to insulin. Developing diabetes is more likely to occur in a dog's more senior years. Female dogs and dogs with Cushing's disease and those on steroid medications are also more likely to be at risk.

About one in every 200 dogs will develop Type 1 diabetes. Due to the destruction of insulin- producing cells in the pancreas and the shortage of insulin, your dog's body will be starved of energy even if she is eating normally. When a dog develops hypoglycaemia (which means the glucose in its blood is too low) the body cells lose their main source of energy, resulting in a severe decrease in the dog's energy levels leading to weakness or even loss of consciousness.

Overweight female dogs are more likely to develop Type 2 diabetes, and while it can occur at any age, we usually see it in dogs around eight years of age. Some breeds such as Samoyeds, Dachshunds, Miniature Schnauzers, Miniature Poodles and Bichon Frise are predisposed to this condition. Symptoms include increased appetite and thirst, increased urination, weight loss and eye problems. Canine diabetes is nearly always treated with insulin injecting and a high-fibre diet.

Feeding dogs with diabetes. Caring for a dog with diabetes can seem a bit of a slog at first but trust me, as the insulin injections and diet changes becomes part of your routine and sugar levels stabilise, it gets easier. The extra care and attention you'll give him may even strengthen your bond. Your dog is more likely to be diagnosed with diabetes if he is overweight and I recommend a high-fibre, low-fat diet because fibre slows the entrance of glucose into the bloodstream and helps your dog feel full. This combination can help your dog eat less and lose weight. But you must make sure your dog drinks plenty of water because fibre takes water from the body, and that can cause constipation and other problems.

Most dogs will be okay on premium brand dry food but your vet may recommend prescription dog food. Your vet will advise you on the best way to transition your dog on to the new diet (read more about transitioning your dog to a new diet in Chapter 6).

But even the best diet is useless if your dog won't eat it — and you can't give a dog insulin on an empty stomach. It can make him very sick. If your dog isn't eating much it may be that he just doesn't like the food or it might be another health problem or diabetes-related so check with your vet.

It's important that your dog eats something, even if it isn't ideal. You can entice him by adding a bit of canned dog food into his normal food or stirring some scrambled eggs or low salt chicken broth into his kibble. Any treats should be low in sugar and carbohydrates. Study the ingredients on dog treat labels and don't buy ones that list syrup, molasses, fructose, dextrose, or maltose. Carrots, snap peas, and cooked pumpkin are good alternatives.

Timing the insulin injections is a balancing act because your dog will be constantly processing food and insulin between meals and injections. Two to three meals a day and twelve-hourly injections will probably suit most dogs but check with your vet about getting the right schedule for your dog. See below for tips on giving injections.

GIVING YOUR DOG INSULIN INJECTIONS

Your stomach might turn at the thought of giving your dog injections; but don't fret, you'll get the hang of it soon enough. It's a good idea to arrange a consultation with your vet for an injection lesson. Your vet can teach you how to draw up the correct dose (accurate dosing is essential in managing this condition), check for air bubbles and administer it in your dog's subcutaneous tissue — usually at the back of the neck, which you lift up to make a tent-like pocket. Take your dog with you, so you can show your vet exactly how you are doing it at home, sometimes owners make little mistakes with dosing and administering insulin and the sooner these are identified the better for your dog's recovery. And don't forget to use the correct insulin syringes and store the insulin correctly – in the fridge!

Regular exercise of the same intensity will also help your pooch lose weight and lower his blood sugar levels. The same length of time and intensity of the exercise is important as an unusually long or vigorous walk could cause a drop in his blood sugar levels. It may take a few weeks to get his blood sugar levels under control so don't give up and be aware that losing weight may lessen his need for insulin, so levels need to be checked regularly.

HYPOTHYROIDISM

An underactive thyroid gland is one of the most common hormone problems dogs have and is reported to affect one out of every 250 dogs. The thyroid hormone controls the body's metabolic rate and in the majority of dogs it is caused by the dogs' own immune system attacking the thyroid gland. The condition is found in a couple of dozen breeds but is especially common in Cocker Spaniels, Dobermans and Golden Retrievers, probably due to their tendency to suffer various immune disorders.

There are no obvious symptoms until a large part of the thyroid has been destroyed; then signs vary greatly from dog to dog but are all mostly related to your dog's slowing metabolism. Signs such as being lethargic and disinterested in walks and normal activities, gaining weight without any noticeable change in appetite, diarrhoea, and changes in their coat and skin (the coat thinning and skin feeling thicker or rougher) are common. Some owners tell me about their dog's sudden change in behaviour such as unexpected aggression, submissiveness, passivity, moodiness, chewing, anxiety, irritability and sensitivity to noise.

Blood tests will determine levels of cholesterol, triglycerides and the hormone thyroxine (T4). Because many diseases mimic hypothyroidism this condition is one of the most over-diagnosed diseases in dogs, so I recommend working closely with your vet to regularly monitor your dog's health, response to treatment and thyroid levels. Dogs with this condition respond almost immediately to a synthetic thyroid hormone – dogs become alert and are willing to exercise more. The outlook is good and the dog is expected to go on and have a normal lifespan.

BENIGN PROSTATIC HYPERPLASIA (BPH)

The most common form of prostate disease found in dogs is known as BPH, which is an enlarged (or hypertrophied) prostate found in uncastrated male dogs. BPH is a common age-related problem which results from excess production of sex hormones. It can be diagnosed as early as one to two years of age in some dogs, but it's said to affect about 95 per cent of intact (uncastrated) dogs by the time they are nine.

It can be asymptomatic and cause no pain at all, while some owners report the dog having difficulty going to the toilet (both urinating and defecating) and having blood in their urine.

Diagnosis is made by physical examination along with a rectal exam, blood and urine tests and imaging. Seminal fluid analysis is also helpful in the reaching a diagnosis. Today samples can also be collected directly from the prostate with the guide of an ultrasound. The most

A good candidate for unwanted litters and prostatic hyperplasia

effective treatment for BPH is to desex the dog as castration completely resolves the problem. Other prostate diseases include cysts, infection (prostatitis) and rarely cancer.

Gastrointestinal diseases

ALLERGIES

Up until the middle of the 20th century allergies were virtually unknown in both humans and dogs but the incidence has since crept up in both. Allergic reactions may occur in different body systems causing various clinical symptoms: on your dog's skin causing itchiness; on the lining of his airways causing coughing, sneezing and breathing difficulties; or in the gastrointestinal tract causing discomfort, vomiting or diarrhoea.

Just like us, dogs can be allergic to many things including foods (beef, chicken, grains, corn), dust mites, fleas, grass, pollen and even the people who love and look after them! Humans shed dander, small flakey pieces of skin, hair and other materials 24 hours a day. These flakes float through the air and can be found are on furniture and clothing in your home no matter how well you vacuum and clean. If your dog is allergic to human dander it means he is allergic to everyone. Because the usual symptoms of human dander allergy are hives, itchy skin, rash, and inflammation, vets will often treat these dogs symptomatically (without allergy testing) and so the specific allergy remain unidentified.

Food allergies may cause no gastrointestinal symptoms but may trigger an allergic response in the skin. One group of allergic disorders is called inflammatory bowel disease (IBD) which affects the gastrointestinal tract. Each dog will experience its own set of symptoms:

- **Allergic gastritis.** A food allergy may cause the dog to periodically vomit bile-tinged mucus. Dogs with this allergy tend to look and behave as if nothing else is wrong.

- **Allergic enteritis.** This is also a food allergy problem and the dog passes loose, watery and smelly stools; sometimes this is accompanied with vomiting.

- **Eosinophilic enteritis.** A form of allergy in which the dog's stools have the consistency of cow manure. The dog may become thin and with a lacklustre coat.

- **Allergy colitis.** If the dog's colon (large intestine) is affected he will suffer from bloody diarrhoea. Food is only one cause of colitis in dogs.

Finding out the specific causes of allergies can be frustrating for the vet and owner and has to be undertaken by trial and error – history of the problem, skin tests, blood tests and special hypoallergenic diets. Some breeds have a predisposition to allergies. Several breeds with predominantly white coats such as West Highland White Terriers, Bull Terriers and English Setters have a higher incidence of skin allergies and Golden Retrievers are more prone to gastric allergies.

DIARRHOEA

Vets view any increase in fluid in a dog's stools as diarrhoea. It's easy to assume that diarrhoea must be related to some sort of gastrointestinal disease and though that's the most commonly the cause, it's not always the case. It can also be caused by problems in other parts of the body, such as the kidney, liver and pancreas.

Most diarrhoea is acute (severe and sudden onset) and causes can include eating off food, allergies or sensitivity to certain foods or ingredients in foods. Food poisoning, parasites such as worms, bacterial or viral infections and certain anti-inflammatory drugs (NAIDs) can also cause diarrhoea. Many causes of acute diarrhoea can be linked to chronic diarrhoea, which is something that develops over a longer period of time.

The vet will try to eliminate specific causes of acute diarrhoea such as diet or drugs. Antibiotics are not routinely used in acute cases unless a bacterial infection is suspected. You should always get immediate veterinary advice if your dog is losing weight despite a normal appetite, has a fever, is lethargic or has blood in the stools. If bloody stools are accompanied by bloody vomiting it could be caused by a bacterial toxin in which case it can be fatal and immediate advice and treatment should be sought. This most often occurs in middle-aged smaller breeds such as Miniature Schnauzers and Toy Poodles.

What to feed a dog with diarrhoea? Depending on the severity of the gastrointestinal issue and the age and condition of the dog, I usually advise giving no food, only water for 12-24 hours. Digestion takes energy and the dog's digestive tract needs a break. When you start introducing food again, boiled or steamed skinless and boneless chicken is the most recommended protein but turkey, white fish and eggs are other suitable protein foods. They can be mixed with white rice. Brown rice is also okay but some dogs have difficulty digesting it. Mashed white potato (boiled or steamed without skin) is a bland easy to digest food which can give the dog a bit of energy. Another way to restore energy is to give a small amount of mashed banana – they're rich in potassium and contain pectin, a soluble fibre that will help bind water in the colon.

Although these options are not bad, my preference is to offer a complete and balanced dog food, prescribed specifically for gastrointestinal health as its guaranteed to be highly digestible and ensure easy nutrient absorption.

FOOD ALLERGIES/INTOLERANCES

When a dog has a food allergy his immune system is hyper-sensitive to something in his food and will have adverse reactions. It will commonly produce a non-seasonal skin itch or, if it affects the gastrointestinal tract, vomiting and diarrhoea. Food intolerance does not affect a dog's immune system but also causes vomiting and diarrhoea. Allergies are related to antigens which are proteins resulting in an immune reaction and inflammation of the skin or gut, these proteins can be found in meat, grains or dairy products. Meat proteins commonly used in dog foods include beef, lamb, poultry, egg, fish and pork. The most common grain proteins are soybean, rice, corn and wheat. The exact cause remains elusive; some commercial foods may trigger an allergic reaction while fresh food using the same ingredient may not.

Short-term treatment is anti-inflammatory medication and topical attention to skin and ear infections. But the best solution is to find the root of the allergy by feeding the dog a completely new diet for at least a month, preferably longer. This is called a dietary elimination trial. If the allergy clears up then comes back on the old diet you probably have the answer. Some commercial manufacturers make excellent hypoallergenic diets and your vet can advise you about these.

All dogs of any breed or mixed breed can develop an allergy at any age but some are more susceptible. They include Cocker Spaniels, Dalmatians, Labradors, Lhasa Apso, Miniature Schnauzers and Shar Pei.

GASTRIC DILATION VOLVULUS (GDV)

This condition is as serious as it gets. The stomach gets distended and bloated with gas and then rotates (volvulus) cutting off its connection to the oesophagus and small intestine, compromising normal blood supply to the stomach. Symptoms include abrupt onset retching, drooling tummy distension and weakness; shock sets in quickly. It is a life-threatening emergency so getting to the vet as fast as you can is imperative, although sadly it has a high fatality rate even with dogs that get immediate medical intervention.

It will be diagnosed with x-rays and the patient will be stabilised with intravenous fluids, removal of the gas from the stomach and surgery to re-rotate the stomach. During surgery a portion of the stomach will be permanently sutured to the body wall to prevent a repeat volvulus. A compromised blood flow may mean that the vet has to remove the spleen and part of the stomach. GDV is relatively common in large, deep-chested breeds although the exact cause is unknown. It tends to run in families and is common in Dobermans, Gordon Setters, Great Danes, Standard Poodles, Irish Setters and Weimaraners.

MEGAESOPHAGUS

Dogs sometimes regurgitate food when a foreign body gets lodged in the oesophagus; this causes a section of the oesophagus to stop contracting properly so that food cannot travel down to the stomach. As I outlined in a previous chapter, dogs will have a go at anything; I have found bones, string, needles and even small toys stuck in a dogs' gastrointestinal tracts and had to removal a remarkable array of hardware from their stomachs.

When regurgitation becomes chronic and worsens over time and the dog starts bringing up food after every meal, the most common cause is an enlarged oesophagus which is called megaoesophagus. It is a rare

Using a doggie dinner table is believed to help the food go down the oesophagus

but inherited condition in some dogs such as Miniature Schnauzers and Fox Terriers and usually diagnosed when pups move from milk to solid food. In older dogs it appears to be an acquired condition with a number of possible causes such as neuromuscular disease (like myasthenia gravis), tumours, foreign bodies as mentioned and more uncommonly toxicity and parasites. It is seen more frequently in German Shepherds, Great Danes, Irish Setters, Labradors and Shar Pei.

If the underlying cause cannot be treated the best method of feeding is by small, high calorie meals given on raised platforms so that gravity can help the food go down the oesophagus.

Sometimes the vet may prescribe a drug to try to stimulate peristalsis to move the food down the tract.

PARVOVIRUS

This is one of those nasty highly infectious diseases for which all dogs should be vaccinated against when they are puppies then revaccinated annually. This canine virus is a very hardy organism that can live outside the dog for months and is resistant to soaps, detergents and disinfectants, but not to chlorine bleaches. It is spread by infected faeces and enters the dog via its mouth, usually as a result of the dog doing something as simple as licking its paw. Once it enters the dog it moves down into the gut, infecting all areas of the dog's body where cells multiply rapidly, particularly the intestinal lining.

In severe cases dogs will experience stomach pain, lethargy, feverishness, vomiting and diarrhoea. It is a life-threatening condition; despite being treated for shock and dehydration from major fluid loss, some dogs die from the diarrhoea and vomiting. Time is of the essence – the sooner the diagnosis, the better the dog's chances of survival. The condition is diagnosed using a special test for detecting parvovirus in the faeces; blood tests are also performed. Antibiotics may be used to prevent secondary infection. Even after they've recovered, they will still have a weakened immune system and will be susceptible to other illnesses. Keeping them away from other dogs (not just to prevent them getting another infection but also because they are still contagious for a couple of months after the initial recovery) and feeding a high-quality, easily digestible diet is really important. It's a good idea to tell your neighbours or friends at the dog park what happened so they know to get their dogs tested if concerned.

PANCREATITIS

This is a painful condition and one of the most common gastrointestinal diseases I see in practice, particularly in middle-aged overweight females. The exact cause is unclear but there is a direct relationship with a low protein, high-fat diet. It also has also been linked to the use of certain drugs such as corticosteroids and diuretics. There are various levels of the condition from acute (where pain causes the dog to tuck up its tummy, vomit and exhibit signs of shock) to mild, which can cause lethargy, vomiting, diarrhoea and feverishness. Acute pancreatitis occurs more commonly in Miniature Poodles, Miniature Schnauzers, Cocker Spaniels and West Highland White Terriers. The vet will aim to control pain, overcome the effects of shock and reduce pancreatic activity.

Feeding dogs with pancreatitis. Once it was thought that the best way to treat dogs with pancreatitis was to have them on 24-48-hour fasts based on the assumption that food passing through the intestinal tract would stimulate the pancreas to secrete digestive enzymes thereby increasing inflammation. Today we know that prolonged fasting can have harmful effects on the function of the gastrointestinal tract, including its role in the immune system. The intestinal tract is lined with cells that depend on absorbing energy and nutrients from food; when a dog doesn't eat, the lining of the intestinal tract changes – the villi (tiny finger-like structures that project inwards from the lining of the small intestine increasing its absorptive surface) shrink. This reduces local immune tissue and allows

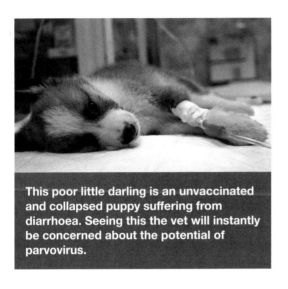

This poor little darling is an unvaccinated and collapsed puppy suffering from diarrhoea. Seeing this the vet will instantly be concerned about the potential of parvovirus.

the intestinal wall to become porous, increasing inflammation, both within the digestive tract and systemically.

Most vets now believe it is best to start feeding pancreatitis patients small amounts of low-fat highly digestible food as soon as the vomiting settles. Effective antiemetic medications can usually control a dog's vomiting within 24 hours. Dietary fat is known to be associated with the development of pancreatitis in dogs, consequently low-fat foods are best. Introducing food after an attack of pancreatitis should always begin slowly. As long as your dog continues to improve, you could increase his food by one-quarter every day so that at the end of four days, he is getting his full daily energy requirements.

Because dogs with pancreatitis need as much nutrition as possible, even when eating in small amounts of food, a highly digestible diet is preferable – one that's low in fibre and made from high-quality ingredients; in fact, it's often exactly the same diet that we recommend for parvo cases. Several pet food manufacturers make low-fat, highly digestible diets for dogs. Most vets carry at least one food like this in their clinics so be guided by your vet's advice. A short-term alternative is a home-cooked mixture of boiled chicken and white rice.

VOMITING

It's normal to think that vomiting is caused by some nasty disease in the dog's gastrointestinal system but that's not necessarily the case. However, while vomiting isn't a disease in itself, if it's persistent it is usually symptomatic of one. First, it's important to distinguish between vomiting and regurgitating: vomiting comes from the stomach or small intestine and is preceded by retching (just like humans, dogs know they are about to vomit) whereas regurgitating starts in the oesophagus (see Megaoesophagus) and tends to happen without warning.

Vomiting may be triggered by an illness outside the gastric tract. It could result from a hormonal imbalance such as Addison's disease or from diseases in the liver, pancreas, kidney, uterus or central nervous system.

The way a dog vomits can give you clues to the underlying problem. Nausea is the first stage of vomiting and your dog may become listless, shiver, hide, yawn, salivate and start lip-smacking. Next your dog may retch without actually being sick. He may then vomit the contents of his stomach. Vomiting and diarrhoea in a puppy is a serious matter – they're susceptible to fluid loss and electrolyte imbalance which can be fatal.

Dogs get rid of a lot of awful stuff they scavenge by throwing it up and some dogs get car sick (see Chapter 14). One vomiting episode in an otherwise healthy dog may be just a bout of mild gastro, usually from eating something they shouldn't have. It might be a good idea to call your vet to tell them what's happened – the appearance of the vomit and any other relevant information. In most cases, if it's just the one-off vomit, they'll advise you to withhold food for the rest of the day providing only water and no human medications – ever. If there is another bout of vomiting or other signs of illness like sluggishness or diarrhoea, its best to get an appointment that day.

For other types of vomiting I advise the following:

Intermittent and persistent vomiting. Food allergies can cause intermittent vomiting but more serious things such as tumours and ulcers can also be the cause so it would be wise to see your vet within 24 hours. Repeated and persistent vomiting may even be caused by a stomach irritation or a serious obstruction, in which case you need to see the vet immediately and as it might be necessary to anaesthetise for surgery, do not give your dog any food or water.

Projectile vomiting. A gastrointestinal obstruction is the most common cause of this type of alarming vomiting and because it is a potential emergency situation you should not delay taking the dog to the vet.

Vomiting blood. Blood in the vomit could indicate something serious such as an intestinal or stomach ulcer or even poisoning and you need to see the vet immediately.

Vomiting yellow foam. In most cases, yellow foam indicates that the dog's stomach is empty of food and the yellow colouration comes from bile. Bile is a digestive fluid that is produced in the liver, stored in the gall bladder and released into the small intestines just below the stomach. There are many medical conditions that cause a dog to vomit on an empty stomach, so a phone call to your vet is always a good idea.

Cardiac diseases

CONGESTIVE HEART FAILURE (CHF)

Heart disease is often a bit symptom vague and only picked up at the dog's annual check-up. Congestive heart disease is when the blood fails to pump efficiently often due to chronic heart valve issues; the heart can compensate, often for years, by increasing in size until finally the blood starts backing up in the veins. This build-up of fluid is eventually forced out of circulation and into surrounding tissues. It can lead to fluid on the lungs which can cause respiratory problems. I should point out here that congestive heart failure is not the same as a heart attack. A heart attack (or myocardial infarction) where the blood supply to the heart is cut off is very rare in dogs.

CHF refers to the inability of the heart to pump blood adequately throughout the body. As a result, blood backs up and fluid accumulates in the body cavities (chest, abdomen or both) further constricting both the heart and lungs and preventing sufficient oxygen flow throughout the body. Though many conditions can lead to CHF in dogs, the most common cause is chronic valve disease, when the valves of the heart degenerate until they fail to function properly. Other causes are dilated cardiomyopathy, defects in the heart walls, fluid accumulating in a sac around the heart, heart worm, infection of the heart valves, called endocarditis, and tumours.

In dogs, there are two main types of CHF.

A mixed breed dog having heart auscultated

Right-sided congestive heart failure (RS-CHF). This occurs when a heart contraction results in blood leaking into the right atrium from the right ventricle through the tricuspid valve rather than being pushed through the lungs and becoming oxygenated, in other words, heading in the wrong direction. As a result, the main circulation system becomes congested with backed up blood and fluid accumulates in the abdomen, interfering with proper organ function. Excess fluid might also build up in the limbs and cause swelling, also known as peripheral oedema.

Left-sided congestive heart failure (LS-CHF). This is the most common type of CHF in dogs and occurs when blood from the left ventricle leaks back into the left atrium through the mitral valve rather than getting pumped into the body's systemic circulation when the heart contracts – again wrong way, turn back! It is a state of diminished cardiac function, causing volume or pressure overload to the left side of the heart. As a result, fluid leaks into the tissue of the lungs, causing swelling known as pulmonary oedema, which leads to coughing and difficulty breathing.

Congestive heart failure can happen slowly or suddenly. There are four stages of heart failure. In the early stage there may be no symptoms although a vet may hear it on the stethoscope. Later there may be breathlessness during exercise and lethargy, things that are often mistaken for the dog's advancing age. The dog may go on to develop a dry persistent cough after the daily walk and at night. Other signs are weight loss, appetite loss and rapid breathing. Symptoms of late stage heart failure include a frothy cough, blue gums and tongue, a rapid pulse, even fainting. Please get to the vet quick smart if you see the early signs of this condition, because once a dog is showing signs of distress because it can't breathe properly, it is a life-threatening situation requiring emergency care.

Various diagnostic tests such as x-rays, ECG, echocardiography and blood tests will confirm the condition. Treatment will depend on the stage of the disease. Drugs such as ACE Inhibitors (medications that slow the activity of the enzyme ACE) can be given to enlarge the blood vessels and reduce blood pressure; diuretics will increase urination, clearing fluid congestion from the lungs and veins; vasodilators are used to relax the blood vessels, helping the heart pump more easily; and in other cases, another type of drug known as a positive inotrope might be prescribed to strengthen the force of contractions in the heart and improve blood flow.

Congestive heart failure affects about 50 per cent of Cavalier King Charles Spaniels, and sadly this is the condition that took my Sasha's life. Other breeds prone to the disease are Miniature and Toy Poodles, Chihuahuas, Lhaso Apso, Yorkshire Terriers and Miniature Schnauzers. It is relatively rare in giant, large and medium-sized breeds.

Apart from the drugs I have mentioned and monitoring kidney function, there are a number of other things I recommend for dogs with this condition. I did all of them with Sasha.

- **Sodium restriction.** I like to put dogs on a low salt diet accompanied by plenty of fluid. Commercially-formulated prescribed diets are ideal because they have low salt products for such conditions.

- **Omega 3 fatty acids.** I advise vitamins and minerals as an option. The science behind them is inconclusive; some vets don't believe alternative remedies work but I believe they help.

- **Restrict exercise.** Some activity is good but anything that leads to excessive panting is too much.

CONGENITAL HEART DEFECTS

These are rare structural abnormalities that a dog may be born with and they will often have a genetic origin. More than 30 breeds are known to be susceptible. The vet will pick up the defects with a stethoscope when listening to a puppy's heart but more specialised equipment will be needed to diagnose the exact form of defect, the most effective being Doppler ultrasound, a special type of echocardiography which can measure the velocity of the blood flow to various areas of the heart. How the puppy will be treated will depend on the severity of the condition.

Patent Ductus Arteriosus. This is the most common congenital heart defect. This occurs where the connection between the aorta and pulmonary artery – necessary before birth to bypass the pup's non-functioning lungs – fails to close down at birth. In this case some of the blood from the left side of the heart flows through the open duct to the lungs. Open chest surgery can close the duct.

Valvular and Septal Defects. A septal defect is a 'hole in the heart', an abnormal opening in the septum which is the wall between the chambers of the heart. When puppies are born with this often the only evidence a vet can detect is a heart murmur. Some pups grow up to lead normal lives; others may not grow as expected and be prone to fainting or don't have much tolerance for exercise. These dogs don't usually survive more than a year.

Dilated cardiomyopathy (DCM). This condition is found mostly in young dogs, sometimes as young as two. It's a disease of the heart muscle in which weakened contractions impairs normal blood circulation, causing the heart to enlarge. The disease is genetic, with Dobermans, Boxers, Cocker Spaniels, Afghan Hounds and Great Danes being in the high-risk category. In Cocker Spaniels and Dobermans, it may also be related to immune system defects.

Although some affected dogs remain symptom-free, over time they will develop severe heart rhythm abnormalities and congestive heart failure; as a result, fluid will accumulate in the lungs and/or abdomen causing it to swell. Symptoms include weakness, lethargy, a cough, loss of appetite and consequent weight loss. Boxers and Dobermans have been known to die suddenly without actually having shown any signs of being unwell.

Diagnosis is made with an ECG and x-rays. Treatment is the same as for Congested Heart Failure. Unfortunately, the long-term outlook for dogs with DCM is poor and the short-term prognosis will depend on response to treatment.

AORTIC STENOSIS/SUB-AORTIC STENOSIS (AS/SAS)

Another hereditary heart disease most commonly found in Newfoundlands, Boxers, Rottweilers and Golden Retrievers and less commonly in Bull Terriers, English Bulldogs, German Shepherds, German Shorthaired Pointers, Great Danes, Mastiffs, and Samoyeds. The aortic valve is the one through which blood leaves the heart and travels to the rest of the body. A narrowing of this valve means the left ventricle of the heart (the chamber that pumps blood through the aorta) must work harder to force blood out through the valve. When the narrowing of the valve is located just under it, it is called sub-aortic stenosis (SAS) and is the most common of these conditions in dogs.

This additional work can have a number of harmful effects on the heart but in many cases, affected dogs do not show any signs and is often initially detected when the vet detects a heart murmur on the dog's routine check-up. In moderate to severe cases, it may be picked up at birth but may not be noted until the pup is six to twelve months old. In severely affected dogs symptoms include lethargy, shortness of breath, and fainting and signs of heart failure such as coughing, laboured and open-mouth breathing. In heart failure, which is more common in dogs with other heart valve problems, fluid begins to accumulate in the lungs. In some severe cases aortic stenosis can cause sudden death.

AS and SAS is diagnosed by x-rays, ECG, and an echocardiogram (ultrasound of the heart) plus routine pathology tests. In mild cases your dog may be closely monitored for signs of the disease getting worse, but medication is not typically needed. In moderate to severe cases, long-term medication can slow the heart rate, allowing the heart to work more efficiently. In some severe cases your vet may suggest a specialist surgical option. Exercise should be restricted in dogs with aortic stenosis, especially those with severe disease.

Skin problems

ABSCESSES AND FOREIGN BODY REACTIONS

Anyone with an active pooch will know that minor surface wounds and irritations are fairly common. There are a number of bacteria that are normal inhabitants of your dog's skin, which are called commensal bacteria. These bacteria can cause a secondary bacterial infection (also known as a pyoderma) if there is a break or defect in the skin causing them to multiply. Most skin infections are caused by the bacteria staphylococcus intermedius and pasteurella multocida, both of which can usually be treated with topical ointments. But if they are left untreated, they can become a painful pyoderma (with characteristic papules or pustules) or abscesses. An abscess can form on virtually any part of a dog's body where the skin has been pierced by any object, such as grass seeds, thorns, cactus spines, glass shards, claws, or a tooth.

The most common cause of a foreign body reactions are certain grass seeds with an insidious shape that enables it to pierce the animal's skin and once in it can only move further into the skin, not backwards.

The most popular spot for seed penetration is between the dog's

A grass seed – the common culprit of foreign body reactions

toes where it forms a lump. The body's immune response to this invader is to form an abscess or a granuloma, which is a mass of granulated tissue, typically produced in response to infection, inflammation, or as in this case, the presence of a foreign substance.

In severe cases, your vet may take a swab test of the infected area to determine the strain of bacteria present and a standard blood test will determine if the infection has entered to the bloodstream. However, in most cases, the abscess is treated by surgical draining and antibiotics.

ANAL SAC ISSUES/ABSCESSES

Your dog's anal sacs are an important part of the way he communicates with his fellow dogs. Every time he defecates, these glands excrete a drop or two of a substance that sends a message to other dogs who sniff it. I have seen a variety of anal sac problems in my practice – they come through the door on a daily basis. The most common sign that something is annoying the dog's anal region is when it starts licking excessively or scooting along the ground (or carpet) on its bottom.

Uncomplicated blocked anal sacs can be emptied by a rectal examination to apply pressure to the anal glands and release the extremely pungent anal gland fluid — I can tell you right now this is not my favourite job! Some dogs need to have this done every couple of months and others not at all. If the anal sac is infected it will secrete a yellow or green pus-filled or blood-tinged discharge. The vet may treat this by flushing out the sac while the dog is sedated or anesthetised, and/or by prescribing a course of antibiotics and anti-inflammatories.

If the anal glands are chronically blocked, they may abscess. In this case the anal glands swell, becoming red and then turning purple just prior to rupturing through the skin around the anus – very painful. The vet will likely need to treat this surgically and will also prescribe oral antibiotics and pain medication for you to take home.

EAR INFECTIONS

There are three different types of ear infections – Otitis externa, Otitis media and Otitis interna. The typical disease process starts with irritation to the skin lining the ear canal causing inflammation, which results in excess wax production and a comfortable environment for yeast and bacteria (normal residents of the ear canal) to overgrow. These microbes can cause significant itchiness and more inflammation, leading to an itch-scratch cycle conducive to self-trauma via headshaking, pawing, and rubbing of the ears.

A sign that your dog has an outer ear infection (Otitis externa) is a waxy, yellow, or reddish-brown ear discharge. Many different things can predispose the ears to the bacteria or yeast which cause infections – allergies, mites, polyps, the overproduction of ear wax or too much bathing or swimming (which can leave excess moisture in the ears). A black and granular discharge, which looks a bit like coffee grounds, usually means the dog's ears are infested with ear mites. However, symptoms of ear mites vary from dog to dog and may include a lot of scratching and ear and head rubbing, excessive head shaking or a dark foul-smelling secretion from the ears.

Otitis media is inflammation of the middle ear structures and usually results from an infection spreading from the external ear canal (Otitis externa) through the tympanic membrane or from migration of pharyngeal microorganisms through the auditory tube. Untreated Otitis media can lead to Otitis internia, which is inflammation of the inner ear structures within the skull. So usually, but not always, it starts externally as Otitis externa then Otitis media and finally lodges, with catastrophic neurological results, as Otitis interna in the brain.

The vet may do a cytology examination on some of the debris from the ear. This is the only way properly diagnose the type of bacteria causing an ear infection and means your dog can be given the appropriate antibiotic the first-time round.

What if it never ends? Chronic otitis is a long-lasting ear infection that can affect any dog, causing itchy, painful, smelly ears. They might be caused by parasites, allergies or growths or a combination of this and other factors such as the ear

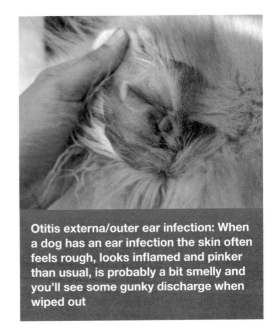

Otitis externa/outer ear infection: When a dog has an ear infection the skin often feels rough, looks inflamed and pinker than usual, is probably a bit smelly and you'll see some gunky discharge when wiped out

shape and environment. And as we discussed above, the condition is progressive and can lead to a rupturing of the eardrum or narrowing of the ear canal. I've had owners in tears over ear infections that just will not go away. Despite our best efforts with diagnostic tests, repeated examinations and ear cleaning and medications, we've lost the battle in these frustrating cases and found that surgery is the only option. There are two surgeries available, a lateral ear canal

---

GIVING YOUR DOG EAR DROPS

If your dog is diagnosed with a condition that needs ear drops – either antibiotics, anti-fungals or a steroid anti-inflammatory — the best way to do this is to lift the ear flap firmly with one hand and with the other place the dropper nozzle into the ear and squeeze firmly so it goes down the ear canal. As soon as the dog feels the trickle go down it will be irritating and he will want to shake his head and consequently splatter the drops all over the room and you!; you have to be prepared for this and use the ear flap as a seal to close off the canal. After that you massage the area below the ear to make sure the medication goes right down to the bottom of the L-shaped canal. After the dog has stopped shaking his head, use a cotton wool ball and clean the area around the ear.

Some vets will give owners a syringe with the correct dose because with all that head shaking it can be difficult to know if enough has gone in. It's always best to get your vet or vet nurse to show you how to do this correctly because administrating ear drops in some dogs is a very fine art.

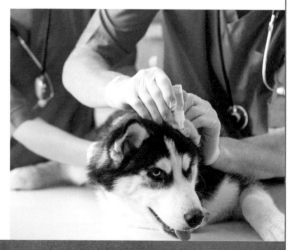

The correct method of administering ear drops

resection and a total ear canal ablation. These procedures are reserved for cases with severe obstructive or proliferative changes to the ear (for example in the case of some cancers) or where extensive medical therapy has proved unsuccessful.

FLEA ALLERGY DERMATITIS (FAD)

Fleas cause dogs to itch but dogs that are allergic to flea saliva suffer long after the flea has munched on your dog's blood. So even if you can't find any fleas on your itchy dog, they may have had a visit from a passing flea. Itching and scratching will be followed by red and raised crusty pimples. The dermatitis may spread to the back legs and underbelly; a vet's trained eye can recognise the symptoms of FAD without seeing the flea. The dog's itching and scratching, a missed dose of prevention, along with some flea faeces or flea dirt on the dog's skin are all a good indicator of FAD. Anti-inflammatory medication will calm the angry skin and antibiotics will be prescribed if the dog has a secondary bacterial infection. However, the important thing to remember is that flea prevention is crucial if you have a FAD-prone dog, and all dogs and cats in your household should be treated with veterinary recommended preventative all year round.

MANGE – DEMODECTIC

Demodex mites are natural elongated-shaped little critters that live in the hair follicles of most mammals, including humans, and unlike most external parasites they are not contagious. They are passed on to the pups by their mother a few days after birth and cause no problems unless the skin's immune protection system fails, which allows the mites to spread excessively and then they develop demodicosis, the demodex mite disease. In puppies and young dogs, the disease is linked to immune suppression and may cause the localised form —mild hair loss, usually around the eyes and mouth — or the generalised form where the area of hair loss is widespread over the dog's body. Older dogs can develop a more severe form of the disease that appears to be associated with an underlying cause such as Cushing's disease, hypothyroidism and diabetes mellitus.

Itching, biting and scratching is symptomatic of a flea allergy

Demodex mites are diagnosed with a skin scaping, using an instrument such as a scalpel blade to mites out from deep within the skin layers without cutting the skin. The vet will then assess the scraping under the microscope to see if the mites are present. Most puppies with localised Demodex disease are free of it spontaneously in a couple of months. In generalised cases, long term anti-parasiticides are usually necessary in either an injectable or oral form. Demodex mites predispose the skin to secondary bacterial infection, in which case a course of antibiotics will also be recommended. Successful treatment in adult dogs is more difficult than in younger dogs.

MANGE – SARCOPTIC

This particular condition is caused by the microscopic scabies mite and is extremely contagious from dog to dog. It is also the most seriously irritating skin disease a dog can experience sending the poor animal into a chewing, licking and scratching frenzy further damaging its skin. Affected areas are typically around the ears and elbows which become inflamed and the dog may lose hair.

To diagnose the condition the vet will take a scaping of skin from affected areas for microscopic examination, but unlike Demodex mites, it is often more difficult to find the mites in skin scrapings because the mites dig in under the skin to lay their eggs so a suspicious vet will treat for sarcoptic mange to see if it clears up. A blood test may detect antibodies to the scabies mite. Anti-mite treatments include oral, spot on or injectable medications; all dogs that have been in contact with the affected dog should be treated. Note – Although different to the human scabies, the dog scabies mite can still affect people, causing itchiness that may last up to three weeks but it generally goes after the dog has been treated. Affected areas are usually those that have been in touch with the dog such as forearms and hands, especially between the fingers.

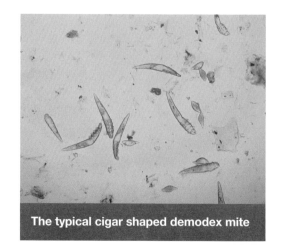

The typical cigar shaped demodex mite

PERIANAL FISTULAS

Also known as anal furunculosis, perianal fistula is a serious medical condition common in mature age German Shepherds and rare in other breeds. In this disease, ulcerating, bleeding and painful tracts of infection develop in the tissue around the anus (perianal); a smelly pus drains from these tracks (fistulas) of infection. In its early stages there may be few clinical signs and the condition may go unnoticed and is only discovered during a routine physical examination. As the disease progresses, the dog will usually strain during defecation, and there will be blood in the faeces. Other symptoms include loss of appetite, excessively licking at its tail and rear end and difficulty sitting. Behaviour changes are common – becoming withdrawn, agitated or even aggressive.

In mild cases, the condition usually improves with a drug regime over several months, but frequently the improvement is not permanent. Antibiotics will be prescribed for secondary bacterial infections. Vets often prescribe a topical ointment and recommend clipping the hair of long-coated dogs and careful bathing. In severe cases surgery is necessary but does have risks.

SKIN ALLERGIES (ALLERGIC OR ATOPIC DERMATITIS)

Finding the cause of an allergy or allergic contact dermatitis will involve taking a history of any pattern in the scratching behaviour throughout the seasons, performing skin tests and blood tests and through trial and error, assessing the dog's response to special diets and environmental changes. Frequent shampooing can remove moulds and pollen spores trapped in the rough coats of certain breeds.

The most effective treatment is sometimes to use drugs to 'turn off' the allergic reaction at its source. These drugs treat the body's chemical reaction to certain external factors and today there are several medications that do exactly that.

The oldest on the market is Atopica (cyclosporine) which works by calming the immune system and for this reason vets call it an immunomodulatory drug. It settles inflammation and itching caused by allergies and I've seen great success with this medication over the years, but it takes time to see results.

Apoquel (oclacitinib) is another option. It's a newer formulation that works at a couple of levels to control the itching. It's fast acting and designed for acute flare ups. Owners usually tell me they can see results on the first day and are thankful to see their furry friend finally get some relief from their allergies.

Finally, there are Cytopoint injections (lokivetmab). This is the newest anti-itching medication on the market and it may be the answer for dogs who refuse to take tablets. It's given by injection every 4-8 weeks and it's very effective. Cytopoint is an antibody (or protein) that blocks the signal coming from the immune cells in the skin that signals the itch. It is a targeted treatment with few reported side effects and I'm seeing great results with it. Cytopoint, like Atopica, is often used for chronic itchiness for extended periods or long term.

While these are great options, there is no magic cure to skin allergies and these treatments are usually costly. Of course, your vet will need to rule out other causes of itching before using these drugs, checking for parasites (such as fleas and mites) as well as making sure there are no underlying bacterial or yeast infections on the skin. They'll also have to rule out food allergies.

This rash is known as lichenification, is a term describing a common skin reaction to chronic disease, in this case chronic allergies. The skin becomes markedly thickened with exaggerated markings and in severe cases resembles elephant skin.

There are no quick fixes in medicine; you have to work closely with your vet to reach find the solution that works for you and your pet. Not every product works for every dog, but with these newer products on the market we usually find one that helps.

Allergy-prone breeds include the Shar Pei and those with predominantly white coats such as West Highland White Terriers, Bull Terriers, Staffies and English Terriers also have a higher than normal incidence of skin allergies.

Chewing and licking feet

Chewing and licking feet are common behaviours and the causes can be complicated. When a dog suddenly starts doing this intensely for extended periods it's natural for an owner to be concerned, so here are a few of the more common reasons why you dog might be chewing their feet.

- Allergies: When chewing coincides with a change of seasons it may be caused by an environmental allergen such as pollen, mould or mildew. Long-term chewing could also signal a food allergy, but determining the exact food ingredient is a process of time-consuming trial and error. Putting your dog on an exclusive hypoallergic prescription diet (that means no other food or treats) for eight weeks is worth a try – speak to your vet.

- Foreign bodies: A thorn, grass seed, pebble or other foreign object lodged in or between the paw pads.
- Sensitivity to soaps, shampoo or chemical substances such as lawn and garden pesticides.
- A cracked claw or a corn - Greyhounds are prone to corns.
- Irritation caused by fleas, ticks or other parasites.
- Dry skin from winter weather or an arid climate.
- A deficiency of fatty acids in the diet.
- Injury or pain from conditions such as arthritis or hip dysplasia.
- A cyst or tumour.
- Autoimmune diseases.
- Hormonal imbalances — too much cortisol or an under-active thyroid.

Some of these causes can be avoided by a few simple things, such as making sure you feed your dog a high-quality, well-balanced diet. However, it should be noted that if a dog is allergic to wheat or meat protein, they'll still be allergic to even the best brands. And assuming the dog's problems are behavioural and not medical, they should also get plenty of exercise, mental stimulation and interaction with people and other dogs. Use preventative flea and tick medication. Bath and groom your dog frequently using dog friendly products making sure you rinse and examine his feet regularly.

Chewing and licking has many causes and just as many treatments. Red flags for a vet visit are new, frequent, persistent, excessive or obsessive foot chewing or licking; limping, bald spots or skin that is red, rough, crusty, swollen, bleeding or warm to the touch; discoloration of foot fur (pink or rust-coloured caused by the compound porphyrin in a dog's saliva); and an area of the foot that is sensitive to touch or has a cut or other wound.

Having covered some of the reasons why dogs chew their feet let's talk about why they lick them. Licking can sometimes be beneficial. Dogs instinctively lick cuts and abrasions (whether on the foot or elsewhere), allowing antibacterial enzymes in their saliva to help clean the wound, ward off infection and promote healing. Have you noticed that your dog wants to lick your cuts? Dogs use their mouth to sooth their own wounds and because you are their companion, an important member of their pack, they'll want to do it to you too. Having said that, I wouldn't encourage it, as they might overdo it and it may not be the healthiest for your dog either.

This chocolate Labrador looks just like my Java

On the other hand, paw chewing and licking can break the animal's skin barrier and interfere with the skin's normal defenses; moisture from saliva can cause yeast and bacterial infections, particularly for dogs with thick fur that retains moisture. Repeated friction from a rough tongue can rub off fur and cause acute dermatitis and lick granulomas (skin lesions). So while the poor dog may have given himself some temporary relief by licking, what he's done actually ends up making things worse. The itch cycle has to be broken with some medications, topical creams or lotions to treat any infections and eliminate the underlying cause. It could also be that a dog licking his feet is a behavioural issue and for more on this see Training and behavioural problems (page 224). This instinctual behaviour is precisely why they are fitted with a buster cone on their head when they go home with stitches!

Respiratory issues

BRACHYCEPHALIC RESPIRATORY SYNDROME

The name means 'short-faced' and is what we see in squashed-faced dogs – French Bull Dogs, Pugs, Shih Tzus, Boston Terriers, Pekinese all have Brachycephalic Syndrome. The condition can come with a collection of problems: stenotic nares, which are very tiny nostrils; stenoic trachea which is a narrowed windpipe; an elongated soft palate; and an abnormal larynx with everted saccules, little sacs that inhibit breathing. Not all Brachycephalic dogs have all these things but even having a couple can make breathing difficult and they snuffle and snore in their attempt to get enough oxygen.

These poor dogs can go through hell in hot weather. Dogs use their tongues for temperature control and a dog without this syndrome would stick its tongue out and pant; the saliva cools the tongue which cools blood and brings down body temperature. Brachycephalic breeds cannot pant properly, and they overheat. I've treated dogs that, even after a short run in a late summer afternoon, have been brought in collapsed from heat stress. See Chapter 14 for more information on heat stress in Brachycephalic breeds.

Chest x-rays and a visual examination, while they are sedated or under a general anaesthetic, will diagnose the extent of the Brachycephalic syndrome. Mild symptoms can be managed with a combination of weight loss, restricted exercise and by avoiding challenging weather. There are some surgical procedures that can assist more pronounced symptoms such as trimming the soft palate or widening the nostrils and the trachea. But it's not a pleasant procedure and these dogs have a greater anaesthetic risk and many are overweight as well which increases the risk further.

COLLAPSED TRACHEA

This condition is found in older-aged, usually over-weight toy breeds such as the Yorkshire Terrier, Chihuahua, Pomeranian and Toy Poodle. It is an anatomical defect that causes the normally rigid structure to weaken and collapse under internal or external pressures. The first symptom will be a honking cough when the dog becomes excited. The vet will want to rule out any other causes of the coughing, but a collapsed trachea will be confirmed with x-rays or fluoroscopy, which allows visualisation of the trachea as the animal inhales and exhales. How the condition is treated will depend on how bad it is. The dog may have to lose weight if the vet believes it has contributed to the condition and be taught how to calm its behaviour, with or without mild sedation; various drugs may be prescribed to reduce coughing, control inflammation and prevent infection. If these drugs aren't helping after a couple of weeks, surgery is recommended. Various surgical

The pug has a collection of problems caused by Brachycephalic Respiratory Syndrome

techniques have been used, but the application of prosthetic rings to the outside of the trachea/windpipe is the current treatment of choice

TRACHEOBRONCHITIS OR KENNEL COUGH

Kennel cough is a broad term covering any infectious condition of dogs where coughing is one of the major clinical signs and is also referred to as infectious tracheobronchitis. The term tracheobronchitis describes the location of the infection in the trachea and bronchial tubes. There are two pathogens that cause Kennel cough – canine parainfluenza virus and the bacterium Bordetella bronchiseptica, both often affecting the dog at the same time.

The cough ranges from a harsh dry, non-productive cough to a moist cough that maybe accompanied by nasal discharge. Affected dogs often develop a fever, become lethargic and lose interest in food. Kennel cough is contagious and thinking about when your dog was last exposed to other dogs in relation to when the cough started will help the vet with the diagnosis. Antibiotics are used to treat the bacteria component of the condition and cough syrups and suppressants are prescribed to reduce inflammation. I recommend all dogs be vaccinated against Kennel Cough. For more on this see Chapter 3.

Eye problems

CHERRY EYE

Dogs have a third eyelid located inside the lower eyelid, also known as the 'nictitating membrane'. This extra eyelid serves as an additional protective layer for the eye, especially during hunting or fighting; it also contains a special gland that produces a significant portion of the eye's protective tear film. When this gland prolapses or pops out, the condition is known as 'cherry eye' because of its resemblance to a cherry. The gland of the third eyelid is normally attached to the lower inner rim of the eye by fibrous material but in some breeds this attachment may be weak, making the gland prone to prolapsed. The breeds most commonly affected include Cocker Spaniels, Bulldogs, Boston Terriers, Beagles, bloodhounds, Lhasa Apsos, Shih Tzus, and other Brachycephalic breeds.

Cherry eye appears as a red swollen mass by the lower eyelid, on the inside of the eye, near the nose or muzzle. It may be large and cover a significant portion of the cornea, or it may be small and appear only periodically, popping up and then disappearing again. You should bring any sign a cherry eye to your vet's attention immediately. The vet may be able to rotate the gland back into its normal position in the third eyelid under local anaesthetic however the problem is likely to recur unless a minor surgical procedure is done to fix the position of the gland. This is critical because the third eyelid gland produces up to 50 per cent of the watery (aqueous) portion of the tear film. Without adequate tear production, your dog is much more

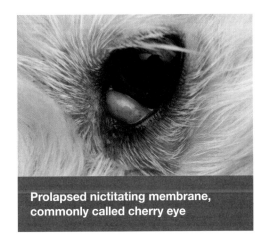

Prolapsed nictitating membrane, commonly called cherry eye

likely to develop 'dry eye' which can seriously impair your dog's sight. In most cases, the gland returns to normal function within a few weeks of surgery.

CORNEAL ULCERS

The cornea is like the window to the eye – transparent and very delicate. Corneal damage is very common because when dogs are running around and playing boisterously, they often get a grass seed or blade of grass in their eye or sand in their eyes at the beach. Of course, rather than doing what a human would do to get something out of their eye, dogs are more likely to crunch it in further while rubbing their face along the floor, until they put a hole in their cornea, known as a corneal ulcers. These abrasions cause localised swelling that may make the corneal surface look hazy, cloudy or opaque, but more often than not the tiny injury is invisible.

It's very painful for the dog and owners usually come rushing in, explaining they were at the beach in the morning and since then their dog's eye has been sore and closed right up. The vet will use a local eye drop anaesthetic to open up the eye after which they put a drop of bright yellow fluorescent dye in the eye so the damage can be seen. Treatment is frequent eye drops (up to three-hourly) and sometimes tablets. They have to wear a plastic cone (Elizabethan collar) on their head to stop them from scratching the eye. The vet will need to closely monitor progress because the condition can deteriorate quickly. If the ulcer doesn't heal with conventional treatment it may be an 'indolent ulcer' requiring surgical intervention.

CATARACTS

In a normal healthy dog, the lens of its eye is crystal clear; when the proteins in the lens become cloudy it might be because the dog has developed cataracts. The problem may be tiny, like a pinpoint, and go unnoticed, or it can grow to the size of the entire lens. Cataracts, which are irreversible, can cause blindness by blocking light to the retina. Most cataracts are hereditary although they can be the result of trauma and metabolic disease. Genetically juvenile cataracts can be found in more than 80 breeds including Boston Terriers, Golden Retrievers, Labradors, Cocker Spaniels, Miniature Spaniels, Miniature Schnauzers, West Highland White Terriers and Siberian Huskies. The onset of diabetic cataracts can be very fast and may be the first sign that the dog has sugar diabetes.

A normal aging condition called lenticular sclerosis or nuclear sclerosis also causes the lens to become cloudy which causes no visual impairment and needs no treatment – a simple ophthalmoscopic examination by a vet can distinguish between lenticular sclerosis and cataracts. There are many methods of removing cataracts and surgery will only be considered if it is likely to restore or significantly improve vision.

An Italian grey hound with cataracts in both eyes

GIVING YOUR DOG EYE DROPS

If your dog is diagnosed with a condition that requires you to give him eye drops you first need to find a comfortable position for the two of you. This will depend on the size of the dog; medium dogs may be happy to sit between your legs, but little dogs may be like wriggly worms and escape, and with giant breeds you may need a helping hand. Then again you

may be lucky enough to have one of those really good dogs who will sit on the floor or table perfectly still as asked. Tilt his head back with one hand under his jaw, just like you would if you would if giving him a tablet. In this position dogs tend to listen better and it's easier to manipulate and hold their head.

The correct method of administering eye drops

Open up the eye with your thumb and forefinger, with the thumb pulling down the bottom lid. Then using the other hand (which is holding the drops) pull back the dog's hair a bit which helps lift the lid so you have a nice open eye into which you put the drops. You are aiming for a single drop in the centre of the eyeball but it's important that the applicator doesn't touch the eyeball because it can create a corneal ulcer. Because eye drops wash away quite quickly, they often have to be given every couple of hours.

If you are applying ointment put a thin strip on the pink area of the lower lid. Blinking will cause the ointment to spread over the eyeball.

PROGRESSIVE RETINAL ATROPHY (PRA)

Here's another genetically inherited disease found in many breeds – 90 breeds are known to get this one; some breeds such as Collies, Dachshunds, Miniature Schnauzers and Cardigan Welsh Corgis can develop it in the first two years of life while others like Cocker Spaniels, Labradors and Golden Retrievers develop it later in life. In PRA retinal cells die and the blood vessels in the choroid layer shrivel; the dog's vision gradually deteriorates and as time goes on he will lose confidence doing things like jumping or walking down stairs. Eventually the whole retina dies and the eye goes blind.

Unfortunately, there is no treatment. The best way to avoid a getting puppy with hereditary PRA is to know that the dog you are taking home has several generations of its ancestors free of the disease. A reputable breeder should be able certify this.

LIVING WITH A BLIND DOG

Keep in mind that a blind dog can still have a very good life. A dog that has gradually lost its sight may remain perfectly happy in its own memorised territory.

If your dog has been diagnosed with a disease that means it will progressively lose its sight, you can test the stage of his sight at home. First, at night rearrange the furniture in a room that he's familiar with then darken the room by dimming the lights then bring the dog in and watch what he does. Then repeat the test with the lights on. A completely blind dog won't find his way around any better with the lights on while a partially-sighted dog will be happier with the lights on and adjust to the new setup.

How dogs handle blindness depends on the personality of both owner and dog. Some owners cope well and make good arrangements to make things as easy and comfortable as they can for the dog; others may find it difficult to adjust to their pet not being able to do all the same fun things. Some more confident dogs may be willing to venture out and do some of the old activities such as having a jog around the block with its owner and having games with the kids in the backyard; a less confident pooch may become depressed and not want to do much at all. If you have a dog losing its sight or already blind, talk through a management plan with your vet.

Urinary tract diseases

URINARY TRACT INFECTIONS (UTI)

Changes to a dog's urinary habits may be due to an infection in the urinary tract or could indicate problems elsewhere. Common causes of urinary infections include simple infections, stones, tumours and some hormonal imbalances. But don't panic, because often there is no underlying disease and it's caused by a simple bladder infection. Typical symptoms of a urinary tract infection (bacterial cystitis) are frequent urination, straining to urinate and changes to the urine itself – colour, smell and volume. If the infection has invaded the kidneys (pyelonephritis) your dog may go off its food, become lethargic, vomit, have diarrhoea, drink more and show signs of back pain.

Diagnosis is made by analysing the dog's urine either in the vet clinic or the lab, where they may perform a culture which will grow bacterial colonies in 24-72 hours and determine the specific type of infection and its response to antibiotics. If the vet is sending urine to the lab for a culture, they will need to get an uncontaminated urine sample by inserting a small needle directly into the dog's bladder. Dogs with a UTI are usually treated with the appropriate antibiotic; dogs with a kidney infection may be hospitalised and treated with antibiotics and intravenous fluids. Dogs with frequent UTIs need to be monitored and the vet will start investigating a possible underlying cause.

URINARY TRACT STONES

While dogs of any age or breed can develop mineral sediments called crystals or mineral stones called uroliths in any part of the urinary tract they are more common in male dogs. Most bladder stones in dogs are made from struvite, calcium oxalate, urate, or cystine crystals.

Different breeds are prone to particular types of stone composition. For instance, Dachshunds and sometimes Bulldogs, get the rarer cystine stone and urate stones occur mostly in Dalmatians. Stones in German Shepherd, Golden Retrievers and Labradors are usually made of silica; Miniature Poodles, Miniature Schnauzers, Shih Tzu, Lhasa Apso and Yorkshire Terriers are all prone to calcium oxalate stones, while struvite stones are mostly found in female dogs.

Stone formation usually starts in the bladder and work its way down to the urethra — kidney stones are not common in dogs. Causes are varied and include urinary tract infections, metabolic disorders and dietary issues. Symptoms include blood in the urine and straining to urinate, although some dogs show no symptoms at all. If a stone is blocking the urethra the dog will strain to urinate without success. This is an emergency situation and you need to get the dog to the vet as soon as possible as the obstruction will need to be removed surgically.

The vet can sometimes feel a large stone when feeling the dog's abdomen and others are found using plain or contrast ultrasound or x-rays. Stones are treated medically or surgically depending on their location, size, and composition. Long-term management such as medication, changes to diet and encouraging the dog to drink more water, is important to stop future stone formation.

RENAL FAILURE

Kidneys do not show signs of failure until at least 75 per cent of their function (eliminating waste from the body) is not working properly. Causes include congenital birth defects, infections, urinary tract obstruction, cancer, heart failure, age-related degeneration, shock (from trauma), immune disease and ingesting toxins such as raisins, grapes and antifreeze.

Vets also see medication-related kidney failure. Some owners when treating their dogs for arthritis with a non-steroidal anti-inflammatory, give them too much without understanding that it can have terrible side effects. Dogs with the most genetic predisposition to developing juvenile kidney failure are Cocker Spaniels, Samoyeds and Shar Peis. Many other breeds share the same tendency but not to the same degree.

Symptoms of acute kidney failure include loss of appetite, vomiting, diarrhoea, lethargy and weakness but these can be an indication of many diseases and any of these symptoms together or individually over a couple of days should trigger a trip to the vet. Dogs become dehydrated and sometimes develop mouth ulcers.

The first thing that vets do is stabilise the dog with medications and intravenous fluid therapy and

Patient on intravenous fluid therapy for kidney failure

once rehydrated will further investigate the possible underlying cause of the kidney failure. Diet management is a big part of the recovery process. Prognosis depends on the cause and extent of the kidney failure and on the efficiency of the treatment. Sadly, it is estimated that about 60 per cent of dogs do not recover.

Blood diseases

ANAEMIA

Red blood cells made in bone marrow carry oxygen around the body and when the red blood cell count gets too low the dog will become anaemic. There are several causes of anaemia, the most obvious being through external or internal bleeding, but conditions such as haemolysis (when healthy red blood cells are killed off prematurely) and suppression of red blood cell production in the bone marrow, are also common causes.

Certain drugs such as nonsteroidal anti-inflammatory drugs (NSAIDs) can cause stomach or duodenal ulcers which may result in internal bleeding as can ingestion of poisonous chemicals or anticoagulant medications (blood thinners such as warfarin). Other causes of anaemia include immune mediated diseases, hypothyroidism, Cushing's disease and some cancers such as leukemia. Fleas, whipworms and hookworm can cause chronic blood loss in puppies and some adult dogs which is why all dogs should always have their worming up to date (see Chapter 3).

The most common symptoms of anaemia are lethargy – your dog will seem to have lost his lust for life. If he is severely affected, he may pant more than normal and his gums become pale and his heart rate quickens. If the dog is bleeding into the gastrointestinal tract (GIT) he may vomit blood or have blood in his stools which may be black and tarry — it appears this colour because it is digested blood, usually originating from the upper gastrointestinal tract. If the bleeding is caused by external trauma (such as internal bleeding from being hit by a car) the vet's first objective will be to stop its flow; the dog may need surgery and a transfusion of blood or blood replacement fluid for heavy blood loss. Once the cause of the anaemia is found and treated the outlook is positive for most dogs.

HAEMOPHILIA

This is a rare genetic condition and only affects male dogs that get the defective gene passed to them by their mothers who are themselves unaffected. The various forms of haemophilia depend on the different coagulation factors needed to clot the blood. Haemophilia A affects mostly German Shepherds and Airedales who may bleed into the joints and stomach. The condition is diagnosed by analysing the clotting times and clotting factors in the dog's blood and the dog is treated with the missing factor in blood transfusions when bleeding occurs.

IMMUNE-MEDIATED HAEMOLYTIC ANAEMIA (IMHA)

Haemolytic anaemia is any condition in which healthy red blood cells are destroyed permanently. There are many causes for the destruction of these cells, such as a rare genetic condition which is fatal in pups and tick-borne blood parasites, but by far the most common cause of haemolytic anaemia is IMHA. When your dog has IMHA, his immune system destroys its own red blood cells. Your dog's body still produces red blood cells in the bone marrow to replace the destroyed cells, but once they are released into circulation, the immune system mistakenly recognises them as something foreign, like a virus or infection, and unfortunately destroys them. All breeds are susceptible to IMHA but Cocker Spaniels, Irish Setters, Old English Sheepdogs and Poodles seem to have more of a predisposition.

The onset of sudden haemolytic anaemia causes red blood cell products to accumulate in the dog's bloodstream. This may cause his gums to go yellow (jaundice) and his urine to go dark brown; the vet will usually find that the dog also has an enlarged spleen. A red blood cell count along with a microscopic examination of the blood will confirm the condition and give the vet an indication of how the dog's system is responding to the anaemia by making new red blood cells. Further tests will determine if it's related to the immune system; only then will the vet know how to treat it. With IMHA the objective will be to reduce the rate of red cell destruction by the dog's immune system. This is done with high doses of immunosuppressant drugs. A blood transfusion may also be administered to replenish the low red blood cell count. The spleen may be removed if it is known to be the source of the cell destruction.

IMHA carries a fair prognosis in most cases, with survival rates ranging from 50-80 per cent. While anaemia itself does not usually prove fatal, the complications of IMHA can be. Thromboembolic disease is the most life-threatening complication of IMHA, with survival rates dropping significantly in these dogs. However, if a dog does well during the acute disease and treatment phase, they usually do very well over the long term. Many can be weaned from the medications over time while others require life-long therapy. Regardless, they usually have an excellent quality of life once the condition is controlled.

IMMUNE-MEDIATED THROMBOCYTOPAENIA (IMT)

In this condition the dog has a reduced number of platelets in its blood – again as result of a confused and overactive immune system. It mostly affects middle-aged female dogs whether they have been desexed or not. Platelets play a necessary role in clotting and lack of them makes thrombocytopaenia, a life-threatening condition with frequent complications including bleeding and bruising. The dog's stools may be tarry and black from gastrointestinal bleeding and there could also be blood in the urine or nosebleeds.

Your vet will need to distinguish IMT from other bleeding disorders such as canine thrombopathia and von Willebrand's disease. Corticosteroids are the usual treatment; sometimes blood transfusions and other immunosuppressant drugs are used. But a word of caution – drug therapy may have to be life-long which can lead to other complications.

German Shepherds between the ages of two and six account for up to 20 per cent of the most serious cases and more than 50 per cent of them will be fatal. The next most at risk dogs are female Cocker Spaniels; the prognosis is fair to good. Less than five per cent of chronic cases are found in small breeds and the outlook is unpredictable.

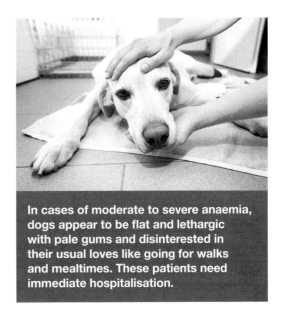

In cases of moderate to severe anaemia, dogs appear to be flat and lethargic with pale gums and disinterested in their usual loves like going for walks and mealtimes. These patients need immediate hospitalisation.

LEUKEMIA

Leukemia is a form of cancer that results in an increased white blood cell count in the blood stream or bone marrow; all forms are uncommon in dogs. Symptoms are general such as weight loss, lethargy and anaemia, and diagnosis is made from testing samples of blood or bone marrow. It is rare that condition is cured, but chemotherapy may give the dog temporary remission. The goals of treatment are to restore proper white blood cell production, reduce symptoms and relieve discomfort. Apart from chemotherapy, steroids, supplements, dietary changes and alternative medicines can help.

VON WILLEBRAND'S DISEASE (VWD)

This is the most common form of canine haemophilia and has been found in more than 50 breeds although it's reasonably rare in all of them except the Doberman. Normal blood clotting depends on the interaction of multiple blood proteins and dogs with haemophilia are born with abnormality of one of these clotting factors. The condition is suspected when the dog spontaneously bleeds from no known trauma or excessively during surgery. The disease is diagnosed by a variety of sophisticated blood tests. It is usually found in young dogs that may get unexpected nose bleeds and blood in their urine and faeces. This disease cannot be cured but active bleeding can usually be controlled with blood transfusions.

Neurological diseases

BRAIN TUMOURS

The most common type of brain tumours in dogs are meningiomas however all brain tumours are rare in canines. Meningiomas are relatively slow growing tumours in the layer of tissue that covers the brain which can displace the surrounding blood vessels and tissue as they grow. There is another type of brain tumour called a glioma which involves the brain tissue itself and aggressively invades healthy tissue and seriously affects brain function. Tumours may also grow on the pituitary gland at the base of the brain. Any dog can develop a brain tumour, especially an older one, but Boxers appear to be at greater risk.

Symptoms will depend on the location of the tumour but seizures, repetitive circling, changed mental abilities, facial twitching and mood swings (unusual behaviour and aggression) are a few signs that need to be checked out immediately. A CT scan or MRI of the brain will be necessary for diagnosis. Primary treatment will involve controlling the symptoms and trying to maintain some quality of life which may involve the use of corticosteroids, anticonvulsant drugs and radiation therapy. Having the tumour surgically removed is a rare option as there are almost always remaining tumour cells which cause the tumour to regrow. Sadly, in most cases there is no cure.

Boxers seem to be at greater risks of brain tumours

DEGENERATIVE MYELOPATHY (DM)

This is a progressive nervous system disease mostly affecting German Shepherds, although it is also found in Labradors and Golden Retrievers as well as some other breeds. This degeneration occurs in the spinal cord, starting in the thoracic region, resulting in demyelination (the stripping of the nerve fibres' insulation) and axonal loss (loss of the actual nerve fibres), and interferes with the communication of messages between the brain and limbs. Early signs generally appear when the dog is about six years of age, starting with a slow loss of coordination with the hind legs which could easily be mistaken for a hip joint problem. With time the weakness turns into a partial paralysis. The condition is painless although the dog may be confused about not being able to feel his paws; dogs maintain control over their bladder and defecation in the early stages of the disease, but control is eventually lost.

The diagnoses of Degenerative myelopathy is a process of elimination. Vets look for other causes of the weakness using diagnostic tests like myelography and MRI. When we have ruled them out, we end up with a presumptive diagnosis of DM. The only way to confirm the diagnosis is to examine the spinal cord under the microscope when an autopsy is performed. Unfortunately, there is nothing that can reverse or even slow down the condition, so the prognosis is grave. Focus should be placed on ensuring the quality of the dog's life, such as good nursing care, physical rehabilitation, pressure sore prevention, monitoring for urinary infections, and ways to increase mobility through use of harnesses, carts and weight management.

DEMENTIA

The correct name for senile dementia in dogs is canine cognitive dysfunction (CCD). I usually suspect the onset of an age-related problem like dementia when an owner reports that their elderly pooch is starting to be disorientated; it may stand in a corner staring at the wall or stand at the wrong place at the door not knowing if they want to go in or out. They appear to lose spatial awareness – they're not blind but start bumping into things in a house where that may have lived for many years. They may start defecating indoors when they have always been house-trained.

As your dog gets older it's a good idea to keep up routine mental stimulation to help keep his brain alert and stave off any possible cognitive issues; puzzle toys and regular outings are great for this. If your old dog starts having some senior moments have a talk to your vet. Some aspects of canine aging are irreversible but the drug Selegeline which is used to delay the progression of Alzheimer's in humans is licensed for use in dogs with CCD. There is inconclusive evidence around giving natural supplements such as melatonin and omega 3s, but they may help. The best advice I have for owners with dogs with CCD is stick to a regular schedule — wake up, feed, go outside, toilet, and off to bed all at the same time each day where possible — as this helps reduce confusion and anxiety for your aging dear old friend.

EPILEPSY

Brain disorders have a range of symptoms; one of them is seizures and the most common cause of seizures is epilepsy. They may be mild, come in clusters or be prolonged and last for several minutes. Generalised or 'grande mal' seizures are characterised by a loss of consciousness and involuntary muscle contractions and can be quite scary for an owner. The cause could be one of a variety of conditions: brain injury, a tumour, heat stroke, low blood sugar or genetic. Partial or 'petit mal' seizures, involving only one part of the body with or without consciousness, can sometimes be so mild that they may go unnoticed. In

Dachshunds have an inherited predisposition for epilepsy

other cases, the dog may exhibit some weird behavioural such as snapping at imaginary things in the air or suddenly indulge in a bit of frenetic digging. Breeds with an inherited predisposition to epilepsy include Cocker Spaniel, Dachshund, German Shepherd, Golden Retriever, Irish Setter, Labrador, Poodles, Beagle, Miniature Schnauzer and Saint Bernard.

The cause of the seizure will be diagnosed using the dog's medical history, blood tests and an electrocardiogram (ECG). If the dog is having frequent fits the vet may prescribe anti-seizure medications called phenobarbital or potassium bromide. These drugs are physiologically addictive and can have side effects; treatment will have to be monitored to avoid toxic blood level.

Paralysis Ticks

Any dog owner who lives on Australia's Eastern Seaboard will be familiar with the blood-sucking arachnid parasites called ticks! There are a variety of tick species that find dogs and humans attractive but the one most attracted to dogs is the Australian paralysis tick (*Ixodes holocyclus*) which causes tick paralysis by attacking the dog's nervous system. The paralysis tick can be, and often is, fatal to dogs. It's important to distinguish the paralysis tick from other kinds; it tends to be light blue to green or grey and vary considerably in size from two to three millimetres. The size of the tick indicates how long it's been on your beloved dog, but it's not an accurate indicator of how dangerous the tick is – a tick the quarter of the size of your little fingernail can kill your dog.

Ticks have four stages of life – egg, lava (six legs), nymph (eight legs — strange but true, they acquire two more legs after a blood meal), adult (eight legs) – and all stages except an egg are toxic. No matter how diligent you are you may miss a tick in its early stages. A tick will grasp onto your dog for a blood feed, burrowing into the skin with its mouth and growing in size the more it sucks; as it sucks it injects a neurotoxin. Early clinical signs are a bit vague but over the next couple of days will progress to classic paralysis. The first symptoms may be loss of appetite and slightly laboured breathing without exercise; then your dog may lose coordination in his hind legs or have difficulty climbing stairs. It may start to choke, hack or vomit. Eventually the dog may not even be able to stand and if left untreated the dog will die from a variety of causes. Unfortunately, some dogs can die suddenly in the very early stages of the disease.

THE CORRECT WAY TO REMOVE A TICK

Small and large tick twisters can be purchased from pet stores, online or from your vet so make sure you have one in the house if you are in a tick-prone area. The following three steps will explain how to use them.

1 *Select the correct size tool for the size of the tick e.g. large hook for medium and large ticks and small hooks for small and tiny ticks.*

2 *Hold the handle between your thumb and index finger and slide the fork end of the tool towards the tick until it is caught between the tongs.*

3 *Lift the tool very lightly and rotate it in either direction two or three times to remove the tick.*

The correct way to remove a tick with a tick hook

If you suspect tick poisoning, there are a few things you can do in the early stages which can make an important difference to the outcome. First have a thorough search of the dog's body, paying particular attention to the head and neck, under its collar and between the toes. If you find a tick remove it immediately using a tick twister or tweezers. The latest evidence says it is better not to kill the tick while it is still attached as it will still inject the neurotoxin.

Other things you can do if your dog is showing signs of tick paralysis is to keep it calm before, during and after removal of the tick. Toxins may act faster in warmer temperatures so keep the temperature neutral. Don't give the dog any food or water and get it to the vet as soon as you can. Treating tick paralysis is an intensive and costly business; it requires sophisticated equipment, experienced staff and often round-the-clock treatment.

Treatment may include sedation, tick antiserum, fluid therapy and in more advanced cases oxygen, suction of the fluid from the throat, tubing of the trachea and possibly general anaesthesia or ventilation to avoid respiratory exhaustion. Breathing problems are the most common cause of death. An important and expensive part of the treatment is an early transfusion of tick anti-serum which binds the toxins in the bloodstream to stop it from entering into the nerve-muscle junction where the toxin causes paralysis. Most dogs will respond well to the treatment and recover to live another happy dog day if they are treated early enough.

Prevention of a tick is better — and much cheaper — than treatment for one, so if you live in a tick prone region make sure you get good advice about the most effective tick product; there are collars, spot application, tablets and sprays.

Snake bites

Having your dog bitten by a snake can be a very scary experience. If you suspect a snake bite you should immobilise your dog and try to keep him as quiet as possible. I advise owners that if they see their dog near a snake, they should assume it was bitten and get down to the vets for a blood test as soon as possible. Because if it turns out it was bitten, the sooner your dog is treated, the better his chances of survival. About 80 per cent of pets survive snake bite if treated quickly but the survival rate is much lower for pets that are left untreated. By the way, don't put yourself or others at risk by attempting to identify the snake. Individual species of snake can vary in colour and pattern considerably and are difficult to definitively identify other than by experienced snake handlers.

Several things will determine what sort of reaction your pet has to a snake bite: the type of snake (some species of snake are more venomous than others); the amount of venom injected (depends of the size and maturity of the snake) and the site of the snake bite are all contributing factors. The head and limbs are the most common site for snake bites on dogs and the closer the bite is to the heart the quicker the venom will be absorbed into the its system and distributed around the body.

At the beginning of summer, when snakes first emerge from hibernation, their venom glands tend to be fuller and their bites more severe because the length of time since the snake last struck can also be a contributing factor. The symptoms of a bite by a tiger or brown snake are varied, however they may show some or all of the following signs.

- Sudden weakness followed by collapse
- Shaking or twitching of the muscles
- Vomiting
- Dilated pupils not responsive to light
- Blood in the urine
- Paralysis in the later stages

Your vet will determine the best course of treatment by assessing the clinical signs. Some diagnostic tests may be necessary. Veterinary treatment will depend on the severity of the symptoms and how rapidly they progress, but usually involve giving intravenous fluids and antivenom to neutralise the snake venom. Some will dogs require multiple vials of antivenom and additional support such as oxygen or help with their breathing. This will continue until the circulating antivenom has been neutralised.

It's important to note that antivenom is not a vaccination or a preventative medication and will not protect your pooch from future snake bites. If the dog gets to the vet promptly, recovery is usually 24-48 hours although it may take substantially longer if the dog has tissue damage to internal organs from toxins in the snake venom. You can reduce risk of snakebite by keeping your dog on a lead during warmer weather, staying on open paths, and by removing overgrown vegetation around your property making it less attractive to snakes.

Heat stress

Dogs can suffer from varying levels of heat stress and it's not something to be taken lightly – if a dog's body temperature gets above 40C the dog is in danger of death from heatstroke unless his temperature is immediately brought down. Dogs keep themselves cool by panting and, to a limited extent, by sweating through their paw pads. But when conditions become too hot, his cooling system will fail and his temperature will rise rapidly and the resultant heatstroke will cause his all-important body systems – neurologic, urinary, circulatory, blood clotting – to begin to fail. At this stage likelihood of recovery is very slim.

Since prevention of heat stroke is vital, knowing and responding to the early warning signs of early heat stress and heat exhaustion could mean life or death of your dog. There are varying degrees of these signs and how obvious or severe they are will depend on how long the dog has been in the heat. I have listed signs to be aware of but there are varying degrees of severity and not all will be present in every case.

- Moving slowly and not keeping up on walks
- Seeking shade and frequent rests
- Seeking water sources for drinks
- Prolonged panting
- Loud or laboured breathing
- Rapid pulse
- Dark red gums and tongue
- Wide, stressed eyes
- General increased anxiety

Those signs may overlap with more severe symptoms.

- Vomiting
- Diarrhoea
- Drooling
- Staggering
- Collapse
- Unresponsiveness or apparent signs of an altered mental state
- Seizures

A common cause of heatstroke arises from dogs left in hot cars or other vehicles, which is illegal and also one of the most easily prevented causes.

Many studies have shown how rapidly the temperature can rise in a parked car to a dangerous level in just ten minutes, even with the windows slightly open and even on relatively mild days. Anybody who has sat in a parked car on a warm summer day will appreciate just how uncomfortable it can be, and just how perilous it can be for small children and animals. And it's important to note that studies have shown having the windows open makes no difference to causing heatstroke in your dog as the temperature in the enclosed space of the car will still be high.

However, be warned hot cars aren't the only place where pets suffer from heatstroke; it can happen during outdoor exercise, play, and even walks on warm or hot days. All dogs need to be protected from heat stress but some dogs are more prone, including elderly and overweight dogs and those with medical conditions such as arthritis, laryngeal paralysis and collapsing trachea. Breeds with Brachycephalic Syndrome are particularly susceptible; even a short walk around the block during the warmer parts of the day can be disastrous for these dogs. A dog that lives outside or spends a lot of time outside during warmer months should be provided with reliable shade, plentiful water, and protection from

According the RSPCA the temperature inside a car can reach 50 degrees C in just five minutes. When the RSPCA conducted this test the temperature outside was 32.5 degrees

hot surfaces. I always advise my clients to consider bringing their dogs inside for their comfort during hot weather.

If your dog has signs of heat stroke it's important to remove it immediately from the hot environment into a cool, well-ventilated area. Give it cool water and take special care to cool its head and body with cold water and a sponge – not freezing water. If the water is too cold, blood vessels in the skin will contract, stopping the cooled blood from getting to the inside of the dog where it's needed most. Clear the dog's mouth of saliva with a soft cloth. Don't put its head in water and if it's unconscious do not put water in its mouth.

Alternatively, you can gently hose the dog outdoors or put him in a sink of water inside or cover him with a wet towel and shower him. Even though taking these steps can be helpful in getting their temperature down, all heat stress cases should be taken to the vet as soon as possible.

Dehydration

A heavy loss of fluid is a serious risk for any dog; it is a common emergency and in severe cases can lead to coma and death. Dehydration is a particular hazard for dogs that have a metabolic disease such as kidney failure or have lost fluid due to vomiting, diarrhoea, heatstroke or burns. Severe dehydration can lead to shock and managing shock takes precedence over any other treatment. Shock may develop quickly or may be delayed for several hours. A good indicator of the level of a dog's hydration is to pinch up a fold of skin; it should fall back into place immediately, so if it takes a few seconds the dog is dehydrated. The level of dehydration can also be indicated by inspecting the dog's gums. Two early signs of dehydration are a pale colour and their 'capillary refill time', which is how quickly blood supply returns when the gums are pressed — more than two seconds is a warning sign.

Other signs of early shock include:

- Rapid breathing
- Anxiety
- Lethargy and weakness
- Sub-normal temperature

The signs of advanced shock include:

- Shallow or irregular breathing
- Blue gums
- Irregular heart rate
- Extreme weakness
- Unconsciousness

If your dog has reached the stage of advanced shock and is still conscious, don't give it any food or water but wrap it in a blanket to prevent any more heat loss. You can try to counter the dehydration in an adult dog that has been having mild bouts of vomiting and diarrhoea for 24 hours or less by giving the dog electrolytic solutions until the illness passes; puppies with vomiting and diarrhoea need to be seen by a vet immediately, Having said that, even for adult dogs it's best done under veterinary supervision. Intravenous fluids may be the only solution in some cases in which case your dog needs to get to the vet immediately.

TIPS ON GIVING TABLETS

There are many health conditions that require owners to give their dogs tablets at home. Many people think the best way to get their dog to take a pill is to sneak it into their food. However, the problem with this method is they cannot be sure just how much of the tablet their dogs have actually ingested and how much remain in the bowl, or has been sneakily spat out when the owner is not looking, so from the vet's point of view it's a bit iffy. Some dogs will swallow it when it's buried in something they like, such as a piece of cheese or a spoonful of peanut butter. A few companies have started making beef-flavoured tablets; once all tablets become tasty and chewable the whole vexed issue can be avoided. In the meantime, vets have a tried and trusted method.

First have the dog sitting; then use both your hands to open up the jaw with one hand on top of the dog's snout and the other on the bottom part of the jaw – it's easier to pry the jaw open if you tilt the dog's head back and point his nose to the ceiling. Once you have a nice open mouth you will see that the tongue makes a little hump; you will need to put the tablet at the back of this hump. As soon as you have done this, quickly close the dog's mouth – because the he will be trying to flick the tablet out with his tongue – stroke his neck downwards to encourage swallowing and blow on his nose. Blowing on the nose makes it itchy and he will want to lick it; but to lick he will first need to swallow, and the tablet will go down.

Sometimes the dog will refuse to swallow and will hold its mouth closed. At the clinic I usually have a little plastic syringe filled with water on hand that I insert it into the corner of the dog's mouth and give a quick flush; the dog will swallow the tablet with the water. You can ask your vet for a syringe if you feel confident to try this at home.

CHAPTER 11

Complementary Medicine for Dogs

The term complementary medicine is often used interchangeably with holistic or alternative medicine. It refers to the many non-conventional and increasingly popular methods of treating a variety of medical conditions and ailments and is often dismissed by the Western medical profession as unscientific. Veterinary medicine is taught under the Western model and yet more and more vets and pet owners are embracing some of these complementary techniques and treatments.

So what do I think about complementary medicine for dogs? My mother is a naturopath and acupuncturist. We have some interesting conversations. My veterinary training has taught me to question anything without hard scientific evidence. I have quizzed her for the rational mechanism behind her work, challenging her on the approaches to see if they withstand my scientific scrutiny. But with time I have learned something… and that is to just shut up because I realise some things just can't be demonstrated through a randomised double blind, placebo-controlled clinical trial. If it causes no harm and people find that these complementary therapies are benefiting them or their pets' recovery and wellbeing, then that is enough for me.

There is more to life than science. With this open mind I have now seen complementary therapies alleviate symptoms of chronic, degenerative conditions. I have seen dogs' post-op recovery time reduced and dogs bound into my consulting room after a round of acupuncture. And probably more than anything, I have been inspired and charmed by owner's commitment to love, care and nurture man's best friend.

So, in the interest of giving dog lovers the best information I can, let's take a closer look at a few of the more popular alternative treatments available for dogs.

Acupuncture

This is an ancient Chinese therapeutic technique used most often to treat pain. It involves applying small-gauge needles to various points on the body to stimulate nerves, improve appetite, increase circulation, relieve muscle spasms, and reduce nausea. The Chinese believe that when an animal or person is healthy, there is an efficient circulation of 'chi' (energy/life force) along well-defined channels (meridians) on the skin. These meridians overlay important vascular structures and are connected to internal organs, muscular and joint structures, and the nervous system. An imbalance or interference with this flow can result in health problems.

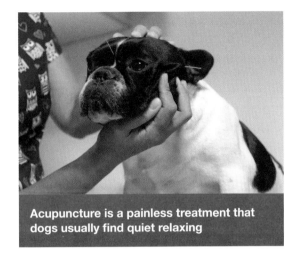

Acupuncture is a painless treatment that dogs usually find quiet relaxing

By stimulating certain points along the meridians, usually with thin needles or a special laser, the practitioner manipulates the chi, activating physiological processes that help the body restore its own health. Again, the results from research on the benefits of acupuncture in dogs are inconclusive but I myself have seen a case where the mobility and spinal posture of a dog with IVDD seemed to significantly improve with acupuncture. And I also feel pretty amazing myself after a session.

Herbal/botanical medicine

Herbalists believe certain herbs and plants have therapeutic value due to their unique combination of ingredients and the use of herbal medicine has increased in popularity in recent years in veterinary medicine. Some vets I know swear that products containing devil's claw and turmeric help reduce inflammation and recommend them for managing arthritis and bowel disorders like colitis. Unlike nutraceuticals, which are isolated compounds of a natural substance, herbs offer a more natural complex of chemicals and may have a broader physiological effect. Because herbs are not regulated in the same way as approved drugs, practitioners must be sure that suppliers adhere to stringent standards of authenticity and preparation.

Homeopathy

Homeopathy is an alternative therapy developed more than two hundred years ago for use in people. The theory behind the practice is that 'like cures like' - that symptoms of disease can be treated with low concentrations of preparations that cause the same symptoms. To be honest, this is a therapy I am most sceptical of as it lacks biological plausibility. But again, each to their own – even members of the British Royal family are known to swear by homeopathy.

Chiropractic

Chiropractic treatment involves applying force to the joints to restore motion and reduce pain and muscle spasms. Chiropractic can be great for dogs that are generally healthy but have musculoskeletal weaknesses, arthritic conditions and back pain. Some vets say chiropractic care is more effective than prescribing anti-inflammatories, claiming that while anti-inflammatories lessen pain and reduce swelling, they won't resolve stiffness or musculoskeletal imbalances. Personally, I don't recommend chiropractic therapy in place of conventional western medicine, but I think when used together it can produce good results. It should be stressed that a veterinary chiropractic therapist must have a comprehensive understanding of animal anatomy and the 'line of correction' as manipulations must be subtle and tactile.

Hydrotherapy

This is my favourite complementary therapy. Canine hydrotherapy is a beneficial alternative to high-impact exercise for dogs with chronic bone conditions or crippling injuries, such as arthritis or cruciate ligament trauma. During therapy, your dog is assisted in and out of a pool to minimise body stress and possible injury. A dog harness is frequently used to help your dog maintain an above-water position. The water in the pool may also be heated; heat application helps alleviate muscular discomfort and pain.

Some hydrotherapy treatments include using underwater resistance jets to create a current for the dog to swim against. Underwater treadmill therapy is a form of hydrotherapy where the dog walks against the force of the water to build muscle. Like water aerobics, moving through water is gentle on joints while requiring muscles to work hard. When I was working in the UK, this was something a lot of my clients did with their dogs. Presumably it was covered by their pet insurance policies. The results I saw were remarkable.

Massage

This is lovely therapy because you can learn to do it at home and in addition to the health and wellbeing benefits to your furry friend, it strengthens your bond. A massage may be a new concept for your dog, but once he realises how great it feels and that you're the one making him feel great, your bond and relationship will be that much stronger.

Massage is said to reduce stress and anxiety, and in cases of injury, massage and physiotherapy can also help to

Hydrotherapy plays an important role in the rehabilitation of dogs with hip dysplasia. The buoyancy of the water means that muscle strengthening can occur with less loading and arthritic pain.

rehabilitate, reduce pain and swelling, heal strains and sprains faster, and keep scar tissue to a minimum. Of course, your vet should advise you on this and you'll need to see trained a professional as if you do this incorrectly you can cause more harm than good. Just like it does for us, massage is thought to promote overall wellbeing and improve body functions by increasing circulation, decreasing blood pressure, improving lymphatic fluid movement, strengthening the immune system, aiding digestion, stimulating the kidneys and liver, and encouraging deeper breathing.

Again, I can't be sure this is all true, scientific studies may say otherwise, but hey it's a lovely activity to do with your doggo. So if it feels right and you both enjoy it, go for it!

Supplements

Here are the six most popular dog supplements.

GLUCOSAMINE

The most popular supplement for dogs is glucosamine, which is an amino sugar found naturally in the fluid around the joints to help build cartilage. Glucosamine is taken from the shells of shellfish and can also be made in the laboratory. Many dog owners and vets believe that glucosamine is effective in treating arthritis in dogs. For older dogs, it may relieve joint pain and improve mobility. Available in many forms — including pills, powders, treats and in kibble — glucosamine supplements are usually formulated with chondroitin sulfate, which occurs naturally in the connective tissues of bone and cartilage.

FISH OIL

The second most common supplement given to dogs is fish oil. Fish oil contains omega-3 fatty acids that are thought to improve coat quality and shine and alleviate skin allergies. There has been some research into whether fish oils are useful in treating arthritis, heart health, and joint health, but results are mixed.

S-ADENOSYL METHIONINE (SAM-E)

This is a chemical that occurs throughout the body and in humans, and it is marketed for use in depression and arthritis, and a variety of other conditions. In pets it is primarily promoted as protecting the liver from damage due to release of toxins, often in combination with milk thistle, although it is sometimes recommended for arthritis. While the theoretical arguments for these uses, especially in the case of liver disease, are plausible, there is virtually no clinical research that the compound actually benefits pets when given as an oral supplement although it may have some possible value in treating age-related cognitive dysfunction in dogs.

ANTIOXIDANTS

Antioxidant supplements are thought to counteract some of the effects of aging, such as memory loss and cognitive dysfunction. They're also used as a treatment for heart disease in dogs and to help reduce inflammation. Found in substances like vitamins C and E, antioxidants protect the body from free radicals, which are potentially harmful molecules that can damage cell membranes and even cause cell death. Coenzyme Q10 is a natural and powerful antioxidant that helps convert food into energy, as well as fighting free radicals.

COENZYME Q10

Like most dietary supplements, coenzyme Q10 is recommended for a wide range of apparently unrelated conditions. In humans it is recommended for a long list of ailments including cardiovascular disease, Alzheimer's disease, migraines, diabetes as well as a general tonic and, of course, the inevitable 'boosting' of the immune system. In dogs it has primarily been recommended for treatment or prevention of heart disease and age-related cognitive dysfunction but there have been no clinical trials for anything specific and recommendations are almost entirely anecdotal.

PROBIOTICS

Given an increase in the use of probiotics in humans, it's not surprising that probiotics have also become popular as supplements for dogs. Probiotics live naturally in the body in the form of yeasts and live bacteria that aid with digestion and intestinal health. As supplements, they're used to treat diarrhoea and other digestive problems. Probiotics come in several forms, including some yogurts, capsules, chews, powders, and in some dog food formulations. Probiotics are great to use after a bout of diarrhoea or a course of antibiotics as they boost the populations of good bacteria present in the gut and help them to out-compete the bad bacteria, keeping the gut and your pet healthy.

While I am in favour of people giving their dogs the best possible treatments there are a few important things to be aware of:

- Always consult your vet before giving your dog supplements because your dog may have an underlying condition that needs medical attention and if your dog is taking a prescribed medication, supplements, even herbal ones, may be harmful.

- If a claim for a supplement sounds too good to be true it probably is. Supplements will not cure cancer or other serious diseases.

- Buy a reputable brand, preferably one that specialises in supplements and has conducted clinical studies.

- Familiarise yourself with substances that are harmful to dogs because some human supplements, like those containing garlic, can be harmful.

CHAPTER 12

Training
and
Behavioural
Problems

L iving with a dog gives us the opportunity to look into another world. In earlier chapters I outlined all the wonderful, wacky and weird things that dogs do in their special canine universe. Yet, as we have seen, they share with us a range of similar needs and emotions from wanting security and love, to expressing frustration and jealousy. A happy and contented dog has successfully negotiated his way in our human environment. He has learnt to socialise with strangers, to curb natural instincts such as biting and aggression, to accept instruction and to have good manners inside and outside the home. But integrating your dog into a mutually satisfying partnership does not come without a bit of effort. Caring for your dog involves more than giving it food and shelter; apart from looking after its emotional and physical health you need to teach it boundaries.

In this chapter I will address the common dog behavioural problems that owners most often ask me about. Every dog will develop habits which you'd rather it didn't have; most are minor and you learn to live with them, just putting it down to their own little 'personality'! Nevertheless, when a dog's behaviour becomes challenging or puzzling it is often mishandled or misunderstood because people forget that they are dealing with a dog and these are actually natural behaviours for a dog! Understanding the reason for the behaviour will help you manage it or train your dog to give it up.

You can also nip the problem in the bud before it becomes entrenched and sometimes that's more about training the dog's human family. For instance, when the puppy is chewing everyone's shoes, train the household to remove all shoes from puppy's reach and give the pup a chew toy.

Basic obedience training

Dogs are pack animals and as such respond to the leader of the pack; when you bring a dog into your house you become the pack leader and he will learn under your instruction. Dogs are acutely tuned to body language and sounds and will quickly distinguish between the different tone of your commands and your physical actions. The best way to start training is to use rewards – affection, toys and treats – for responding correctly to your commands. Have a treat ready to give immediately and accompany it with heaps of praise. Slowly cut down on the number of edible rewards so he's not always expecting them; eventually the dog will do want you want for praise alone.

Never save the best reward for last; if you do you are setting the dog up to want the training session to be over so he can have the treat. The response to disobedience – using stern words such as 'no' sharply and momentarily separating yourself from the dog – should also be instant.

Puppies are easier to train than adult dogs who may take longer to accept you as the new pack leader; but be patient – he'll learn if you are consistent in your training. Most dogs will carry out your commands because they have a desire to please you and it's also in their interest to do so — remember I said that dogs are great opportunists! Keep lessons short; a minute or two several times a day is enough for a puppy. If you train before his mealtimes you will have four opportunities a day; as he gets older and the number of meals gets less, train when he wakes up or after he has gone to the toilet. Older dogs can concentrate for longer periods, but 15 minutes is usually more than enough for most dogs.

To help with training your puppy it's not a bad idea to book him into some puppy classes which are a bit like pre-school for little children. Try to get the puppy's whole human family to attend some of the classes but make sure any children are supervised. The classes will last for about an hour, and ideally should have a restricted age group — preferably under 16 weeks — with bolder dogs separated from more timid types during free play time. A course is usually about six weeks; ask your vet to recommend one or ask someone with a well-behaved dog!

Dogs are easily distracted, so the best place to begin command

Nothing beats a loving stroke from your owner

training is the place with the least external distractions – your home. Start with the basic words – 'sit', 'come', 'stay' and 'lie down' – then once your dog understands and reliably responds to the basics, it is ready for walking to heel, which is traditionally on the left side. You can start lead training down your hallway and once your dog is following commands inside you can move outside to the back garden, eventually graduating to the street or local park.

TEACHING 'SIT' AND 'STAY'

Teach your dog to sit first by getting down in front of your pup and holding a treat as a lure. Put the treat right in front of his nose and slowly lift it above his head. As you do this he will probably sit as he lifts his head to get at the treat. Allow him to eat the treat when his bottom touches the ground. Repeat this one or two times and then remove the food lure and use just your empty hand, but continue to reward the puppy after he sits. Once he understands the hand signal to sit, you can begin saying 'sit' right before you give the hand signal. Never physically put your puppy into the sitting position; some dogs find this confusing or upsetting.

A puppy who knows the 'stay' command will remain sitting until you ask him to get up by giving another cue, called the 'release' word. Staying in place is a duration behaviour. The goal is to teach your dog to remain sitting until the release cue is given, after which you start adding distance.

First, teach the release word. Choose the word you will use for release, such as 'okay' or 'go'. Start with your puppy in a sit or a stand position, toss a treat on the floor, and say your word as he steps forward to get the treat. Repeat this a couple of times until you can say the word first and toss the treat after he begins to move. This teaches the dog that the release cue means to move his feet.

When your dog knows the release cue and how to sit on cue, put him in 'sit', turn and face him and give him a treat; pause, and give him another treat for staying in a sit, then give him the release cue. Gradually increase the time you wait between treats (it may help to recite the

Good boy!

227

alphabet in your head and work your way through it). If your dog gets up before the release cue, don't worry it just means he isn't ready to sit for long periods so go back to a shorter time.

After your dog can stay in a sit for several seconds, you can begin adding distance. Get him to sit and say 'stay', take one step backwards, then move back to the dog, give him a treat and use your release word. Continue building in steps, keeping it easy enough for the dog to feel he's being successful. Practice both facing him and walking away with your back turned, which is more realistic.

Gradually increasing the distance is also good for the 'sit' because the more deeply he learns it, the longer he can remain sitting. It's important not expect too much, too soon; training goals are achieved in little steps, so you may need to slow down and focus on one thing at a time. Sessions should be short and successful.

LEAD AND HEEL TRAINING

Your dog must understand 'sit' before you start lead and heel training because it's always the start off point and also a very basic and important command. When you are teaching your dog to 'stay' be careful not to over praise when you release him from the stay position – too much 'good doggie' may over-excite him causing him to bounce and jump around at the end of the session. 'Stay' training, like any type of training, should only be attempted when you have your dog's full attention. If your dog is more interested in other dogs or children, his mind is elsewhere.

If your dog is distracted while you are teaching it to walk on a lead, use your left hand on its collar to bring it back into the heel position, get its attention with a food treat and continue. If the distraction is overwhelming, command it do something you know it will do – 'Sit'. Verbally reward it and wait until the distraction action has passed.

When you are training your pooch, stand upright, be consistent and use a combination of verbal and hand commands. Try not to get annoyed and repeat the same commands over and over; if it's not working out, take a break. Sometimes training can be frustrating for both the owner and dog. If you're being consistent and following the steps exactly and not getting anywhere - consider some other training resources, there are a number of methods to train a dog to do these commands, maybe you'll find tweaking the steps a little will help your puzzled fur baby understand what you're actually on about.

If other family members are involved in the training, make sure you are all on the same page by using the same words and signals so you don't confuse the dog. If the dog stubbornly refuses to comply with your command, it's better to take a break and do something different and go back and have another shot at it later.

Training more than one dog

If you have more than one dog, trying to train them together is virtually a hopeless task. Train them separately, keeping the other dog or dogs out of earshot while you train one at a time.

While living with multiple dogs in the home can be wonderful it can sometimes be challenging as you manage their behaviour in certain situations. Dogs being pack animals want to get along with each other and if they become aggressive it is usually only in the initial phase as they compete for the top dog position and negotiate relationships within the pack. Handling more than one dog in the house successfully depends on you having a good understanding of doggy interactions to avoid the dogs becoming stressed.

Feeding in multi-dog households

Possession aggression over food – one of biggest issues in multi-dog households – can be triggered when dogs are fed different foods, or if one dog just feels entitled to more food than the other. If you don't take steps to stop it, food aggression can result in injuries — not to mention an unhappy household of dogs.

One of the biggest issues in a multi-dog house usually revolves around feeding time. You have to be diligent with supervision while they are eating to prevent fights. It's important to teach the dogs manners and a good place to start is to use the seniority of the dogs. By this I mean the one that has been with you the longest – he should know your routine and be well-trained. Feeding him first will help the newest or youngest learn their place although this jostling for top dog position may pop up again if the younger dog wants to assert his rights as the dominant dog as he gets older. And that's okay, it's not uncommon for changes in pack hierarchy to occur.

You can begin to train dogs to wait their turn at dinner time by first teaching them 'treat manners'. Teach each dog separately to take the treat only when his or her name is called. Then add one dog at a time, offering the senior dog a treat first by saying his or her name. Ask the dog to sit before taking a treat. It doesn't matter how many dogs you have – two or 10 – ask them all to sit at the same time, then call a dog's name and offer that dog a treat. The aim is for each dog to wait patiently to hear their name called.

Training multiple dogs to have peaceful mealtimes requires patience, but it works if you are firm and consistent. Training is done in four stages of a few days each.

Stage 1. Place each dog in separate, but adjoining, rooms when you feed them closing the door in-between so they can't see each other while they're eating. They won't fight over food if they can't reach the other's food. Feed both dogs separately like this for a few days.

Stage 2. Open the door separating the dogs at mealtime and stand guard in the doorway while they eat; do not allow either dog to leave his bowl and head towards the other dog. When they don't react towards each other, reinforce their positive behaviour with lots of praise and a treat after they've finished their meals. If one dog approaches the doorway and will not stop, close the door between them. Feed them this way for a few days.

Stage 3. At mealtime put both dog bowls into one large room, placing them as far apart as you possibly can. Praise the dogs for not interacting with each other while they are eating. Arm yourself with a large metal baking tray and spoon. Stand between the dogs and watch for signs of possessive aggression e.g. a long stare, growling or baring teeth. If the aggressor exhibits any threatening behaviour, bang loudly on the large metal tray to startle him or place it directly in front of his nose to stop him from approaching the other dog.

Stage 4. Daily move the bowls a little closer together to train the dogs to eat their food without arguing over it. If they start fighting again, move the bowls farther apart and if necessary, restart the process at Stage 2.

Barking

Dogs bark for many different reasons; they also howl and whine which is their way of communicating something. They bark when they're alert and excited, or as a warning of danger or when they're bored and seeking attention which is probably the most common cause of neighbourhood complaints. And sometimes it's actually a neighbourhood dog thing – one dog will bark a response to another's bark setting several dogs off at the same time. Not everyone enjoys this cacophony of dogs talking to each other. However, most dogs that bark excessively for long periods do so simply because being left home all alone is the pits for a dog, and they could be suffering from separation anxiety: 'Hey! You guys forgot me! Hello? Why am I here by myself?'

Unless you are dedicated to solving the problem I usually suggest owners seek the help of a professional dog behaviourist to do the training. I have put together a few methods that can help and while all of them can work, you shouldn't expect overnight results. The longer your dog has been practicing the barking behaviour, the longer it will take for him to learn new ways.

- Discourage the barking behaviour by removing whatever it is he is barking at. For instance, if he is barking at people or animals passing the house bring him inside or if he's inside looking out the window, get block out blinds or put him in another room.

- Ignore your dog's barking for as long as it takes him to stop then when he does reward him with a treat and praise. Any attention you give him while he's barking only rewards him for being noisy. Don't talk to him, don't touch him, and don't even look at him until he finally calls it quits. If he barks for an hour and you get so frustrated that you yell at him to be quiet, the next time he'll probably bark for an hour and a half. He knows that if he just barks long enough, you'll give him attention.

- If some external stimulus is the cause of your dog's barking gradually desensitise him to it by getting him accustomed to it.

The first thing to do if you have a barking dog in the neighbourhood is to speak to the owners and try to come to a solution. With a cooperative and conscientious owner, your support and feedback as their neighbour can help resolve the problem.

Start with the thing that makes him bark, such as another dog for example, at a distance. It must be far enough away that he doesn't bark when he sees it. Feed him lots of delicious treats. When you think he's ready for the next challenge, move the stimulus a little closer (perhaps as little as a few inches or a few feet from the previous point) and if there's no barking, reward again with treats. If the stimulus moves out of sight, stop giving your dog treats. You want your dog to learn that the appearance of the stimulus leads to yummy treats. Repeat the process multiple times and be aware that it may take days or weeks before your dog can pay attention to you and the treats without barking at the other dog.

- Teach your dog to bark on command. Give him the command to 'speak', wait for him to bark two or three times, and then stick a tasty treat in front of his nose. When he stops barking to sniff the treat, praise him and give him the treat. Repeat this process until he starts barking as soon as you say 'speak'. Once he can reliably bark on command, teach him the 'quiet' command. In a calm environment with no distractions, tell him to 'speak'. When he starts barking, say 'quiet' and stick a treat in front of his nose. Praise him for being quiet and give him the treat. Once he knows the 'quiet' command, practice it in increasingly distracting situations (such as a knock at the door) until he stops barking immediately when asked to.

- When your dog starts barking, ask him to do something that's incompatible with barking such as lying on his bed. Once he stops barking, toss a treat on his bed/mat and tell him to 'go there' or the phrase I've always used is 'into bed'. When he knows going to his designated spot earns a treat, get someone to knock on the door while he's on his bed or mat and use the 'stay' command; if he gets up and starts barking when you open the door, close the door immediately and persuade him back to sitting quietly in his spot. Repeat this until he stays on his mat in silence when the door opens. Reward him when he does!

- Make sure your dog is getting sufficient physical and mental exercise every day. Depending on his breed, age, and health, your dog may require several long walks as well as a good game of chasing the ball and playing with some interactive toys. A tired dog is less likely to bark from boredom or frustration at being left alone for several hours at a time. If the entire household is out all day arrange for a dog walker. Doggie day care is a good option but it's not cheap – can be around $50 a day, which is not dissimilar to the cost of my kids' day care!

A couple of things to remember when training your dog not to bark: don't yell at him to be quiet (no point in both of you barking at each other), be consistent and enlist the whole family in the training so as not to confuse the dog. Stay positive.

Mounting or humping

As a vet I have often had to discuss various elements of dog behaviour which owners find embarrassing – one of them is mounting. Owners often assume mounting is sexual in nature and will stop when the dog is desexed – then become concerned when the behaviour doesn't stop and even more alarmed when the dog humps visitors or its behaviour alarms young children.

However, while it is a normal behaviour, many dog owners do not consider it acceptable. It may be sexually based or a display of dominance (especially around visitors and children) but without knowing the context of a dog's behaviour it's hard to be precise about the reason for it. Anxiety and arousal are probably the two main causes if the dog is mounting objects or people, however it is less likely to be associated with establishing dominance if the dog is also mounting inanimate objects.

Mounting is a form of out of context behaviour in response to an internal emotional conflict. It could be the response to an exciting event (e.g. playing with a new toy) or they might mount a visitor as a way of demonstrating their insecurity about their interaction with that person. When we look at mounting in this context, we can see it as a release of tensions around a particular event and not just a demonstration of hierarchy in the house where the dog lives.

There may also be an element of attention-seeking in mounting – a new human in the house, how exciting, look at me! Mounting can also be anxiety about being punished for something the dog doesn't understand. For instance, if the misdemeanour (digging up the garden, going through the rubbish bin) took place sometime before the pack leader got angry about it, the poor dog will only be confused because it will not understand what it is being punished for. Mounting can also be sexual in nature and both male and female dogs can continue this behaviour even if desexed.

Motivation for mounting can be anxiety, excitement, sexual, dominance and self-soothing, which is a bit like masturbating with a favourite toy or blanket — both male and female dogs self-soothe. So, what can be done about it? If the vet has neutered the dog and the behaviour continues, there are a number of different approaches to discouraging the behaviour depending on the owner and the dog. Understanding the reasons for the dog's mounting may make it easier to manage. Some owners decide to live with it if it's occasional and not harmful. My approach is to suggest the owner redirect the mounting behaviour to an object or even better distract the dog from the behaviour by encouraging another activity. If your dog likes to mount other dogs when you're out and about, try avoiding situations in which it could happen – for instance dog parks.

Chewing

Chewing stuff is a natural canine behaviour but it drives people crazy; it can also be dangerous if dogs chew electrical cords. I've treated dogs that have received electrical shocks; they get major burns around their lips and some suffer from pulmonary oedema (fluid on their chest) from the shock.

Mouthing and chewing are normal puppy behaviours as they curiously explore their new world; when they are teething, they will be looking for something to chew at all times. When your puppy chews something they shouldn't, take it away from them and offer something alternative to chew on and they'll eventually learn what's appropriate to chew and what's not. Sometimes when puppies are mouthing humans in a playful way, they may start to get a bit assertive and inflict pain; when they do this make a noise that sounds like pain (like a yelp or an ouch!) and take your hand or body part away. If the mouthing/biting continues, repeat your response and walk away, ignoring him until he settles down.

Malamute puppy enjoying a good ol' chew

Dogs also chew from boredom; that's when they go to work on your house. Encourage your dogs to chew appropriate things – their toys or rawhide bones – and keep your personal items away and electrical cords and wires out of reach. If you do find your dog chewing the wrong thing you need to correct the behaviour while they're doing it. A sharp clap with 'Hey!' or 'No!' – right then and there. Or you can bang a rolled-up newspaper to make a noise (but not to hit them with!) giving them an instant association between chewing the wrong thing and a loud noise.

Digging

Digging is a normal dog instinct and a genetic component in some breeds such as Jack Russell Terriers and Wire Haired Fox Terriers, while most Miniature Poodle's couldn't think of anything worse – some wouldn't even step on dirt, let alone dig in it.

Boredom, anxiety and fear can also make dogs dig. Sometimes they'll employ an evolutionary method to cool themselves down; on a really hot day they'll dig away the top soil to find the cooler earth underneath to lie on. And sometimes they dig to hide possessions, toys, bones or some smelly bit of rubbish they have taken a liking to.

If digging is a problem (and it might be if you've just planted a row of lovely plants in your garden) you should initially say 'no' and provide an alternative activity to divert his attention. If he continues you could block the hole with a rock or his own faeces (that should deter him). If you have a spare spot in the garden you could let him have his own special digging pit and encourage him to use it by burying one of his toys for him to find.

Separation anxiety

Separation anxiety is among the biggest and most concerning behaviours in dogs. In the dog world, packs stick together for mutual protection and it isn't natural for the pack to be split for lengthy periods of the day so it's something dog owners have to manage if they have to leave the dog home alone. Some 'please don't go' whining is normal when you leave the house. But true separation anxiety is when as you're preparing to go – you get your shoes on or your keys out – the dog starts to panic – pacing, whining and generally boo-hooing. The dog is terrified that you might not be coming back.

Have you ever had the misfortune of coming home to find it semi-destroyed and messages in your letter box or under your door complaining about your dog barking and howling for hours on end in your absence? If so, you're dealing with your dog's separation anxiety – a mild term for a pretty destructive and difficult behaviour that has even led some desperate owners to surrender their dogs for re-homing or have them put down. Once the separation distress was quite uncommon but today few households have someone home regularly during the day to keep the dog company.

However, before trying to modify a dog's behaviour it's important to correctly identify it as separation anxiety. You need to rule out normal puppy behaviour, play, fear, or a way of working off excess energy or a reaction to outside noises. If a dog urinates in the house when left alone as well as when the owner is home, it's more likely a housetraining problem than a separation issue. However, a dog urinating in his crate when the owner leaves the house, but who is fine holding it through the night, is an example of possible separation anxiety. Separation-related destruction is usually directed toward escape efforts – chewing or clawing at or through doorframes, windowsills, and walls. If the destruction is more generalised throughout the house – chewing cushions, clothes and bedding – it may point toward one or more of the other possible causes such as boredom or lack of exercise, rather than an isolation issue.

There are a number of things you can do to minimise your dog's separation-anxiety behaviour but having a dog with a strong emotional response to being left alone will need patience and commitment. It's hard work but if you succeed in helping him be brave about being alone you'll both reap rewards. It's best to set yourselves up for success from the outset and this begins when you bring a new dog or puppy home and start a program to help him be comfortable with being alone for

Oh, this can't be happening again!! She's driving out the driveway. I knew it! How could she do this to meeeee!

gradually increasing periods. This will help to assure him that it's not necessary to panic: you haven't abandoned him; you always come back. Here's a few other behaviour modification pointers.

- Give your dog a decent walk or other energetic exercise before you leave. A tired dog has less energy with which to be anxious and destructive.

- A few minutes before you leave, give him a juicy, chewy treat to take his mind off your imminent departure.

- Keep your departures and returns calm and emotionless. If he gets excited and jumps all over you when you return, ignore him and walk away. When he finally settles down, greet him very calmly.

- Mix up your departure routine by also doing them when you are not leaving such as rattling your car keys and then settling down to watch TV. Or change the pieces of your departure routine, such as eating breakfast before you shower or putting your briefcase in the car while you are still in your pyjamas; in this way his anxiety won't build to a fever pitch as he recognises your departure cues.

- If you are considering adopting a second dog to see if it helps settle your dog's anxiety, first try borrowing a calm, stable, compatible dog from a friend, to see if it makes a difference.

- Ask your vet about anti-anxiety plug-ins, medications or environmental sprays.

I am often asked if it's good for dogs to go to doggy day care. I say it's not suitable for all dogs. It can be good for dogs with separation anxiety but if you are doing it every day you are not teaching the dog how to be alone for lengthy periods. It's a bit of a balancing act. A friend of mine has a dog with separation anxiety and when she has to go anywhere for a few hours she drops the dog at her mum's or with a friend. But a clingy dog is going to be in trouble if the owner has to go into hospital or goes on holiday. Sometimes I think it's far better to have a dog trainer come in and teach the dog that they can trust other people and it's okay to be alone.

Inappropriate toileting

When your dog begins to wee and poo when and where it shouldn't, it's a problematic behaviour, especially if it's in your in house or worse, when you are visiting someone else's house with your previously perfectly toilet trained darling dog. The first thing you need to do when this happens is to see the vet to rule out any medical causes such as urinary tract infections or urinary incontinence which sometimes affects older dogs or a gastrointestinal problem.

Puppies are always going to toilet inside until they're over 12 weeks of age. Young dogs should not be expected to stay at home for long periods without being able to relieve themselves. In this case look for other solutions such as a local dog walker or a friendly neighbour who might be happy to take him out. But when this behaviour suddenly starts in older toilet trained dogs you have to look at causes. A dog trainer would investigate various causes, such as excitement urination or submissive urination, where dogs will urinate if they are submissive and confronted by a larger dog. It could also be attention seeking or lack of proper training. You may have got the training right, but something happened to upset the dog's emotional state, such as moving house or a new person moves into the house. In these cases, training needs to be reinforced.

Escaping

If you have a dog and a yard, make sure it is fenced securely to prevent escaping. Owners frequently underestimate the height of a fence a dog can scale if it is determined to get out; dogs of either sex that have not been desexed will be especially eager to run off and find each other when a bitch comes into heat. It is normal for a dog to want to escape sometimes to explore the world but if he continues to run off you may need to assess whether he has enough stimulation at home to amuse him when he's at home alone. Make sure he gets enough exercise before you leave home.

Some dogs are naturally inclined to wander and others suffer from separation anxiety and are desperate to find their owners. Sometimes it's hormonal and sometimes it is related to

Some dogs will do just about anything to escape from an approaching storm

the dog's history; for example, a rescue a dog that previously lived on a farm and roamed around visiting the neighbouring farm houses on a daily basis would find it difficult to settle in a small city garden. The only method of keeping a wandering dog safe is to keep him inside.

Owners of dogs whose inclination is to escape during thunderstorms or fireworks need to provide a higher level of security during storms and certain celebrations.

Eating dirt

Why do dogs eat dirt? Actually, it's not uncommon behaviour, many dogs engage in this odd dining habit which dog owners often find disgusting. Dogs eat dirt for a variety of reasons. If your dog is a puppy, dirt eating may be just normal, exploration behaviour. Puppies explore the world with their mouths, and yes, that includes tasting dirt! Sooner than later, they learn that dirt isn't really that tasty, unless you dropped something yummy on top of it of course!

Another common reason dogs eat dirt is boredom. If a dog is confined in a back yard and there is nothing better to do, he may entertain himself with a bit of digging and dirt eating. Dogs need exercise and mental stimulation and failure to provide those can lead to destructive or even harmful behaviours. Make sure your dog has access to fun toys and make time to engage him in fun games to take his mind off the dirt. There may also be a chance that the dirt-eating behaviour is a way of gaining your attention, especially if he is bored and under stimulated.

Any form of pica (which is eating something they shouldn't like poo or dirt), may indicate underlying problems such as an obsessive compulsive disorder, anxiety, or other mental problems which have developed from painful past experiences or are due to genetically inherited behaviours. More commonly this behaviour is thought to reflect either a minor mineral or vitamin deficiency, a gastric upset or irritation, or even something simple like the animal smelling a delicious food scrap on or in the ground. I usually advise owners that if they see it once or twice to not to worry about it. However, if it seems compulsive or excessive, to take the dog to your vet and be sure that the dog is on a complete and balanced diet.

Coprophagia (eating poo)

It's not uncommon for dog owners to tell me they have been horrified to find their precious pooch eating his own poo. Eating the faeces of other animals can also be part of their scavenging behaviour. Dogs are attracted to the smell, texture and taste of foods – regardless of whether we consider them to be appropriate or not. As dogs interpret smells differently to humans, it's important to remember that poo isn't necessarily an unpleasant smell to a dog. In fact, poo is an odour that dogs are consistently attracted to when exploring their environment. So, if poo is attractive enough to your dog, you may find your dog eating it.

Vets refer to dogs eating faeces as coprophagia. It's natural for female dogs to ingest their puppies' poo while they are cleaning them. Other than that, it may be a behavioural problem but it's important to rule out a medical cause before a behavioural diagnosis is made. Medical problems that decrease the absorption of nutrients can increase the appeal of a dog's own stool. Some possible medical causes include:

- Underfeeding or eating a poorly digestible diet
- Digestive enzyme deficiencies
- Parasites
- Vitamin and mineral deficiencies and malnutrition
- Diabetes, Cushing's disease or thyroid disease
- Some medications containing steroids

Your vet will identify anything medical and fixing it may include providing a more digestible diet or switching to a high bulk or high fibre formula. Adding enzyme supplements to your dog's diet may improve digestion and absorption.

Coprophagia in puppies is quite common and generally clears up by adulthood. However, dogs of all ages may indulge in coprophagia and some common non-medical causes are:

- Curiosity and playfulness. Poo-eating may attract attention from owners which encourages the dog to keep doing it.
- Copying other dogs. Puppies may mimic the behaviour of their mother or other dogs that are doing it.

- Incorrect training. Sometimes owners attempting to toilet-train their dogs by sticking its nose in their poo when they've done it inside, this may actually encourage coprophagia.

You can stop coprophagia by consistently limiting and preventing access to poo as much as possible with thorough cleaning and supervision when your dog is outdoors. You should also discourage your dog from sniffing and eating other dogs' poo (the poo that irresponsible dog owners have left behind) and distract and deter him from sniffing his own poo before you bag it.

Feet licking

When dogs lick their feet and any underlying medical condition has been eliminated, it is often a behavioral issue. It can be a sign of anxiety, depression, stress, boredom or a canine compulsive disorder, which is a dog's version of human obsessive-compulsive disorder – OCD; the repetitive action may be a form of stress relief. It may come down to a bit of attention-seeking; for instance, if what your dog is doing is driving you crazy, reacting to it can inadvertently reinforce it. Make sure your dog is getting plenty of exercise and plenty of stimulation.

Ask your vet about the temporary use of a head collar (aka Elizabethan collar or cone) to discourage this using or bitter topical spray as a deterrent.

Biting and aggression

Biting is an instinctive canine behaviour and part of pack mentality. Beyond a puppy's nipping explorative behaviour, there are quite a few reasons for biting, all of them aggressive. Some dogs are predisposed to an aggressive tendency and unless properly socialised may act on that tendency. Early socialisation – to humans, to other animals, to strangers and to a whole raft of external experiences — will greatly reduce a dog's likelihood of becoming aggressive. Dogs become aggressive for a reason that is obvious to them but not always obvious to us. It's important to understand that aggression will not disappear on its own. It has to be contained, reduced and eliminated and for this you may need professional help

The following are nine different types of aggression.

DOMINANCE AGGRESSION

This type of aggression is the most common reason why dogs bite their owners and for that reason it's the most important. Dogs who always get their way usually just become spoiled brats and that's something we can handle. But for some dogs with a more aggressive personality, this life of luxury without leadership or consistent rules creates a furry monster that aggressively claims ownership of everything they want – food, toys, sleeping places and attention. Dominance aggression is something I take very seriously, particularly because it is very dangerous around children (as dog bites tend to focus on the head and neck).

Most dogs are very unimpressed with the head bucket, while others, like this long-haired Chihuahua, grin and bear it

Signs that your dog is dominant aggressive include aggressive responses to your eye contact and resistance to your commands to vacate sofas and beds. If your vet cannot find any medical reason for this behaviour (sometimes medical issues trigger or exacerbate dominant and aggressive behaviours), you will likely need to work closely with an experienced animal trainer or behaviouralist to overcome this dangerous behaviour. Increased exercise and regular obedience training may be effective in reducing aggressively dominant dogs.

Unfortunately, while behavioural therapy and training are excellent, they are not always sufficient to resolve dominance related aggression, and in those cases anti-anxiety or antidepressant medications may also be required. In addition, it is likely the dog's owners will need some training to reassert their position as head of the pack. For example, after an aggressive incident, attach a lead to the dog's collar and remove him to another room to temporarily isolating him from the rest of the family. A minute is enough. Never use physical punishment as it could make matters worse – a firm tone of voice, facial expressions and body language should give him the message that you are the boss.

INTER-DOG AGGRESSION.

This a type of dominance aggression and occurs when a dog is overly aggressive towards other dogs, in the same house or elsewhere. I am often asked where this behaviour originates. There can be several reasons; a dog may have become overly aggressive due of past experiences, including abuse and neglect. For example, it may not have socialised with other dogs as a puppy, or it may have had a traumatic encounter with another dog. Rescue dogs often have an unknown history and sadly some have been retrieved from situation where they have been encouraged to exhibit aggression such as, for dog fighting and to protect drug dens.

When the dominance aggression is between two dogs in the same home, they tend to be relatively equal in size, sex and weight. But if they are not, don't be tempted to take the side of the underdog. While it might be instinctual as their leader, it can cause more harm than good if the owner shows compassion for a weaker dog by punishing the more dominant dog. Other reasons for aggression are fear, wanting to protect territory and social status, or a painful medical condition. Dominance aggression towards people or other dogs is less likely if the dogs are desexed.

SEX-RELATED AGGRESSION

Aggression over sexual urges can happen in both male and female dogs. In non-desexed females it may occur only twice a year when the dog is hormonally active. Aggression between non-desexed males can happen all year round but is more likely if they were allowed to play rough-house games as puppies and were not corrected.

FEARFUL AGGRESSION

Aggression due to fear is the most common reason why dogs bite strangers. I have been bitten by dogs in the clinic because they're afraid. Fear biting is more usual in dogs that were not properly socialised as puppies. Take your puppies to the vet, dog parks, cafes, dinner parties, even your work if your allowed, to get them used to the big wide world as early as you can. Signs of fear – growling, teeth-baring, body posture – should be nipped (!) in the bud before they turn into fear biting.

PREDATORY AGGRESSION

This very basic form of aggression is potentially present in all dogs. Some breeds – terriers, herders and hunters – are genetically prepared for chasing prey and biting it once caught. Not surprisingly these are the breeds that come in for emergency treatment for snake bites.

TERRITORIAL AGGRESSION

This sort of aggression is about your dog protecting its patch – your home, your car or even you. Never let an aggressive dog stand between you and their owner, because they'll do what they can to protect the owner. Your dog could show signs of territorial aggression if he thinks a stranger presents a threat. There's nothing inherently wrong with the family dog alerting you that someone has come to the door, but it shouldn't be aggressive. Again, early socialisation by introducing your dog to visitors when he's a puppy should help with friendly greetings. However, if you got the dog as security for home, train it to bark, not bite. The correct role of a security dog is to deter threats not to be used as a weapon.

FOOD AND TOY AGGRESSION

Some dogs become very possessive over food, toys, or even bedding; they show aggression if someone tries to take them away or move them and may bare their teeth and growl. Remember, in the wild, dogs never knew where or when their next meal would be, so it's very instinctual for them to scoff their food down and to protect it from anything that approaches. Your dog should be taught that it's acceptable for you to touch or move its food bowl while he's eating. The RSPCA suggests that one way of overcoming food possessiveness is to put several bowls of food down and while the dog is eating, take one of the bowls away, then replace it and take another one away. In this way the dog becomes less stressed by the removal of food and is rewarded by having it returned without exhibiting aggression. You can use a

This is a not so subtle warning to steer well clear

similar approach with toys by offering a treat when attempting to take something off the dog and returning the possession after the dog has given it up. Breeds like German Shepherds, Rottweilers, Dobermans, and Chow Chows were selected for guarding traits. Though typically their guarding was for property or livestock these guarding instincts can spread to other things/resources.

HEALTH-RELATED AGGRESSION.

It's natural for a sick dog to become aggressive and to bite if something hurts. Certain medical conditions, such as an under active thyroid or arthritis in an old dog and dementia are the most common. However, dogs are like humans, any condition that causes stress or pain to a dog can cause them to become aggressive.

LEARNED AGGRESSION

Once taught, aggressive behaviour is hard to get rid of. The owner is responsible for a dog's actions. If you deliberately train your dog to bite and it bites someone, you are legally responsible.

And a special request on behalf of all the vets of the world, if your dog has been aggressive to strangers or bitten a vet in the past, please advise the vet clinic us as soon as you arrive.

A NOTE ON MUZZLES

Something I have commonly found in my practice as a vet is that dog owners, even those with dogs that have a history of biting, are hesitant to train their dogs to wear basket muzzles.

Owners worry that it's either cruel to the dog or that others will think the dog is much more vicious than it is. My advice to these owners is to be responsible. If your dog already has a bite history, whether with people or dogs, your first step should be conditioning your dog to wearing a muzzle.

Rottweiler with muzzle. Muzzling should not be used in place of training

Muzzling your dog should not be used in place of training so seek help from an experienced trainer to come up with a behaviour modification and training plan.

Yes, muzzling is cruel if the wrong muzzle is used and it does not allow the dog to pant; the muzzle needs to fit properly, and the dog needs to be acclimatised to wearing it. A muzzle should not be used without first addressing any underlying issue; that is laziness. Nor should muzzles be used to stop your dog from barking, chewing, or eating things off the ground or for a puppy that is play biting. Work with a trainer for tips on how to deal with those issues.

The following are a few things to remember when using a muzzle:

- The muzzle should fit properly. Make sure you purchase the right size and style muzzle for your dog. It should be well-fitted and comfortable, allowing for panting and ideally drinking water and eating treats. Contact the manufacturer directly for assistance in sizing your dog.

- Create a positive association with your dog to their muzzle. Go slow and introduce it in a fun way. Make it a game with lots of treats! It's 'party hat' time!

- Mesh muzzles or any muzzle that holds the dog's mouth closed and prevents panting should not be used except for extremely short periods of time or in an emergency. These muzzles can cause a dog to overheat quickly, especially in a stressful situation.

- Always use a muzzle in combination with training. Muzzles are not a replacement for addressing the issues your dog is having; finding an experienced trainer and working with them to help your dog is a must.

Scary sounds

Besides thunderstorms there are many sounds that scare dogs – fireworks, smoke alarms, people yelling, squawking cockatoos, vehicles backfiring and high-powered motor bikes. Little Sasha was afraid of jet skis when we lived on the boat. Fear is a normal emotional response to a real or perceived threat or situation however fear can escalate to a phobia, an exaggerated and irrational response to a noise that can completely emotionally cripple a dog. Thunderstorm phobia in dogs is real, common and shouldn't be ignored; it can turn a calm dog into a pacing, panting, shaking, quivering mess, desperately seeking somewhere safe to hide; it's even worse for dogs who already have fearful behaviours such as separation anxiety.

The interesting thing about thunderstorm panic attacks in dogs is that they often happen completely out of nowhere. Vets don't really know what the triggers are, but we suspect they are set off by a combination of elements prior to the noise of the thunder and lightning such

Dogs hide from thunderstorms

as barometric pressure changes, static electricity and low frequency rumbles that humans can't hear. One theory is that dogs experience painful shocks from static build-up before the storm and the long-haired coats of some breeds are an ideal for a static charge. While I'm not so sure of this theory, I have to admit it does seem like the long-haired breeds such as German Shepherds, Border Collies and Golden Retrievers appear to suffer more than short-haired breeds like Greyhounds, Boston Terriers and Dachshunds for example.

Most dogs don't grow out of thunderstorm phobia on their own and unless your dog is only mildly affected it can be difficult to fix without the help of an animal behaviourist. But there are things you can do to reduce a dog's distress during stormy weather. Not being dogs we don't always know when we are going to be struck by thunder and lightning but some places in Australia have distinct storm seasons such as the tropical regions of the far north between November and April. The following are a few tips to help your dog survive storms and other noises.

- Train the dog to be calm when there is no storm. Many owners make the mistake of only trying to comfort a dog that's whimpering and clinging to them like Velcro but rewarding your dog for this behaviour it will only encourage it. While it is okay and necessary to comfort a dog when it's phobic (this is different to naughty/mildly anxious) time must also be invested in training the dog when it's calm, because, just like children, dogs don't learn when they are frightened.

  Practice trying to get your dog to settle on your command when there is no storm. Get the dog to lie calmly at your feet inside with a special lead on (different to your normal walking lead). Praise the calm behaviour and at the first sign of a storm, put the special lead on and tell your dog to 'come and lie down here'. Once trained to do this the dog will know what to do. Distract the dog with some music that makes it difficult to hear the storm and its favourite toy, patting it and giving it treats as long as it remains calm.

- Give the dog a special safe place to hide when a storm comes on. Let him choose the place –it could be his crate, or a bathroom, maybe a shower cubicle where tiles may mute the noise outside. He should be able to come and go freely because being shut in somewhere might make him more anxious.

- Desensitise him to the sound of storms by playing a recording of thunder noises at a low enough level so he's not frightened. Give him treats while listening and over weeks and months gradually increase the noise, stopping if he shows any sign of anxiety. The goal is to get him used to thunder noises although there's no guarantee of the amount of success when he encounters a real storm because there may be other factors associated with the storm that effect his behaviour.

- If your dog is particularly anxiety prone, ask your vet about anti-anxiety medication. The vet can help you work out a management plan that includes anti-anxiety medication during the storm season, some behaviour modification and desensitisation.

Storms can affect some dogs so severely that they escape and run mindlessly kilometres and kilometres in sheer terror, often found the next day in neighbouring suburbs or surrounding districts, battered, bruised and shaking. If you have an outside dog who is storm phobic, always let them inside before the storm hits. And make sure they are microchipped and have your phone number clearly marked on their collar. I have known owners of storm phobic dogs who have convinced their bosses to be able to leave work early every time they see black clouds building – ahh, the things we do for the love of dogs.

Lip licking

Lip licking is part of a dog's body language. If you notice your dog licking his lips when you correct him sharply for unwanted behaviour, it's safe to assume that it's a stress response. I sometimes see it in the clinic when the dog is uncomfortable, particularly if he doesn't know me. If your dog is licking his lips out of stress, try to distract him in a positive manner such as giving him a simple command and give him a treat when he follows it. Avoid comforting him when he seems uneasy because this can actually reinforce his fear or anxiety.

Lip licking and showing the whites of the eyes are typical signs of a nervous or uncertain dog

Lip licking is also an appeasement gesture when dogs are confronted by something they consider a threat and sometimes they lip lick and yawn when they are frustrated or confused. Owners may notice this behaviour during training sessions when their dogs are having trouble understanding what is expected of them. Take this as a sign to wind up the lesson. At the next lesson try to break down the training into smaller segments so it's easier for your dog to learn.

Dogs can also lick their lips for medical reasons such as nausea, dental disease or mouth pain. Other causes could be gastroesophageal reflux, sudden dietary changes, intestinal obstruction or pancreatitis. Lip licking combined with nausea and vomiting are often secondary to other conditions like liver disease, kidney disease or Addison's disease. If in doubt about lip licking, see your vet.

CHAPTER 13

Human Behaviours

Sleeping with your dog

P assionate dog owners are divided on the issue of dogs in the bed. In my introduction I wrote about how I was so desperate to have my new little puppy Sasha sleep with me that I took my bed to her. If dogs could talk they'd give you many reasons why they want to sleep with their pack leader – they're lonely, it's cosier than their own bed, entitlement, it's roomy enough for a good stretch, it smells good (of you) and they just love you and if you loved them why would you expect them to sleep on the floor.

As a vet I have heard both sides of the argument – owners who would never dream of allowing the dog on the bed and those who have slept happily with their pooch for years. Some dog behaviourists say allowing your dog on your bed sends mixed messages, lowering your pack status to be equal with his. As far as I'm concerned it is a personal choice. It may be a good way to bond with your dog but don't forget setting rules and boundaries. After all it's your bed — not your dog's.

Apart from bonding there is also some evidence to suggest our brains subconsciously interact, even in sleep, and the peaceful waves emitted by your beloved pooch can influence your brain for the good. On the negative side there are a few health and safety issues such as the other things your dog might bring into the bed – fleas, ticks and ringworm. It is not a good idea if you have young children because even the best-natured dogs might snap in self defence if a child bounces on the bed. Owners have also been known to be bitten in bed. I've heard stories of marriages

Sometimes having your dog on the bed is a comfort; other times it can create relationship issues

in strife because the family dog has assumed the role of leader of the pack and dominates the bedroom as well.

I recommend that you have your pack relationship well established before considering allowing your dog to sleep with you. This means educating darling doggie that sleeping with you is a privilege not a right, and that when you say 'off' he must obey. Puppies need to learn how to sleep alone so they don't grow up clingy. (See Crate Training, Chapter 4). If your dog is clingy and co-dependent or suffers from separation anxiety, he should not be in your bed. A dog who suffers great stress when you are away needs to practice feeling secure when not in your direct presence. An ever-present shadow whining outside the bathroom door needs to learn how to be comfortable with separation. Sleeping curled up against you all night only feeds this co-dependence.

Outmoded communication

What we know about canine behaviour has changed significantly over the years, yet despite new knowledge, many people still cling to disproven beliefs about dogs and dominance and their relationship to wolves. Using outmoded philosophies can lead to dogs being handled and trained in the wrong way which results in fearful and/or aggressive behaviour. One example of inappropriate 'training' is staring into a dog's eyes to let the dog know 'you are boss'. This intimidating body language can make a dog very uneasy. If you love dogs it's important to understand how a dog sees the world and relates to other dogs and people.

Training has evolved to emphasise positive reinforcement and kinder methods of getting dogs to behave the way we want. Dogs do best in an environment where they are taught to do what you want them to do and rewarded and praised for good behaviour. Training that focuses on punishment, which dogs find threatening and unpleasant, can lead to even more inappropriate behaviour.

Anthropomorphism

Anthropomorphism is when we attribute uniquely human characteristics to non-human creatures such as our dogs. It's a natural human tendency that is almost unavoidable, and something we need to be conscious of when we are dealing with our dogs. We often put very human ideas and feeling into our dog's heads — and they don't really belong there.

Expecting dogs to think like humans is fairly widespread among their owners and right now there are more dogs than ever before in Australia so there's a lot of anthropomorphism going on. Every year we spend millions of dollars on our dogs. We buy them expensive collars (My dog likes to show off to his mates), comfy beds (What – an outside kennel? My dog would hate it) and commercial foods that smell good to humans ('Home made gravy – yummo!'). We hold birthday parties for them with balloons and doggie cakes; we put them in doggie day care so they don't get lonely; we seek out the best groomers for their haircuts and nail trims; we dress them up in mini jackets and tutus and put bows in their hair and, when they get over-anxious, we medicate them.

Much of the training based on pack theory could actually be an exercise in anthropomorphism. I mean, are dogs really keeping a mental tally of who is in charge based on who walks in front of whom or enters a doorway first? Are dogs really in a constant battle with us for supremacy? Or is this just something insecure humans worry about? Many house-training issues end up being anthropomorphised. People believe that a dog rips up the cushions because he's angry when his people have gone out for the day. And of course, when they come home they believe the dog knows he's been naughty because they misinterpret the look on the dog's face. By evaluating canine behaviour using human values we risk misinterpreting our dog's emotions and motives and turning minor behavioural issues into chronic ones.

Anthropomorphic dog owners can improve their relationship with their dog and ultimately the dog's behaviour if they make an effort to understand their dog's

Birthday parties for dogs a well-meaning idea that some owners think dogs love. But in all honesty, the best treat for your dog on his birthday is a day of your undivided attention. The personalised dog balloons and pup-cakes are more for the human guests.

unique emotional makeup. While leaving a sackful of Santa dog treats under the Christmas tree is not a crime, loving dog owners should be careful that their actions don't interfere with boundaries and effective positive reinforcement. When a dog's behaviour is unacceptable – he's hyped up, obsessive or attention seeking and we give him a hug and tell him it's okay, it's comforting for us to think we're soothing the dog but often the dog gets the message that we approve of the inappropriate behaviour.

I'm not saying anthropomorphism is bad so long as what you are doing is not harming your pet or interfering with what should be a harmonious relationship. But next time you communicate with your dog with a little 'kissy, kissy for Mummy' perhaps remind yourself that you are talking to a different species and it's perfectly okay to treat your dog like a dog.

♥

CHAPTER 14

Travelling With Your Dog

As your dog is considered part of your family, why wouldn't you want him to come along on the family holiday? And most dogs love to come along – no show without Punch. My Sasha loved driving places with us, happily came on a couple of flights with me and adapted to a life on the water when my family had its yachting adventure around the coast of Australia.

But travelling isn't for everyone, or every pooch. It's normal for dogs to value their territory (something vets call the home range), it's here they know where they can find food, water and shelter easily. And most importantly it is home to something most precious to them – you! Dogs may have mostly evolved to be cautious and remain close to what is familiar. Some might like to explore, but chances are they'll enjoy much more if it's with you.

Travelling with pets isn't difficult if you understand 'best practices' and adhere to all the rules and regulations regarding taking animals on various modes of transport

Travelling by road

When you're out shopping for a new car your pet's safety probably isn't usually the first thing on your mind. But it's a fact that some cars are a little more pet friendly than others. A vehicle that's roomy, square at the back, equipped with fold-down seats and a power-operated tailgate will make it much easier for your dog to get in and out of, especially if he's large. Cargo barriers can also come in handy when you want to keep dogs separated from the passenger areas.

The main thing about driving around with your dog is keeping him restrained. An unrestrained dog is not only a distraction for the driver — it can become a deadly missile flying straight into the windscreen if you brake suddenly or are in an accident.

Restraints are mandatory in Australia; driving with a dog on your lap (or even sitting unrestrained in the back seat) is illegal with stiff fines and the threat of loss of licence and demerit points if you are caught. In fact, the Australian Prevention of Cruelty to Animals Act also says that any pet injured because they weren't restrained can cost the owner a fine of several thousand dollars and the prospect of jail time. The same act penalises drivers who transport untethered dogs in the back of a ute. I've seen horrendous injuries inflicted to dogs that have jumped out the back of a hurtling ute. I'll never get those shocking images from my mind.

There are a few things to bear in mind when shopping for the most appropriate car restraint for your dog. The two basic types are harnesses that attach to seat belts and box-shaped transport containers, otherwise known as pet crates. A crate must be properly secured and be big enough to let your pet sit erect and comfortably lie down. If your dog has been crate-trained as a puppy he will be familiar with it and happy to travel in it.

If you are buying a seatbelt-attaching harness make sure you get one that fits your pooch properly. Harnesses are meant to be used only in the back seat because harnessed dogs in a front car seat are at risk of injury if the airbag deploys in an accident.

If you're buying a new car, you might want to consider your dog's safety as well as the human family members

When people ask me if it's okay to let a dog stick its head out of a car window, I tell them 'Only if the car is standing still'. Airborne dust and debris can damage a dog's eyes. It is okay to open the window a crack for ventilation, but it shouldn't be open wide enough for their head to poke outside.

Travelling with dogs in vehicles is a bit more complicated than just securing them in their crate or harness and cruising happily into the sunset. If you are going on a road trip you need to put a bit of thought and preparation into the process. For instance, if you were planning to go into the bush, you should be aware that dogs are not permitted in Australia's National Parks and that regulations regarding where pets are permitted have a habit of changing, so contact the relevant authority to get the latest advice before setting off.

To make sure you have an enjoyable and stress-free experience on a trip that includes camping or caravan parks, start investigating pet-friendly parks before you leave home. Once you've found one where you want to stay, it's a good idea to call them to discuss their specific pet policies because they do vary from park to park. Despite a pet-friendly status, some parks won't let pets inside cabins.

On arrival be sure to do the right thing and follow camp rules. The actions of inconsiderate dog owners may cause holiday parks to ban dogs, punishing the responsible dog people. For the safety and comfort of other park guests keep your pooch under control at all times.

CAR SICKNESS

Dogs that don't travel in the car very often may suffer from car sickness, which makes long journeys unpleasant for everyone involved. It may be better to start off with short car trips and gradually build up to longer journeys. This will also help to reduce any anxiety that may contribute to their car sickness. Many puppies start off with car sickness which they simply grow out of as they get older. If possible, avoid taking a young puppy on very long drives if they are showing signs of anxiety, discomfort or nausea.

Take regular driving breaks to allow your dog to stretch its legs, have a drink of water and a pee every two or three hours. This will make him more comfortable during the drive and less prone to car sickness. Don't feed the dog an unfamiliar diet while travelling as it may upset his tummy. In severe cases, have a chat with your vet before you leave as there are medications that can help. But if your dog does get carsick (or is known to have the occasional toilet accident on long drives) it might be prudent to invest in waterproof seat covers and/or rubber floor mats for extra protection. Feed dogs two to four hours before you leave – not ten minutes before they hop in.

OTHER NECESSITIES

Keep in mind that if you are visiting remote areas it may not be possible to find the usual food your dog eats, especially if he's on a special diet, so bring whatever food he'll be eating (but obviously not fresh meat unless you have fridge storage). It's also necessary to pack plenty of drinking water (taps aren't always easy to find) and don't forget separate food and water bowls. Other basic necessities include poo bags, medications, leads, grooming items, a big towel (in case your pooch goes for a swim or gets caught in the rain), his favourite toys and a familiar bed or blanket. Also ensure your dog is wearing identification with your current contact details.

Just because you're comfortable in the front seat doesn't mean your dog is just as happy in the back; check on him regularly to ensure he's okay and make sure there is plenty of air flow; stop for regular toilet breaks and the occasional exercise break. Use the lead when you let a dog out in a new place to make sure he can't run off.

If you are travelling in the summer or to places where temperatures are known to be warmer than your dog is used to, you need to remember that dogs are less efficient than humans at regulating their body temperature in warm weather. Dogs only sweat minimally through their nose and paw pads. Make sure your dog has access to clean, cool drinking water, and limit exercise to cooler times of day, such as early morning or late afternoon. Choose roadside rest areas with plenty of shade. If you stop at a roadside cafe for coffee and something to eat, never ever be tempted to leave your dog in the car on a hot day because you 'won't be long'. Temperatures can rise to dangerous levels very quickly and it is illegal to leave your dog alone in the car.

If your dog has a medical condition that may require urgent attention, it may be prudent to look at the areas with veterinarian services along the way so you are prepared in the event of an expected emergency. Having pet health insurance is a good idea as is carrying all relevant medical records and vaccination certificates.

Travelling by air

There are a number of important aspects to be aware of when considering transporting your pet by air, both domestically and internationally. Not all dogs are suited to travel by air and some airlines will not take certain breeds and have strict conditions for others. In these cases, owners should investigate other available modes of transport, preferably where the animal can be supervised directly while travelling.

DOMESTIC TRAVEL

Qantas has some specific rules about transporting dogs on domestic flights. Among the dogs it will not permit on any Qantas, QantasLink or Jetstar service are American Pit Bull Terriers and puppies under eight weeks of age. American

Staffordshire Terriers less than 12 weeks old are able to travel on all domestic sectors provided it is in an approved wooden dog crate. If the American Staffordshire Terriers is more than 12 weeks old, lodgement for travel can only be made through a pet transport company. Guard or racing dogs or those that are part of the police or defence forces are not classified as pets and have to be transported as live animal freight.

There are rules and regulations around transporting your dog by air

Full bred Brachycephalic dogs – Pugs, Pekinese, Boston Terriers, Japanese Chin and French, British and English Bulldogs — cannot travel on any Qantas, QantasLink or Jetstar service flights of more than five hours in length and no more than two sectors (i.e. two connecting flights) at a time. For increased air flow and comfort, they must also travel in an approved crate, twice the usual minimum required size. These same breeds are only permitted on international flights longer than five hours if the owner completes an indemnity form against the airline due to the high-risk factor.

Virgin Australia will only accept animal bookings through accredited pet agents for both domestic and international flights. More than 18 international carriers will transport pets but they must be carried according to the International Airline Travel Association (IATA) Live Animal Regulations which includes special crates. Under certain conditions, some overseas airlines allow dogs to travel in the cabin but in Australia all pets must travel in approved containers in the hold.

Approved containers must provide adequate ventilation; along with the surrounding temperature, poor ventilation is a major cause of heat stress which can be fatal. The dog must have good shelter/shade to protect it from the weather. I cannot emphasis enough the importance of being aware of heat stress and the necessity of minimising the risk. Any dog is susceptible to heat stress but the ones at increased risk include: the obese; the Brachycephalic breeds; heavy-coated breeds; those with respiratory, cardiovascular and/or brain disease; and animals travelling from a cooler climate to a warmer climate. Very young or very old animals are also be more susceptible.

Your pet should be fit and healthy and able to cope with being confined for an extended period. An airport is an unfamiliar and noisy environment which can cause some animals to become stressed and agitated. It is advisable to get your vet to assess your pet for air travel and make sure its vaccinations, worming and flea treatments are up to date. Airlines usually require a certificate to say the dog has been vet checked. I would not recommend air travel for anxious or stressed animals. Sometimes I advise a light sedation, but every drug has side effects and I suggest the owners administer a trial dose at home well before travelling so respiratory and heart rates can be monitored – sedating an animal that can't be monitored for effects is not advisable. IATA does not recommend sedation for international flights.

Before you place your pet in the container and lodge them, make sure they have had plenty of opportunities to go to the toilet and stretch and exercise. Remember, your pet will be confined in its container from the time of lodgement until he is collected by you at the destination. You could give him a light meal a few hours before he leaves although food is not normally needed for domestic flights. Choose a crate that has a water container inside it with outside access for filling.

Note: Avoid bringing your dog into Australia during the months of December through February as the temperatures in the cargo hold during that period can be too high for your pet.

INTERNATIONAL TRAVEL

The process of moving your dog to another country or bringing your dog to Australia is a complicated process and a lot depends on the country you are going to or coming from. The more disease-free the country is, the tougher the regulations to get the dog in which is why it's difficult to bring pets into Australia and penalties to pay of you don't follow the rules — remember US actor Johnny Depp and the illegal entry of Pistol and Boo?

If you have already been through the process of taking your dog overseas when relocating, you will be familiar with the lengthy and complex procedures involved in moving animals from country to country. Rules do change from time to time and for more detailed and up-to-date information it's best to contact the Australian Department of Agriculture. However, as the whole business of moving will be stressful for both you and your pooch it might be worthwhile enlisting the services of a licensed pet transport agent; being in experienced hands can help take the worry out of the details.

Bringing dogs to Australia

Here are the major rules that must be followed if you are bringing a dog into Australia.

MICROCHIP

Your dog must be microchipped with an International Organisation for Standardisation (ISO) non-encrypted microchip. This microchip number must be present on all importation documents.

RABIES VACCINATION

This is not required for pets born or residing for at least six months in Group 1 countries: New Zealand, Norfolk Island and Cocos Island, and Group 2 Countries: American Samoa, Bahrain, Barbados, Christmas Island, Cook Island, Falkland Islands, Federated States of Micronesia, Fiji, French Polynesia, Guam, Hawaii, Iceland, Japan, Kiribati Mauritius, Nauru, New Caledonia, Niue, Palau, Papua New Guinea, Samoa, Singapore, Solomon Islands, Kingdom of Tonga, Tuvalu, Vanuatu, Wallis and Futuna.

Dogs coming in from all other countries require rabies vaccination a minimum of 30 days before a rabies titer test (FAVN) which is performed by a licensed veterinarian. You can apply for an import permit into Australia after this titre test is done. The titre test is valid for 24 months.   Vaccines for Distemper, Hepatitis, Parvovirus, Para-influenza and Bordetella bronchiseptica are recommended and valid for the entire post-arrival quarantine period. Dogs entering from the United States must be vaccinated against canine influenza and it is advised that dogs entering from other countries also receive the vaccination if it is available. Dogs must be treated against Brucellosis, Ehrlicia canis, Leishmaniosis and Leptospirosis. Dogs that have visited Africa must have treatment for Babesia canis.

PUPPIES

Unvaccinated puppies are not permitted to enter Australia. Import requirements include microchipping and rabies vaccination not earlier than three months of age. Puppies should wait a minimum of 30 days after rabies vaccination prior to having their titer test, which would bring the minimum age of import would be ten months.

IMPORT PERMIT

A permit is valid for 12 months after issue date. (Not required for pets entering from New Zealand or Norfolk Island.)

HEALTH CERTIFICATE

A dog travelling from the USA or Canada requires a USDA or CFIA endorsed Veterinary Health Certificate done within 72 hours of entry. Other requirements apply for other departure countries.

INTERNAL AND EXTERNAL PARASITES

Your dog must be treated against internal parasites twice with the second treatment administered within five days of departure. Dogs must start treatments for external parasites 21 days prior to Ehrlichia blood sampling.

NON-APPROVED COUNTRIES

There are a number of countries that are not approved for direct import of dogs but you might be able to get around this by first moving the dog to what is known as a group 2 or 3 country which is an approved rabies-free, absent or well controlled country. (Consult the Australian Department of Agriculture for full list of countries and requirements.)

QUARANTINE

All pets entering Australia enter as air cargo at Melbourne Airport and all (except those from New Zealand or Norfolk Island) are subject to 10 days of quarantine at the Mickleham Quarantine Facility at Melbourne. It is advisable to make reservations for your dog as soon as you receive his import permit. When entering Australia from another country via New Zealand, dogs must be quarantined in New Zealand first and then remain there for 90 days after quarantine prior to entering Australia.

BANNED BREEDS

Australia has legislated to ban the import of the following breeds: Dogo Argentino, Fila Brazileiro, Japanese Tosa, Pit Bull Terrier, American Pit Bull Terriers, Perro de Presa Canario or Presa Canario. The American Staffordshire Terrier is not banned from import in Australian legislation. The banning laws only apply to pure bred dogs and not apply to cross breeds or mixes. Wolf and dog crosses are also not eligible for import.

ASSISTANCE DOGS

The Department of Agriculture and Water Resources manages the biosecurity risk associated with bringing all dogs, including assistance dogs, to Australia. Anyone applying to import an assistance dog must provide evidence that meets the department's assistance dog eligibility criteria. According to the Australian Commonwealth Disability Discrimination Act 1992 eligibility criteria is the provision of evidence that their dog is trained to assist a person with a disability and meets the appropriate standards of hygiene and behaviour for an animal in a public place. The laws around assistance animals vary between countries and people should not assume their dog will comply with the department's criteria, even if the dog is recognised as an assistance dog in the country of export. A permit is not required to bring in an assistance dog from New Zealand but conditions apply.

TAKING YOUR DOG OVERSEAS

If you are planning to take your pet to live in another country, you will need to apply for an Export Permit and supply a Health Certificate. As you have to meet all the requirements of the country you are locating to, again it may be best to enlist the services of a licensed pet transport agent for the country your pet is travelling to.

Pets on public transport

Every state has different rules regarding the circumstances in which your pets can travel on public transport; assistance dogs and police/security dogs are allowed on all forms of public transport anywhere in Australia.

Transport New South Wales rules that dogs are not permitted on trains or platforms; they can however travel on a bus or light rail at the discretion of the staff if contained in a box or crate. In metropolitan Melbourne dogs are permitted on trains if they are on a lead and muzzled and only in a crate on buses and trams. Regional Victorian trains also allow small animals to board as long as they are kept in a box or crate.

In Queensland, pets are allowed on buses if they are restrained in a box, basket or suitable container, which in the case of dogs would mean very small ones. The Northern Territory has similar restrictions except dogs are not permitted on trains or in taxis but there are a number of pet taxi services available if you book ahead.

In South Australia dogs are allowed on buses if restrained in a box, basket or suitable container, while only assistance and service dogs are permitted on public transport in Perth.

As you can see, the rules vary greatly from state to state, so always check online for the most up to date information. And remember – if your pooch is allowed on board, be sure he is well behaved and that you clean up any little indiscretions.

Introducing your dog to public transport from an early age means they'll be calm, well-behaved and socialised. Dogs like this are welcome out and about in public places.

Pet sitting and boarding

Not all dogs enjoy travelling and you should always put the comfort and wellbeing of your animal first; in some circumstances taking your pet with you is impractical, especially if you own several pets. In that case, you need to decide who will be looking after your pets while you are away. You may be lucky enough to have family or friends who don't mind taking on a four-legged house guest or two.

Vets are always a good source of advice about boarding options in your area, and some even provide boarding services themselves at their vet clinics. Choosing a house sitter or pet sitter may work out cheaper than paying kennel fees because most house sitters will look after your home for free in exchange for the accommodation they receive in return. An advantage of this is that your dog can stay in a familiar environment, which will be less stressful for them. Some pet sitters will take your animal into their own home for a daily fee. They will be dog lovers but always check out their references. It's also worth ringing your local RSPCA because some RSPCA shelters offer boarding services.

If you're leaving your pet in a boarding kennel you should have a look at the facilities in advance. While it's good to check out online reviews, remember to take them with a grain of salt because after all it's the internet! Once you have found a suitable option, book a time to visit before your trip. Ask to take a tour, and make sure the boarding facility is clean and well ventilated and the dogs look happy.

Before committing to a boarding kennel, speak with the staff and give yourself peace of mind that your pet will get the best possible care while you're away. Have a check list of questions:

- What vaccinations does the kennel require?
- What facilities will your dog has access to?
- What exercise will your dog will receive?
- What food will your dog be fed?
- Can you bring your own food?
- What is the ratio of staff to animals available to care for and play with your pet daily?
- If your dog is on medication are the staff able to administer it as instructed?
- What is the company's protocol for handling medical emergencies?
- Has the kennel had a history of its dogs escaping or getting into fights?

Once you have decided you have found the right place and booked your pet's stay, double check with your vet to make sure your dog is up to date with their vaccinations and flea and tick medications. When you drop your pets off, don't skimp on the details or instructions for the staff. This is a member of your family so make sure the kennel is fully aware of specific personality traits and potential areas for trouble. Leave multiple methods for contact in case of an emergency.

Whether or not a dog enjoys travelling depends a lot on the dog and its life experience. Does travel remind them of fun-filled trips like going to the beach, camping or visiting a farm or fear-filled ones like being dropped at sterile boarding kennel or getting needles and nail clips at the vet? In my experience most dogs are happiest at home.

CHAPTER 15

Children and Dogs

Dogs love children and children love dogs – mostly. But not every dog is right for children and not every child is right for a dog. I have already related how much I longed for a little dog when I was a child and how the day I finally got Sasha was the happiest day in my life – I still feel fuzzy when I think about it. Children and dogs can be best friends and there is nothing sweeter than seeing a child playing happily with his or her dog, however as a vet, and now the parent of two little boys, I am especially conscious of the potential issues around children and dogs.

Due to a child's small size and unpredictable behaviour there are several things every pet owner or parent should know about children and dogs. Many of the problem dog/child interactions I have come across in my clinic have involved children under six years of age. If you have small children you should think very carefully before choosing a new dog (See *Choosing the Right Dog*, Chapter 5). If you are adopting a rescue dog, by-pass large dogs that have been bred as guard dogs or have a history of being aggressive or biting; likewise, those big high-energy dogs that can knock children over. If you are getting a puppy be aware that cute puppies grow into adult dogs which may have behaviour traits not suited to small children.

Sometimes a dog is purchased because the parent thought it would be good for the kids or parents were worn down by the child begging for one – just like I did with Sasha. Often the parents did not really want the dog and were not totally committed to caring for and training the dog. My father did not want a dog in the house so I had to prove I was responsible and would look after it properly by walking a neighbour's dog for months before I was allowed to have Sasha. But by then I was nine and many children at that age or older, are ready to begin developing a rewarding relationship with a dog – the right dog at the right time. While dogs can help teach a child responsibility, patience, empathy, and compassion, no young child is capable of properly training or completely caring for a dog; you, as the parent, are always ultimately responsible for any pets in the house – after all you're the one footing the food and vet bills.

Rules from the start

Remember that if you are bringing a puppy home, everything is new to him and no matter how desirable it is to cuddle and play with him, he needs several days to adjust to his new environment away from his mum and siblings first. Put a list of do's and don'ts around the new dog on the fridge. An important decision is where the dog will sleep (See Crate Training, Chapter 4). Even though my Sasha slept with me as a puppy, I don't advise a puppy sleeps in the bed with children – I wasn't a vet when Sasha was a pup and I now know behavioural and a few medical problems can arise from this practice

Just as the dog has to be trained how to treat the new family, children have to be trained on how to treat the new dog. Good relationships can be established by following some good training methods and taking common sense precautions against a nip or a bite – a very undesirable event. Many cases involving dogs biting young children could have been prevented with more knowledge of canine behaviour. It's important to understand the actions that might cause the family dog to snap or bite. One of the tragic outcomes of a bite is that the dog, who may have never exhibited any aggressive behaviour before, may have to be relinquished to a shelter, where he has a low probability of finding a new home and may end up being euthanased.

When dogs bite children it can be from fear or aggression, but many times it is more likely to be a 'warning bite' usually to the face or hand and while traumatic for the child, is often not of a serious medical nature. While any dog bite is extremely serious it is important to distinguish between the natures of bites to prevent problems in the future and to do this it is necessary to understand the pack behaviour of canines. When a dominant dog is unhappy with a subordinate dog, he will use a series of body positions

I remember begging Mum to let me stay home from school so I wouldn't have to leave little Sasha. I think I was the one with separation anxiety!

to signal that he is unhappy, and the subordinate dog better toe the line. If the subordinate dog doesn't obey, the dominant dog will growl and possibly bare his teeth. If the subordinate dog still refuses to obey, the dominant dog will snarl and quickly bite the subordinate dog. The bite is not necessarily intended to injure but used as a stern warning and punishment. This is very similar to what happens when children are bitten because dogs will almost always consider small children equal or lower in the pack hierarchy.

Dogs and small children should never be left alone unattended. Even the sweetest most passive dog and a well-behaved child cannot completely be trusted alone. It is important to remember that in the dog's mind the family is a pack unit and, in most families,, one or both of the parents are considered the pack leaders and the dog is subordinate to them and young children subordinate to the dog. So, the dog may refuse to obey the child's commands or 'accidentally' bump into the child and knock her down. Unfortunately, children are not usually able to interpret the dog's language, nor is the dog capable of communicating in any other way so the interaction may escalate to growling at the child when the child is near food or toys, or even baring his teeth and biting when the child approaches or tries to play with him.

In the unpleasant situation that your child is bitten, and the skin is broken, the wound should be thoroughly cleaned, and you should seek medical attention that day as subsequent infections are common, and they may require a tetanus vaccine. In some cases, people are hospitalised for intravenous antibiotics. If they are immunocompromised, infection risk is even greater.

Tips to keep kids safe

Here are a few tips to keep kids safe from dogs and dogs safe from kids.

- Dogs want to eat in peace. Don't let children muck about with the dog's food.
- Children should be taught to interpret a dog's anxious, threatened or uncomfortable body language as there is usually some warning signs before a dog growls, snarls or bites a child. These include lowing the head or body, tail tucked between legs, averting eyes, yawning, lip licking or what is known as 'whale eye' when the dog turns his head away but keeps looking at the child or the perceived threat.

- Children should be taught to leave the dog's toys alone (unless it's part of a known fetch or catch game). Dogs can be possessive of their toys so you could train the dog to be tolerant in case the child picks it up. By training the dog to give up their toy for a reward they will willingly give the child the toy instead of feeling possessive.

- Teach children not to get in the dog's face. Putting your face into a dog's face can be irritating to the dog; it may even be perceived as threatening because you are not respecting the dog's personal space.

- Dogs need a safe location where they can be away from kids and excitement, such as their crate.

- Children should avoid annoying the dog while it is sleeping or resting.

- Children don't like rough handling – nor do dogs. However, dogs can be trained to tolerate, sometimes even enjoy, boisterous handling so that they are not reactive when the child accidentally hurts the dog, but in general children should be taught to be gentle with pets.

- Teach children that climbing, riding or stepping on a dog may irritate, even hurt it.

- To a sound-sensitive dog excessive noise like loud screaming, yelling and children's shrieks might indicate danger to them, especially if they are not accustomed to it.

- Not all dogs enjoy being hugged like a stuffed animal. Puppies can be trained to like cuddles and hugs but while it's important for children to know the interaction their dog likes they should also be aware that other dogs might not have the same tolerance.

- Parents should teach their children to read the signs of a fearful or anxious dog and to back off.

- Don't let kids feed the dog scraps from the table. If the dog begs remove him from the dining room.

- Never allow the dog to jump up on anyone. Teach the child to raise their knee and turn their hip towards the dog when it jumps. This behaviour should be trained out of the dog when they are young – ignoring them while they are jumping up is the key.

- Adopt a zero tolerance for any dog growling or aggression and undertake strict obedience training for the dog.

Once the children understand the rules of kindness to their pet they can be taught appropriate games to play such as those that involve tossing and retrieving balls or toys that the dog is willing to share. Older children can be part of the dog's daily exercise regime by walking him on a lead. It is up to adults to make sure that the dog has lots of positive associations with the kids such as letting them give food rewards for the dog's calm, well-mannered behaviour, such as 'sit' on command. But regardless of how good the interaction between child and dog, adult supervision is important because behaviours can be misinterpreted in a split second.

ZOONOTIC DISEASES

Zoonotic diseases are those transferred from animals to humans. When a dog licks its bottom (which they do every day when self-grooming) or eats or licks its poo, there is a strong possibility that pathogens, such as worms, fungi or bacteria, will be transferred to the human when we, as doting dog owners, get licked on the face, particularly kids who get licked straight in the gob! Regular household worming of both the dogs and the humans and good hand washing practices is a must when you have dogs and children living together.

New babies and dogs

Dogs are very in tune with their human family, so an event as monumental as a pregnancy will have alerted the dog that something is up. A pregnancy affects the entire household. You may feel excited, anxious, or worried. Remember, your dog will pick up on your emotions and mirror them. But just because your dog has picked up on the new feelings hanging in the air, doesn't mean that he understands what they mean.

In the months before the birth it's a good idea to establish yourself as the household's 'top dog' and smooth out any of its bad habits which you don't want to have to deal with when the baby comes home. If you need help, hire a professional trainer to work with you. Any work you put in before the baby is born will be appreciated when you bring your newborn home to a calm, well-behaved dog.

Condition your dog to understand that there is an invisible barrier around the nursery that he may not cross without your permission. Eventually, you can allow your dog to explore and sniff certain things in the room under supervision with you deciding when he needs to leave. Repeat this activity a few times before the baby arrives. This will let your dog know that the baby's room is off-limits and must be respected at all times.

To introduce your baby to your dog, start by taking your dog on a long walk to work off your dog's energy. On returning, wait at the doorstep; make sure your dog is in a calm-submissive state before bringing him in. When he goes into the house, he will instantly recognise a new, somewhat familiar, scent in the house. Whoever is holding the baby, either mum or dad, must be in a completely calm state. At this first meeting let your dog sniff the baby at a comfortable distance. Eventually, he can be allowed to get closer and closer to the baby. In doing this, you are teaching the dog to respect the baby as another member of the family pack.

As a newborn baby's interaction with the family dog is minimal, most problems tend to begin when the baby starts crawling or turns into a toddler and begins invading the dog's space. When your child is in the exploratory state, it is important to supervise all interactions between child and dog. Once your child is old enough to learn right from wrong, teach them not to bother the dog, yank its tail, pull its ears etc. These lessons based on mutual respect cannot begin early enough. Too many children inadvertently provoke an otherwise peaceful dog, simply because they are unsupervised, or their parents don't give them proper instructions.

Don't forget about the dog when your baby is born. A dog does not need toys or special attention to feel important; you simply need to maintain the routine, providing daily walks and consistent loving care. This will help your dog feel secure and enable him to relax about the new baby. Sadly, I see this problem often and I understand it; I have two little boys and I know how hard it can be. But it is not okay that the dog gets forgotten, or suddenly

A dog should only be allowed in the baby's room with your permission

A gorgeous moment captured between a little boy and his dog. It's the parents' job to teach kids that while your dog might love cuddles and having his muzzle stroked, other dogs may find this behaviour scary enough to bite.

gets kicked out, going from an indoor to outdoor dog.

Never assume your dog will or will not pose a problem just based on breed alone. Dogs are not always predicable – we have all heard stories about those lovely gentle dogs that 'wouldn't hurt a fly' who have unexpectedly given a child a bite. The key to keeping your baby safe is leadership. Ask yourself if you can control your dog at all times in all situations? If, after working with a professional and on your own, you still have doubts about the safety of your baby with your dog, then finding your dog another home to protect the wellbeing of both your child and your pet is a decision you may have to make.

CHAPTER 16

Doggie Trivia and Other Tails

Do dogs have belly buttons?

Like us, dogs are placental mammals, so yes, because dogs have umbilical cords they have to have belly buttons. However, the position of the belly button on a dog is different to that of a human – in both male and female dogs the naval is flanked by nipples. Having less hair than dogs, humans are used to having their belly buttons more visible whereas a dog's belly button is only obvious for a short time after birth; the mother removes the umbilical cord from her puppies and the tiny scar is rapidly obscured by fur.

If you have a short- or medium-haired dog, you can check out the location of his naval by looking for a tiny thin scar located just below the end of his ribcage, and just above the start of the abdomen. The only time you'd have reason to give a dog's belly button any serious thought is if something goes wrong during his puppy development such as umbilical hernia – a condition where something that should be securely positioned inside the body bulges out. Normally, a wall of muscle seals itself after birth at the spot where the umbilical cord was connected. In dogs a hernia happens when the small opening created at the time the umbilical cord is severed doesn't close over or heal properly.

Although they can occur in any breed, certain dog breeds are genetically predisposed to develop umbilical hernias which can either be complicated or uncomplicated. A complicated hernia is one in which contents of the abdominal cavity, such as a loop of intestine, have passed through the opening in the abdominal wall. These hernias are more troublesome and can be life-threatening if the internal

A large and very obvious umbilical hernia. They are often only a fraction of this size and first noticed by the vet during their puppy vaccinations.

organs or intestines become entrapped. I get these patients into surgery as soon as possible.

An uncomplicated umbilical hernia is associated with a soft swelling in the umbilical area that contains a small blob of fat but no internal organs. This swelling may be variable in size and may come and go. Uncomplicated hernias don't have any impact on the dog's wellbeing and are easily corrected at the time of desexing. While umbilical hernias can occur in any breed, Airedale Terriers, Basenji and Pekingese have a certain predisposition for them so owners of these breeds should inspect their puppies' tummies and get to the vet if they suspect a hernia.

Why do dogs have tails?

Have you ever stopped to wonder why dogs have tails? Or why they wag them. Many animals have really useful jobs for their tails – horses and cattle can flick off flies, monkeys can swing from trees, squirrels use them for balance on branches – but does a dog's tail have a practical use? Not surprisingly, the tail is more than just a happy wagging appendage; depending on the breed and the purpose for which it was bred, tails can be used to maintain balance during strenuous physical activity, assist in swimming, and provide insulation against cold weather. They can also be used to communicate.

Because tails seem to wave about easily it might be logical to assume that they are made of a flexible material such as cartilage. Actually, dogs' tails, regardless of their shape and size are extensions of the spine. The bones of the tail (vertebrae) are bigger at the base and get smaller toward the tip. Soft discs cushion the spaces between the vertebrae and allow flexibility. The tail muscle and nerves facilitate tail movement (and even play a role in bowel control). The number of tail bones varies by breed or mix, but there are typically anywhere from five to 23 coccygeal vertebrae.

The longer the tail is, the more exposed it is to damage or trauma and believe it or not a short, tight curled tail is really an inherited deformity arrived at through generations of breeding practices. It is most common in Brachycephalic breeds such as the little Pug or the spike-eared French Bulldog. This condition is called hemi-vertebra which literally means literally 'half of a vertebra'. The vast majority of dogs with this genetic anomaly are asymptomatic, but a few may suffer from rear-limb weakness and incontinence.

What about docking tails? I am firmly against this inhumane practice for cosmetic purposes. Not only does this inflict unnecessary pain on the animal but it means the dog will lose its ability to communicate with its tail and no longer be able to use it for balance as they run and swim. Just because dogs such as Doberman pinchers and Weimaraners traditionally had their tails docked, doesn't mean it is right to keep on doing it. This

Why do dogs wag their tails?

is particularly relevant to backyard breeders who dock tails without anaesthetic! Let's not forget the tail is actually an extension of the dog's spine.

As I mentioned, dogs also use their tails to communicate, both with other dogs and with their owners. Body language is an important part of a dog's self-expression and the tail is a far more subtle organ of communication than barking, whining or howling. There are a multitude of dog tail signs; we may think the way a dog carries his tail or how he wags it are distinct signs but in fact the two – wagging and carriage – frequently work in collaboration to convey specific details about mood and emotion along with a particular message. You can learn a lot from a dog's tail if you put your mind to deciphering its mysterious patterns.

There are three main ways a dog carries his tail: A dog with the tail tucked between the hind legs can be considered fearful or socially submissive; when a tail is carried horizontally, straight with the line of the back, it represents a relaxed or indifferent dog. A dog with his tail held upright or pointed towards his head might be excited, alert, or preparing for action.

Dogs' tails wag in each of these positions, and at all degrees in between. How fast the tail wags, the sweep of its arc, and even which side — to the left or to the right — all work together to deliver the intended message in all its complexity. You can attempt to get an idea of what your dog is trying to 'say' with his tail, not only by its position and wagging action, but also by knowing where your dog holds his tail normally and working from there.

Getting to the point

Tails are not the only way dogs communicate a message. The act of pointing, where the dog becomes motionless with his nose towards an object and one front leg raised off the ground, is normally associated with dogs that have been bred and trained for hunting. These breeds were first bred in Europe a couple of hundred years ago to sniff out birds and freeze in the pointing position, which showed the hunter where to find the prey.

Hunting breeds are not the only ones who will point and you might even see this tendency in your own dog; certain breeds do seem to lend themselves to being trained to point.

Kissing and smiling

I am a big fan of the smiling dog – it gives me a warm fuzzy feeling because I know the dog is happy. And what about the sweet, comforting feeling of baby puppy kisses? But hang on, do dogs really smile? Or kiss? Surely the reality of being kissed by a dog is just to be licked. Let's explore the contours of your dog's mouth and learn a few facts about dog anatomy and a bit about behaviour along the way. While dogs can't talk, their mouths can still tell us how they are feeling.

LIPS

Dogs do have lips but they're very different in form and function than the ones that adorn the human face. Despite apparent differences, one common feature is that, like a human's lips, a dog's lips form a continuous protective circle around the outside of its mouth. A dog's lower lip is simply the lower lip, but the upper lips are called 'flews.' The flews vary in length from breed to breed. Heavy-muzzled, big-drooling breeds such as Bulldogs and Mastiffs have long, low-hanging flews draped over their upper jaw-line; along with voluminous facial hair in other dog breeds, the flews can completely obscure a dog's lower lip. The lower lip is lined with finger-like protrusions, which may have some function in gripping food, providing some friction as opposed to a slippery smooth lip.

CHEEKS

The cheeks of a dog and the cheeks of humans are very different. A dog's comparatively longer jawline is balanced by smaller cheek capacity, whereas our cheek and lip muscles work together, providing suction that keeps food and water in our mouths. When you run your tongue over the roof of your mouth you will feel ridges; the ones in a dog's mouth are much larger and more pronounced. A dog's tongue and hard palate perform a similar function to our cheeks and lips combo but are less precise – one reason so much falls out of their mouths when they eat and drink.

LIP COLOUR.

While it might seem that all dogs' noses and lips are black, they are not. However a dog's nose and the outer lining of their lips are usually the same colour. Melanin is responsible for all eye, skin, and coat colour variations in dogs except for white and pink, which are not colours themselves, but denote lack of colour. The darker a dog's lips and nose are, the more melanin in their genetic make-up. The most common nose/lip colours, from least to most melanin, are Isabella (dusty), liver (brown), blue (grey) and black. But genetics can be capricious and inconsistent which explains why some dogs have spotted noses and lips. Darker noses and lips give much better natural protection from the sun.

SMILING

The corners of a dog's lips are called commissures and they can tell you as much about a dog's state of mind as a wagging tail can. Dogs often pull back their commissures resembling a 'smile' in two ways: the 'submissive or tense smile' which is not a smile at all, but actually closely resembles a snarl, with the front teeth bared behind tight lips; the next time your dog growls, notice how the corners of his lips tighten up. If his ears are back, his body is still and the commissure forms a c-shape, he is not happy.

The other is a 'relaxed smile,' the mouth is usually slightly open, lips are flaccid and eyes are soft.

Does a dog smile to convey happiness in the way that we do? Perhaps a better interpretation of a doggie smile is that its lips are flaccid, especially at the site of the commissures. So combined with his sparkling eyes and lolling tongue, the loose contours of your dog's lips could be telling you that if he's not smiling he's at least contented and relaxed.

DO DOGS KISS?

Dogs do not kiss each other, nor can they be said to kiss their owners in our anthropomorphic interpretation. Owners plant kisses on their dogs willy nilly but do dogs like being kissed? Maybe some do. Look to your dog's body language for cues — is his posture welcoming your kisses? Where is he holding his tail, does he lick his lips when you approach for a kiss or do the corners of his mouth tighten? Your affectionate smooching could be making him nervous!

While it may be satisfying to show your love for your darling pooch by kissing it on the lips, in my opinion it's probably not the best idea. Although most human and canine respiratory illnesses such as the common cold aren't zoonotic (meaning we can't infect one another) there's another reason to keep a bit of distance between your mouth and your dog's (or anyone else's dog) – think about all the rather gross places dogs' tongues go on a daily basis.

If there is one dog that looks like he's always smiling it has to be the beautiful Golden Retriever

Kennel cough is a potential concern in terms of transmission to humans as it can cause respiratory infections. However, this is quite rare and largely confined to high-risk individuals, such as those with a weakened immune system, or who have had their spleen removed, or those who already have underlying respiratory disease of another kind, and pregnant women. The evidence of transmission of Bordetella bronchiseptica from pets to people is relatively weak and circumstantial and it is not clear whether the human Bordetella infections in these cases were truly due to contact with a pet.

Does your dog love you?

How do you know if your dog loves you? Many people think that when their dog licks their face he's saying 'I love you'. Sounds plausible but it's not necessarily true. There are many reasons why dogs lick humans and each other and none of them have the romantic connotations of human kissing. If a puppy licks your face the little dog is more likely to be requesting food. When an adult dog licks your face it is more likely to be acknowledging that you are in charge. Here are a few ways your dog will tell you that he loves you.

THE SHADOW

One clear indication is physical proximity – sitting on your lap, leaning on you, nudging you and can't take his eyes off you. Yep, he loves you. When a dog is feeling affectionate and non-threatened by his owner, he will move closer to indicate that he feels love and trust, but if he moves further away, he is sending the opposite message. Once you bring your new pooch home you quickly get the message that your life will never be quite the same again. The new member of the family will follow you everywhere – even to the bathroom. Your dog doesn't necessarily have to touch you but wants to keep you within sight. So, if he sits at your feet while you watch TV, talk on your phone or work on your computer, it is a sure sign that he's attached himself to you.

JUMPING

Another sign that he loves you is when he jumps up on you; this is something that most people train their dogs not to do as it can be annoying. But it's just a sign of delight in seeing you.

BOTTOM FIRST

One unusual sign that your dog loves you is when he turns his back on you. Sounds a bit weird but in canine language it's actually a sign he trusts you. A dog that was uncomfortable would never turn its back on someone he thought might be dangerous so if he pushes his bottom into you, don't worry, it's another sign of affection.

DOWNWARD DOG

When your dog stretches towards you with both paws together it might not just be because he's having a stretch after waking up from a nice snooze; this behaviour is a way of telling the person that he loves that he's happy to see you. However, it's important to note that a dog that wants to be with you all day and every day and exhibits fear and anxiety when you leave the house is not necessarily a sign of love. This dog could be suffering from separation anxiety.

Why do most dogs have brown eyes?

In spite of the fact that dogs come in many different shapes, sizes and colours, it may seem a bit strange that the majority have brown eyes; a few breeds do have blue eyes. Eye colour is determined by the pigmentation of the iris – the circular structure surrounding the pupil, and this tends to vary according to the concentration of melanin in the front layers of the iris, hence the more the melanin concentration, the darker the eyes. The melanin concentration is much less in dogs with blue eyes.

Melanin is also responsible for the colour in a dog's skin and coat and protects the skin cells from harmful ultraviolet radiation by trapping light rays. Without melanin, dogs would be albino – white coats and pale, pink skin. However, unlike albino rabbits and rodents, albino dogs don't actually have pink eyes (or irises); albinism in dogs is more likely due to lack of pigment around their eyes which can give the eyes a pinkish look. Dogs with white coats and dark eyes or noses can sometimes be confused as albino, but unless they have pink noses and pink skin around their eyes, they are not albino, just white-coated. There are other coat patterns that can be confused for albinism such as merle and piebald which result in something similar to albino; among the breeds where this is mostly found are Great Danes, Dachshunds, and Border Collies.

Most puppies are born with blue eyes which gradually changes to its permanent colour when melanin production kicks in, usually by about two months. If the eye colour doesn't change the pup will keep its blue eyes. Dogs with merle coats are unlikely to go dark because the merle gene dilutes the pigment. Some breeds will have varying shades of brown according to their genetic make-up. For instance, all dogs with liver coats have amber eyes. The amber eye colour can range from a light brown to yellow or almost grey. The gene dilution in the liver-pigmented Weimaraner gives its eyes the 'gray ghost' look. Amber eyes are also seen in blue-coated breeds and sometimes dogs with black pigment have amber/copper eyes.

A playful Dalmatian

CHAPTER 17

At the End of Your Dog's Life

When Is the right time for euthanasia?

As we get near the end of Love your Dog, we reach what I consider one of the most significant chapters, the end of a dog's life. Euthanasia is the term vet's use when they end an animal's life with an injection, and it is the most common way dogs die. Around 50 per cent of dogs are euthanased due to incurable illness or old age and about two percent of euthanasia is done for dogs with behavioural problems. The rest of the dog population dies from natural causes, accidents or illness.

Euthanasia is a really difficult journey for everyone, including the vet. During my early years as a vet I don't believe I did a very good job performing euthanasia. I felt an incredible amount of discomfort and anxiety about the whole procedure and worried myself sick that something might go wrong or the owner would think I wasn't being compassionate enough. I can look back now and see I wasn't putting myself in the owner's shoes; people were crying and I just wanted to get this horrible part of my day done – get them out of the clinic so they could grieve with their family. I didn't understand how important my role was as a councillor.

Over the years I came to understand what a huge responsibility it is to be involved in the decision making around the best and most peaceful way to end a dog's life; in many ways it's an honour to be part of it. And I completely changed my perspective about euthanasia. Where once I rushed the procedure, just giving someone a quick hug at the end of it before moving on to the next patient, today I spend as much time as bereft owners need. The longer I practiced as a vet the more bad euthanasia stories I heard – the vet didn't take the time with them or didn't explain what was happening; I never want to be that vet.

People love their dogs and ending the life of a family pet can be a very traumatic event. A vet does not want to influence someone to keep the dog alive longer than they feel is fair, but sometimes vets may do this because they are medically trained to treat sick animals and they may hope that a health problem can be resolved. Personally, I always work carefully with the owner to make the right decision; everyone has their own philosophy about how much medical intervention they want for their dear old dog, or even a younger dog with a life-threatening illness. Most people do not want to prolong a pet's life beyond what's fair, but vets do have a responsibility to educate people on any reasonable options available.

Sometimes a family makes the decision at home and book their dog in to be euthanased just because it's old and sick without any prior veterinary advice. This can be a tricky situation for a vet who knows the condition is treatable. Unfortunately some people think vets want to keep dogs alive to make money out of treatment; I can tell you as a vet I find this most upsetting because my intentions, and that of all the vets I know, are always honourable – I never want to keep an animal alive if its quality of life is very low, but on the other hand I don't want to put it down too quickly if it's life can be improved with the right treatment.

Vets often have long-term relationships with clients because they have been treating their dogs since they were puppies. Relationships like that are very special because you've created a rapport with the pet owner over the years and they trust you and so it's often easier to come to a joint decision about what's best for the dog. But when a vet is meeting a client with a dog they want to put down for the first time, the vet has to gather a lot of initial information and create a mutual understanding about the right decision at a very serious moment, and most vets find that challenging.

When people ask me if 'the time is right' I spend time asking a few questions to get an idea of what is really going on with the dog.

Loving an old dog makes you realise that true beauty is not covering up the grey but embracing the silvery softness of every strand. Senior dogs have a composed and tranquil presence.

IS YOUR PET IS EATING?

Dogs generally are quite motivated by food, so going completely off their food can be a sign that they have sort of given up and they don't really have the will to push on. Lack of appetite is not the only consideration as many dogs become anorexic or go off their food when they're sick – but it is one clue up for discussion.

IS THE DOG COMFORTABLE?

Is it stiff and sore and sometimes yelps in pain when touched or jumping into the car. People often describe a dog in pain as not 'being himself' because the animal can't really tell you about any pain they are experiencing, and their natural energy and spirit tends to mask it. But there's another reason that dogs mask pain – evolutionary survival; canine instinct warns pain is a weakness that makes them prone to predators.

So, we'll talk about how comfortable they think the pet is, and also their enjoyment of activities. We expect old dogs to be slow and arthritic – they're no longer energetic little puppies; but when their favourite person comes to do the door, do they get up and walk over? It might be slow, but do they still have that desire to greet a favourite person. If you say 'let's go to the park' or to the beach or to their favourite place – do they get up?

IS THE DOG SLEEPING?

Sleeping also is an indication of a dog's level of comfort. An uncomfortable dog is usually agitated and up a lot at night because they are sore, probably going to the owner's bedroom every few hours to be taken out to toilet or because they're sore. That's another indication that they're not comfortable.

When a dog gets towards the end of its life and is no longer interested in food or going to its favourite place, and when their owner comes home and their tail wags but they can't get up for a proper greeting are all signs that that the pet's quality of life is poor.

WHAT ABOUT TOILETING?

Hygiene is a major thing for a dog; I am always concerned if the dog is too sore to get up for the toilet – a dog should never have to sleep in its faeces. Mobility is very dependent on the owner; some owners will want to put a dog down if it has to lose a leg or is paralysed because they believe its life is compromised. Others will import ambulatory wheels from the US, take the dog for physio three times a week, willingly help with toileting, wiping the dog's bottom and treating any urinary rashes.

HOW TO ASSESS QUALITY OF LIFE

You and your vet can assess the quality of life of your terminally ill pet's life by taking into consideration the following factors:

- Hurt or pain
- Hunger
- Hydration
- Hygiene
- Happiness
- Mobility
- More good days than bad

There are no hard and fast rules, consequently a vet can never make assumptions because so much depends on the owner and their beliefs around pet care. Often it comes down to how they were brought up to interact with animals; for instance, if they were raised on a farm, they probably have more clear and assertive ideas about a dog's role and what is fair for a dog. Whereas people in the city who have always had house dogs may see them more as a family member and they're happy to do the nursing care. Either belief is fine; a vet just needs to be sure what the client wants.

Once I feel confident that the owners understand what is best for their dog I ask them to go home and talk it over with the rest of the family. They need to digest their decision because it's not one they want to rush. Then ideally, we like them to come back when they're ready for the euthanasia procedure; it might be the same day if the dog is in a critical state, or it might be in a couple of weeks and in the meantime we might give the dog some pain relief, physiotherapy or put them on a drip if they are dehydrated. Some people ask if they should just let their pet die naturally and, depending on the condition of the dog, I usually explain that euthanasia is more humane because dying naturally often involves suffering.

Palliative care

This is the care that is delivered as a dog approaches the end of his life if owners choose not to treat the disease due to the dog's age or if the dog's disease symptoms have progressed to such an extent that they interfere with the activities of the dog's daily living but they are not yet ready for euthanasia. This is not the same as veterinary palliative medicine which is a philosophy of care in which a decision has been made to stop trying to cure a life-limiting illness; some diseases can be managed long term without any hope for a cure such as diabetes, chronic kidney disease and congestive heart disease.

Incurable cancer is an example of the principles and practices of veterinary palliative medicine. Palliative medicine in the face of terminal cancer depends on the dog and type of cancer. Your vet will discuss the expected course of the disease and how it will affect your dog's quality of life and daily activities. This is crucial because it allows everyone to participate in the palliative care planning – the dog's lifestyle is important in defining good quality of life versus poor quality of life and enables the vet to work out individual therapy. It is essential that the family understand what will happen during the course of the disease and their pain management and comfort goals for the dog as death approaches.

Pain management is crucial; the vet will determine which medications and nutritional supplements will give your dog the maximum comfort. The vet may also recommend other things such as physiotherapy, acupuncture, massage and therapeutic laser to relieve musculoskeletal pain. Palliative care may also involve modifying the home environment because his balance and ability to move normally may be compromised — here are a few suggestions to help him get about safely.

Old dogs spend more time sleeping

- Non-skid floor surfaces can make moving around the house easier for the dog. In non-carpeted rooms, you can create non-skid floors using rugs and the spongy interlocking floor tiles often found in children's play areas and gyms.

- Raise the dog's food and water dishes onto something – such as a brick or two depending on the dog's size – just above elbow height. This will minimise the risk of back pain when the dog is eating and drinking because the spine will be in a neutral position. If the dog is not very mobile, it may be best to place food and water bowls in front of him wherever he is most comfortable resting.

- Make sure the dog is supervised when going up and down stairs by blocking access. If carrying the dog is not an option, you can use a sling to help him. All you need is a large bath or beach towel that is strong enough to support the dog's weight. The towel must be long enough to pass under the dog's belly and be pulled up on either side of him as handles for you to hold on to. It often helps to add a lead to the dog's collar as it assists in the manoeuvring and also reminding him you want him to try to walk. When you walk, do it slowly and gently alongside your dog; never rush a dog with mobility problems. For large, overweight and giant breeds you will need a person on either side of the dog, each holding the towel to manoeuvre him smoothly along together.

- If a dog's mobility is seriously limited, it's a good idea to keep him feel engaged with the family he loves by making comfortable places for him rest near the centre of the family activities.

The euthanasia procedure

Once the decision has been made to euthanase their dog, owners are often worried about whether or not they should be there for the procedure. That's another personal decision. I don't believe dogs know they are going to die so there is no right or wrong here. But I definitely find that in the presence of its owner a dog will generally feel calmer and more secure. So, if you want to be sure that your dog to be calm until his final breath then staying with them is a nice way to achieve this. Of course, there are some situations where this is not possible; if the dog is aggressive or has been in an accident. If an owner simply cannot bear the thought of witnessing the procedure, I am completely respectful and empathetic to that as I know most vets are – it can be disturbing for some people or at the least too upsetting.

Another question I am asked relates to the presence of children when the dog is euthanised, especially if it's the children's dog. It depends how well they understand death. Probably at around the age of five they have some concept of things dying. Personally, I think it's good for them to be there because it helps them process what's happening. It would be a big shock for a child to come home from school and find out that their dog has gone. I welcome older kids and take the time to discuss the procedure very gently with them, making sure they're ready to witness it; I make it known that if they get upset, it's okay go outside. Sometimes the whole family comes to say goodbye to their dear old friend and that's a lovely thing. I think it is good idea for them to keep the collar and some people ask for a lock of the dog's hair.

When the owner brings the dog into the clinic there is initially some paperwork; there's a permission form to be filled in and while we do invoice ongoing clients, most people pay on arrival because it means they can leave immediately afterwards as people are often too emotional to talk to anyone.

While any paperwork is being done, a nurse and I will take the dog into the consulting room where we place a catheter in a vein. Before we start the procedure, I will have a further discussion with the owner (and anyone else who has come in to say good-bye) to make sure everyone has digested the decision and I think it's important to warn people what to expect. The dog may lose control of his bowels and bladder during the procedure, so we usually cover the lower part of the body with a blanket or towel. Often people are quite shocked at how quick it can be – five to ten seconds; they will be watching as the vet gives the injection and suddenly their dog's head gets heavy and they drift off. I also explain that there can be a change in their breathing – like a big gasp – beyond their last breath; it's called agonal breathing and sometimes there's a few of these gasps which can be a bit disconcerting. Anything unexpected is to be avoided during a big loss like this.

We inject the animal with a high dose of phenobarbitone, a very strong anaesthetic coloured bright green so it can't be mistaken for any other medication. I ask the owner to hold the dog's head as he will lose strength and in the first few seconds drift off to sleep and eventually pass away. In terms of dying it's an easy way to go – quick and painless. But for many owners it's very difficult to watch and the memory of this experience can stay with them for the rest of their lives.

What happens to the body?

There are several options for disposal of the dog's body. Most people choose a routine cremation; the dog is cremated with other animals and they don't get the ashes back.

Another option is a private cremation where the dog is cremated by itself; it costs more but the ashes are returned to the owner who can pick an urn or a special box to put them in. Some people want to take their pet home to bury, like I did with Sasha, especially if they are in rural or regional areas; it's a little more difficult in cities where there are strict laws about burying pets. If the owner can't take the body home immediately, the vet will keep it refrigerated at the clinic until they can. It actually goes in the freezer, so they need to be prepared to collect a stiff, frozen body, which in itself can be upsetting.

Anyone who wants to bury a pet in their backyard needs to make sure they are in an area where it is permitted and that they follow all the requirements e.g. depth of grave, usually about a metre so it cannot be dug up by other animals. It should also be wrapped in something biodegradable like cotton pillowcase or wool rug (avoid synthetics or sealed containers). They should be sure that the animal is buried in an area with bush land or ornamental plants, not food crops. Consideration should be made for future plans for area (could there be a subdivision or pool going in sometime in the future?). It's nice to mark the location with little tree or shrub perhaps a slab or stone painted by the children or marked with a poem or prayer. However, organising anything like that is often too much for an emotionally attached owner, so having a neighbour or close friend do it or electing cremation is often a better option for everyone.

The grieving process

Grieving is a deep emotion and the significance of losing a beloved pet is probably under-appreciated in our society or at least not discussed enough. So, when it happens many people are shocked by the impact it has on them. Sometimes they feel embarrassed to talk about how they feel to other people because they fear the reality of the loss may not be fully appreciated. It may also be fobbed off as a bit of a joke; a workmate who might say, 'Oh, so-and-so didn't come to work today because their dog died' or dismissed by another, albeit well-meaning person, who will suggest sadness can be instantly solved by getting another dog.

How an individual feels about their dog is a big deal and it's important to be respectful of that relationship and recognise that it may be very different to someone else's. For instance, someone who has five kids and lives on a farm is going to have a very different relationship with their dog compared with a woman that lives alone in the city with no kids and a dog she nurtures like a child every day. It's important to be empathetic and not judge someone else based on how you feel about your own dog.

The heartbreak many people feel is real and the depth of it is often unexpected; people get home from the vet's and think they might be sad for a few days. But I've known clients who tell me months later that, 'Every time I walk in and see his little scratches on the floorboards I want to burst into tears' or 'I can't bear to look at the part in the fence where he chewed'. Arriving home can be a big hurdle for people; that little joy bomb that used to greet them and bring so much warmth to the home is no longer there; now coming home feels empty.

I remember when I returned home to Mum's after Sasha died – I was at vet school in Brisbane – and sat down automatically expecting to have a little soft fluffy pooch snuggle at my feet as she used to do and I would get a jolt remembering that she had died. So, I understand why people put their dog's bowl down with food, then realise their dog's not there. This is a normal response and it's all part of grieving.

Some people want to pack up their dog's belongings pretty quickly and have them out of sight. I tend to not advise people to throw these things away; sometimes it's better to do that a bit later rather than on the first day. I encourage people to write poems or stories about their pet; another ritual that can be quite therapeutic is to toss their ashes over a beach or park where they loved to run around or to plant a tree in their memory. A ritual in which the whole family is involved can help with the grieving process. For children it is a good way of learning about life and death and of letting go. And don't forget that if you have other cats or dogs they might be sad too, missing their friend and not understanding where it has gone.

Any conversations with the vet about dealing with grief should be done before or after the procedure, preferably not on the same day because most people want to leave immediately afterwards, often in a numb state. When owners do have the foresight to ask me what they should do when they get home, I do make some suggestions. I also caution that while talking about the loss is important, outside the family circle the depth of this loss it may not be fully understood. Nevertheless, the more it is discussed in the wider community, the more the significance of the human-animal bond will be realised.

The way an animal dies plays a big role in how grief is processed by the owner. If it's an unexpected death such as being hit by a car or a sudden fatal illness many people go into denial and in disbelief and try to go on as normal, reaching to pat their pets or feed them. Anger is another common troubling emotion. The mourner wants to find blame and goes home to stew and – just as people look to the medical profession for answers to unexpected human deaths – they sheet blame at the veterinary profession. They come back and say they have read something on the internet that could have saved their dog – why weren't they told about it. It's a difficult situation for the vet. I have found that trying to explain why the decision to euthanase was the right one is often a fruitless as they are not interested. Their thinking is emotional, not logical. Sometimes you have to let people be angry. I have been the recipient of angry reactions, but they are not common and more than compensated by the messages of gratitude from owners thanking me for the care I took of their dog both in life and at the time of death.

Getting a new dog

At the time of losing a beloved family pet, many people tell me that they will never get another dog, but statistics reveal another story – more than 75 per cent of those who lose a dog to death will get another dog, and sometimes within months. But getting a new dog is an individual decision; the time has to be right and there's no definitive answer about when this might be. There is no doubt that moving on after the death of a dog is difficult. Every person deals with the death of a pet differently however, closely assessing your feelings can help you decide when the time is right. For instance, if your dog was run over by a car you may feel a sense of guilt and need to work through this for some time before getting a new dog; however, if your old dog died of natural causes or you made the decision to end his life to stop his suffering, there will be grief but no guilt and you may want to take on a new dog sooner. Being mentally and physically ready to welcome a new dog into your home will make the transition easier on both you and your new pet.

When thinking about getting a new dog there are a few things you should consider:

- Do you have time for a new dog? Remember the time you spent training and socialising the old one – are you up for that again.
- Are you actually happy without a dog? There may have been things you were putting off while caring for your old and possibly ailing dog? Maybe now is the time to do that trip around Europe!

- Why you want another dog—what purpose will a new dog have in your life? If you're getting a new dog just to fill the void of losing your old one, or to ease the pain, it's probably better to wait because a new dog should not be considered a replacement. A new dog will have a different personality and quirks, and you will need to build a whole new relationship with it.

- Do you live with other people? Other members of the household should have a say – are they ready to welcome a new dog? The decision should be one you make as a group and once you have all agreed to get a new dog, you can then discuss details such as what sort of dog and who will make the final decision if you can't agree on a particular dog!

- Don't forget any other pets you have in the house. Remember, other pets grieve too and may be feeling sad and lonely without the departed dog. If your remaining pets are not ready to accept a new dog it can cause disharmony in the house. Watch your remaining pets closely following the dog's death. Look for subtle changes in personality, activity level and appetite. Only when you are confident they are back to their normal selves should you consider bringing a new dog home and when you do make sure you introduce all pets to it gradually and carefully.

Once you have decided to proceed on the journey with a new dog there are a set of different things to consider:

- Think about choosing a different breed or a different sex; you may be tempted to make comparisons between your old dog and your new dog if they look similar, which is not fair on the new dog.

- How are you physically these days? Your health may have changed since you got your last dog. If your old dog was a large breed and needed a lot of physical activity, do you have the same energy level to cope with the needs of a big dog? You might be better off choosing a smaller breed that is compatible with your current circumstances.

- List the qualities you want in a dog taking into consideration your current situation such as your health, your living arrangements and family situation. Start with the most important qualities and work down.

- If you got your last dog as a puppy, why not adopt an older dog from an animal shelter; there are hundreds of wonderful dogs out there looking for new homes. As long as you know what you're looking for, you will probably find a suitable dog at a shelter near you.

Choosing a new dog may take some time and you may have to visit more than one shelter and look at a lot of dog profiles online before you find the one that the best fit for you. Shelter staff are usually quite knowledgeable about different breeds and can probably help you with personality traits of the dogs waiting for new homes. Many dogs in rescue groups have been living in foster homes and the foster carers can usually give you a pretty good idea of what to expect from each dog. Sometimes the decision is out of your hands – a certain scruffy dog will give you 'the nod' and bingo, you're in love.

Right, you've got the new dog along with a whole set of new responsibilities that came with it. It might be a good idea to approach this as if you were getting a dog for the first time. His needs will most likely be many and sometimes unexpected. He'll need time to adjust to a new environment and may have some anxiety problems if he's been mistreated in his former life. Some training will be necessary and possibly more exercise than you are used to, especially if your previous dog was a slow old senior. If you had many years with your previous dog, his care may have become a matter of routine for you. Therefore, you should make sure you are prepared to make adjustments to your routine if necessary.

As your new dog settles in you start introducing it proudly to the neighbourhood and the other dogs in the dog park. You will reminisce about your beloved old dog with family and friends, knowing he can never be replaced, but in your heart, you also know that you and your new dog are already sharing a new and special love. Life goes on and the love lives on. The human-canine bond is a beautiful thing.

A Vet's Perspective

Most people have a very romantic idea about being a vet and there's a lot to love about being a vet, yet vets in Australia are four times more likely than the general community and twice as likely as other medical professions – doctors, pharmacists, dentists and nurses – to take their own lives. That's one vet suicide every 12 weeks. For this reason I thought it important to give you a bit of background about the men and women who choose to treat and care for sick and injured animals.

Being a vet is considered the 'dream job' for animal lovers and, as you would have read in my introduction, it is why I had my eyes firmly set on this path from a young age. But becoming a vet is not for the faint hearted and anyone who decides to tread this path needs to be aware of the bumps in the road. I have enjoyed my years as a general practice small animal vet – no two days are alike. I see a huge range of diseases, injuries and other health problems in a variety of animals using state of the art diagnostic tools to determine the best plan of action. I never know what will come through the door on any given day and that can be exciting.

There's so much to do and learn. Playing detective as I investigate and evaluate each case can be challenging but also rewarding. Animals can't explain what is bothering them, so vets have to work things out based on physical examinations, laboratory tests, and what the owner tells us. Being an advocate for a voiceless animal is truly a dream come true. And the humans on the other end of the lead aren't bad either! Owners are people from all walks of life and the animals they bring to see me have their own personalities, which often resemble their owners! I have met a variety of interesting and inspiring people through my work and I have grown to love my clients and the friendship we develop over the years. Having the opportunity to educate and advise owners about looking after their pets is something I have always loved, so much so, that I also do it online through my YouTube videos, social media posts, blogs and speaking at community events and in the media.

The best thing I have ever done ever as a vet is to own my own practice. Running a business is hard work but it also brings a special feeling to walk into a veterinary clinic and know it is your own – that five hard years of study paid off. People who graduate in veterinary science can go on and pursue a speciality such as a species-specific practitioner. Others become anaesthetists, behaviourists, emergency and critical care vets — these are the night owls that love living on the edge. Veterinarians can specialise in many areas – dental, dermatology, pathology, internal medicine, or do research at universities. Vets also work for drug companies or become clinical pharmacologists. There are veterinary orthopaedic surgeons, radiologists, ultrasonographers and toxicologists. Those into exotic animals go into zoological medicine and work in zoos; the options are endless and it's a challenging and exciting career.

So why are vets taking their own lives?

Despite the perception, it's a difficult and extremely demanding job. The average shift for a vet is ten hours and if you add the after-hours service, the working day can creep up to 12, even 15 hours. So long hours coupled with low pay, high university debt, compassion fatigue, work overload and poor work-life balance add up to a potent mix. But what makes this mix particularly dangerous is access to drugs that can take your life in an instant. If you've a bad day, it's right there – it's too easy.

And it's not difficult for me to picture a vet's bad day. Alone in the clinic after everyone else has gone home, reflecting on another day that has had endless difficulties and demands; maybe there is ongoing financial, mental and emotional strain and perhaps things aren't good at home – when people have poor work life balance home life usually suffers and I see an awful lot of divorced vets. A vet at the end of such a gruelling day may make a bad decision in a temporary moment of hopelessness which results in permanent devastation.

Vets deal with a lot of death and grief. And if a vet is good at what they do they are very empathetic and put themselves in the client's shoes when they have to put their beloved dog down. And it's not unusual to euthanise five animals in a day. What is worse for the vet is if you don't agree that the animal has to be euthanised, but you still have to do it. In this country vets euthanise more than 100,000 dogs every year — not because they are sick, just because they are unwanted.

On the one hand it is very easy for a vet to be seen as a hero – 'He saved my dog's life' a grateful owner will tell everyone in the neighbourhood. Vets feel an obligation to keep on being that hero. On the other hand, it is common for vets to have to deal with some unreasonable demands from owners. Clients use emotional blackmail and will even abuse a vet who is trying to do their best for a sick animal. People complain about the cost – even on late-night call outs complaints are often made about the fee making a vet who has got out of bed to travel to attend to a sick or injured animal feel under-appreciated for their trouble.

There is an erroneous public perception that vets' overcharge. The reality is that vets are just not paid enough. Vets are about the lowest paid profession in Australia – after finishing a five-or-six year rigorous degree the base wage is around $55,000 and the average annual income of a vet today is about $75,000, about half that of a doctor or accountant.

It is very sobering how these problems have rippled through our profession, causing vets to leave in droves. In data released in 2019, the Lincoln Institute, an industry body that looks after the interests of veterinarians said that vacancies for vets in general practice had doubled in the last five years and it was also taking almost twice the time to fill those vacancies. The unprecedented shortage of vets was not about the lack of graduates; it was the alarming rate of attrition after five or six years of practice.

It costs about $1-2m to buy a clinic with all the specialist diagnostic equipment and many vets, still burdened by their university fees debt, struggle to make their practice profitable; for those that are profitable, it is often because owners are not paying themselves an appropriate salary.

In an attempt to shift these frightening statistics and keep vets in the industry, the Australian Veterinary Association is initiating wellness and communication programs throughout Australia and has set up a dedicated helpline for vets.

I have a particular passion for helping vets create a balanced lifestyle — a sustainable one that allows them to enjoy a lifetime as a veterinarian, even if it means occasionally stepping outside the vet clinic, as I have done with projects such as this book and my workshops and role as a trainer. Communication is the key to being a successful practicing vet – communication among the veterinary team and also with our clients. You can have all the veterinary knowledge in the world but if you cannot explain it clearly to the pet owner or if you struggle building trust and rapport with them, all that knowledge is wasted.

To help address some of the issues that are emerging and to encourage vets to find more joy in the in this profession I developed a 10-hour continuing education program for veterinarians recognised by the Australian Veterinary Association. This five-module course covers the keys to running an effective consultation, including various communication skills, models and the techniques; it also teaches vets the most compassionate way to have difficult conversations and break bad news to pet owners. The aim of the course is to help vets build a better connection with pet owners; a good connection makes it easier to develop a shared treatment plan that takes into account the owner's beliefs, values and ideas. In the final module I share a variety of ways vets can take better care of themselves, not only at work and between consultations but also at home.

Dedicated veterinary professionals play an important role in fostering beautiful human-canine connections. We need them to keep our little four-legged mates healthy and happy. And even more so, they need you to be the caring loving owner that you are! When things get difficult, I think we can all get something out of remembering one of the dog philosophies – gratitude; dogs are great at saying thank-you, even for the smallest gift. We humans tend to look to the future, waiting for something better to come along – we think 'If I just had that then I'd be happy'.

Acknowledging life's every little miracle, like dogs do, is a good lesson for everyone to learn.

www.drclairestevens.com

♥

Appendices

Animal cruelty

According to the RSPCA, animal cruelty can take many different forms. It includes overt and intentional acts of violence towards animals, but it also includes animal neglect or the failure to provide for the welfare of an animal under one's control. In addition to this, it is important to remember animal cruelty is not restricted to cases involving physical harm. Causing animals' psychological harm in the form of distress, torment or terror may also constitute animal cruelty.

As a result of there being so many possible forms of animal cruelty, state and territory animal welfare legislation does not attempt to define it in an exclusive way; rather, animal cruelty is described generally as any act or omission that causes unnecessary or unreasonable harm to an animal. Most Animal Welfare Acts will provide particular examples of cruelty. These may include:

- torturing or beating an animal;
- confining or transporting an animal in a way that is inappropriate for its welfare;
- killing an animal in an inhumane manner;
- failing to provide appropriate or adequate food or water for an animal;
- failing to provide appropriate treatment for disease or injury; and
- failing to provide appropriate living conditions.

State and territory animal welfare legislation prohibits all forms of animal cruelty and imposes obligations on all animal owners to provide for the welfare needs of their animals. Breaching animal welfare legislation is a crime. Serious cases can result in large fines and imprisonment. The penalties for animal cruelty in each state and territory can be found on the Knowledgebase:
kb.rspca.org.au/What-are-the-penalties-for-animal-cruelty-offences_271.html

State and territory animal welfare legislation is listed on the Knowledgebase:
kb.rspca.org.au/What-is-the-Australian-legislation-governing-animal-welfare_264.html

If you believe you have witnessed a case of animal cruelty, please report it immediately to your local RSPCA Inspectorate. To help an animal or report pets requiring care as a result of domestic violence: 1300 ANIMAL (1300 264 625). Ninety-seven per cent of the RSPCA's national funding comes from the community. You can help by contacting: 1300 RSPCA1 (1300 777 221) or 07 3426 9972.

Pet insurance companies

I recommend comparing the market for the best insurance policy for you. Here are some of your options.

1300 Insurance 1300insurance.com.au/pet-insurance

Australia Post auspost.com.au/pet-insurance

Australian Seniors Insurance Agency www.seniors.com.au

Bondi Vet Pet Insurance bondivet.com/petinsurance

Bow Wow Meow Insurance bowwowinsurance.com.au

Bupa www.bupa.com.au/pet-insurance

Guardian Insurance www.guardianinsurance.com.au

Guide Dogs Pet Insurance www.guidedogsinsurance.org.au

HCF www.hcf.com.au/insurance/pet

Insurance Line www.insuranceline.com.au

Kogan Pet Insurance www.koganpetinsurance.com.au

Medibank Pet Insurance www.medibank.com.au/pet-insurance

MiPet www.mipetinsurance.com.au

Pet Barn Pet Insurance www.petbarn.com.au/services/pet-insurance

Pet Insurance Australia www.petinsuranceaustralia.com.au

Pet Secure www.petsecure.com.au

Petcover www.petcover.com.au

PetMed www.petmed.net.au

PetPlan www.petplan.com.au

PetSure www.petsure.com.au

Prime Pet Insurance www.primepetinsurance.com.au

Prosure www.prosure.com.au

RACQ www.racq.com.au/insurance

Real Insurance www.realinsurance.com.au

RSPCA www.rspcapetinsurance.org.au

Woolworths Supermarket insurance.woolworths.com.au/pet-insurance.html

Suggested reading

A Modern Dog's Life, How to to do the Best for Your Dog by Paul McGreevy (Workman Press 2010).

Bones Would Rain from the Sky: Deepening Our Relationships With Dogs by Suzanne Clothier (Grand Central Publishing 2005).

Cesar's Way by Cesar Millan (Harmony 2006)

Dog Sense: How the New Science of Dog Behaviour Can Make You a Better Friend to Your Pet by John Bradshaw (Tandor Media 2011).

Inside of a Dog: What Dogs See, Smell and Know by Alexandra Horowitz (Scribner 2009) , Former No1 NY times best seller.

Making Dogs Happy by Paul McGreevy and Melissa Starling (Murdoch Books 2019).

The Dogs that Made Australia by Guy Hull (HarperCollins 2019).

The Genius of Dogs: how Dogs are Smarter than You Think by Brian Hare and Vanessa Woods (Dutton Adult 2013).

The Other End of the Leash, Why We Do What We Do Around Dogs by Patricia B. McConnell (Ballantine Books 2002)

Australian laws concerning dogs

pets4life.com.au/state-government-pet-laws-in-australia
This website lists the various government pet laws, state by state.

Useful websites

www.rspca.org.au/ For all creatures great and small, including DOGS!

www.dogzonline.com.au/ Index for dog breeders, puppies for sale, rescue dogs and older dogs needing homes, as well as dog semen for sale!

www.dogculture.com.au/ Website to sell travel gear for dogs, but a great resource for off leash parks and beaches in Australia and tips for travelling and camping with dogs. Also lists community dog event

www.australiandoglover.com News, pet care advice, product reviews, book club, travel, upcoming dog events and much more.

www.dogster.com/ Dogster magazine's website, excellent dog advice.

www.petmd.com/ Vet authorised and approved articles and videos for pet care.

www.bringfido.com For pet friendly accommodation in Australia and around the world.

www.akc.org/ A great source of expert advice on health care, training, breeding and A-Z of dog breeds.

www.animalplanet.com Although the Animal Planet website features all kinds of animals, there is plenty to please dog lovers, including dog facts, a dog breed selector quiz and lots of dog care tips.

www.lifewithdogs.tv/ This American site touts itself as the 'world leader in dog news and entertainment'. Here you will find the latest in dog news, information about dog training, articles about dog health, a fan photo gallery, and more.

www.vetstreet.com/dogs/ Another US site, this one offers just about everything you will ever need to know about caring for dogs, along with many other pets. Find guides to pet wellness, information on how to keep your dog healthy, articles on training and understanding pet behaviour.

moderndogmagazine.com/ Modern Dog Magazine– This is the 'Lifestyle Magazine for Dogs and their Companions' where you will find loads of anything and everything dog-related.

Australian dog events and pet expos

There are literally dozens of fun dog events all over Australia every year and you can find out about upcoming events on websites such as www.dogculture.com.au and www.australiandoglover.com.

You can choose from dog festivals and get-togethers, pet and animal expos, pet markets and charity fundraiser events at dog-friendly venues around Australia. Here are some of the bigger dog events around Australia.

Dog Lovers Show

dogloversshow.com.au/

Held annually in Melbourne, Sydney and Auckland, this is the nation's biggest celebration of everything dog related.

Million Paws Walk: Walk to Fight Animal Cruelty

www.millionpawswalk.com.au/

A national activity day by the RSPCA that is held annually in May. Dog owners take their animals walking on designated routes in various cities and towns, with the aim to get around 250,000 animals nationally (hence 'a million paws'.) Owners pay a small contribution that goes to the running of local RSPCA animal shelters. The RSPCA arranges for water troughs and 'poo' disposal bins at various places around the course.

Royal Melbourne Show – All Breeds Championship show

www.rasv.com.au/dogs/

Australia's leading dog competition, with more than 3,900 entries across 200 breeds competing over nine days during the Royal Melbourne Show.

Royal Queensland Show (Ekka)

www.ekka.com.au/competitions/animals/canine

The Canine Competition presented by Black Hawk is one of Ekka's largest and most popular competitions and attracts an average of 2,400 entries. From Border Collies and Chow Chows to French Bulldogs and Poodles, up to 217 different breeds are on show at Ekka. Judges fly in from overseas to put the canine competitors through their paces. Some of the world's best examples of breed will be on show as exhibitors take to the floor for the toe-tapping Dances with Dogs.

Royal Sydney Show

www.rasnsw.com.au/sydney-royal-competitions/competitions/dog-show-sydney/general-information/

This popular Sydney Dog Show is part of the Royal Easter Show, held annually by the NSW Royal Agricultural Society at Sydney Olympic Park. During the 12 days of competition of the Easter Show, thousands of dogs will compete in conformation, obedience, agility and sweepstake competitions.

The Royal Adelaide Show

theshow.com.au/show-entries/competitions/dogs/

Dog conformation, agility, flyball and grooming show.

Perth Royal Show

www.perthroyalshow.com.au/competitions/competition-entries/dogs/

More than 2000 dogs are judged annually at the Perth Royal Dog Show. Dogs from all over the country arrive to show off their best form. Dozens of breeds are on display from adorable poodles to the majestic Great Dane and each day different groups will parade in front of international judges on the lawn outside the Dog Pavilion.

Royal Darwin Show

darwinshow.com.au/enter-online/

Competitions for conformation, obedience, agility and Rally O. Judging groups including toy, terrier, gun dog, hound, working dog, utility and non-sporting dogs.

Bendigo Dog Show

www.bendigoshow.org.au/event/bendigo-and-eaglehawk-kennel-clubs-annual-dog-shows

A huge country event that attracts more than 3,000 dogs annually.

Sydney's Mardi Gras Dog Show

www.mardigras.org.au/doggywood

Dogs and the LGBTIQ+ of Australia celebrate.

Index

Acknowledgements

I have to start by thanking my husband, Christian. Thank you for being the one person I can share my wildest ideas with and know I'll have your full support. You are my number one fan and I am so grateful to have someone on this planet that just gets me – flaws, quirks and all. Thank you for being an amazing father to our boys and entertaining them for countless hours while I worked on this book.

My mother, my best friend and inspiration. For the first time in 34 years I am speechless. I can barely find the words to express my thanks for all the kindness, love and support you have always given me. I look at you with my sons, being the most wonderful Nonna I could ever imagine, and I can't help but thank my lucky stars. We are all so fortunate to have you in our lives. Thank you for believing in me, in this book, and every other abstract idea I have!

My father, you have always been the person to keep me level-headed. Thank you for showing me the value of hard work, planning and sacrifice. I know it is you I have you to thank for my determination, focus and rationalism. I promise I will be instilling these values in the next lot too!

My sisters, Luzena and Renae, I remember every single time you have led me, protected me and loved me. I am forever grateful.

I want to thank Libby Harkness for believing in me. You have been a huge support and mentor over the past year. I have grown to truly love your lessons in literature, grammar, history and other important things like Oliver Twist.

I would also like to thank the team at Woodslane, for all their hard work and kindness.

There are many other people I would like to thank: my gorgeous friends, family members, and the incredible tribe of women I have in my life; the list is enormous. You know who you are.

Thank you.

Woodslane Press

Sydney for Dogs
By Cathy Proctor
$29.99
ISBN: 9781925403541

Travelling with Pets on Australia's East Coast
By Carla Francis
$34.99
ISBN: 9781925868340

Melbourne for Dogs
By Julie Mundy
$29.99
ISBN: 9781921874826

WOODSLANE PRESS